# Music and the Classroom Teacher

# MUSIC and the CLASSROOM TEACHER

James L. Mursell
*Teachers College, Columbia University*

SILVER BURDETT COMPANY
New York · Chicago · San Francisco

*Printed in the United States of America*

# Preface

IN THIS BOOK I HAVE TRIED TO SHOW HOW
the classroom teacher can deal with music adequately and
fruitfully. This is an issue which is being discussed very
actively today, and many people find it baffling. How can
the classroom teacher, with comparatively little musical
training, do anything worth while with music? That is the
question to be considered.

Everything depends upon the point of view. If we regard
music as a technical specialty, then the average classroom
teacher cannot do much with it. But if we say that the
technical aspects of music are far from being its most important aspects, that music reading in particular is of comparatively minor importance, and that what children ought
to have are varied musical experiences and activities involving no specialized difficulties or problems, then everything changes. The expert will still be needed to guide, to
stimulate, to coordinate, to provide resources and ideas.
But the classroom teacher will find herself fully able to
organize the indicated experiences and activities with enjoyment and benefit both to her children and herself.
Those feelings of hesitation and inferiority with which she
so often contemplates working with music will be dis-
sipated. A range of rewarding and indeed delightful service will open up before her. And she will be able to make

her classroom a much better place by bringing music into it.

So the key to answering the question as to what the class-room teacher can do with music is the adoption of a certain point of view. In this book I have tried to explain and defend that viewpoint, and to show how it works out in practical procedures.

                                                        JAMES L. MURSELL

# Contents

# CHAPTER ONE

# Why Music for Your Children?

## I

IN THIS CHAPTER I PROPOSE TO PRESENT a nine-point answer to a question that is of great practical importance. Why should you give music to your children? You as a teacher have every right to ask this question. You as a classroom teacher also have a right to an answer that is sensible and convincing. But before developing such an answer, I want to begin with a two-fold discussion of the question itself.

1. Why music for your children? Giving music a proper place in your classroom is bound to make demands upon you, and you already have to cope with many demands. Your teaching day is crowded. You have an exacting round of planning and preparation. With all that you have to carry, why give time and thought to music? What claim has it to any such recognition on your part? What rewards does it offer to your children, and perhaps to you, which should make you reckon energy devoted to it as well spent? Why weave the strand of music into the already close-knit fabric of your work?

It is obvious that for any busy teacher these issues are exceedingly practical. These questions are perfectly fair and reasonable. You have every right to raise them. Indeed I believe it is even your duty to do so. Your time, your energy, your ability are by no means unlimited, as you very well know. You do not want to hoard them like a miser; but you do want to utilize them for the best advantage of your children. This means that you have to economize, to make certain choices, to select, and in some cases to reject, if you are to do your best work and to render your most effective service. What, then, are the claims of music? Ought you to undertake it, along with everything else? If so, why?

You have every right to a convincing answer. Indeed the supreme condition for your own effectiveness as a teacher is your own belief in what you are doing, and your zeal for doing it. This is true of all teaching, everywhere, but it is particularly true of teaching music in an elementary school classroom.

To be sure, there are plenty of classroom teachers who do, in fact, teach some music without raising the question *why*. They teach it because it is in the course of study, or because the administration insists upon it, or for some such reason. But this is not likely to lead to much satisfaction for them, or much benefit to their children. When you teach anything at all, including music, simply because it has to be done, you are most unlikely to teach it well. You may use procedures which some expert has told you are correct, taking a good deal upon himself when he did so. You may be a successful disciplinarian and handle your group quite well. So far, so good. But there still will be something lacking, which is indeed by far the most important thing of all. A vital spark, a living drive! These come only from your own conviction and enthusiasm. A teacher's conviction and enthusiasm are worth more than all the methodologies ever invented and all the devices for classroom management ever hatched. You must bring music to your children because you yourself believe that it should be brought to them, if its living values are to be realized in your classroom.

Furthermore, teaching which you do only from an external sense of duty, or because of a wish to conform, is not likely to be rewarding to you. There is a deep and wonderful satisfaction in feeling the response of a group of children to something you want very much to give them, and in receiving the impression that sometimes comes with irresistible force, assuring you that the good you are doing here and now will live on in your children's lives, in the years that are to come. But how can this deep satisfaction ever be yours unless there is something about music that you yourself really want to give? This, surely, is impossible. On the other hand, once you perceive how many benefits, how much joy, how much fulfillment music can convey to your children, both here and now, and also later on, you will find a deep and abiding joy in bringing it to them. You will find yourself looking forward to those times in your teaching day when your classroom will be filled with music. This is the best possible guarantee that such moments will be repaying both to your children and to you.

All this is true because of the very nature of teaching itself. Effective teaching is not the clever use of a bag of tricks for getting this and that into children's heads. It is the revealing of possibilities otherwise undreamed of, the transmitting of a vital spark, the projecting of an influence making for happier and better lives. You cannot teach anything well unless you feel in your heart that here is a message you long to deliver because you are convinced that it is worth delivering. This applies to all teaching everywhere, and most emphatically it applies to the teaching of music. The worth-whileness of your work depends

absolutely upon your own sincere, inner, personal conviction of its value. This is the first and most important
reason why asking and answering our great question, "Why
music for your children?" is of such commanding practical
importance to you.

2. The question is important, in the second place, because it is my sincere conviction that the moment you see
clearly *why* it is worth while to bring music to your children you will also see clearly *how* you ought to do so—at
any rate, in principle. The question *how* seems to many
classroom teachers a very serious stumbling block indeed.
They are at home with most other subjects, but with music
they feel at a loss. There seems to be something mysterious and baffling about it. They do not know how to handle
it properly, and very often they think that they cannot do
anything with it.

But suppose we find that there is a list of specific, tangible, understandable values that children can get from
music. Then surely it will not be so very difficult to see
what must be done to help children realize those values.
That is to say, the proper line of approach at once becomes
evident. You want to bring certain benefits to your children through the use of music. Obviously you should set
about doing so as directly as you can. You see that, in
certain definable respects, music can be a helpful influence
in your children's lives; and your job shapes up into
making it such an influence. In short, the moment you
have a good answer to the question "*Why* bring music to
your children?" you are well on the way to answering the
further question, "*How* bring music to your children?"

You need an answer to both these closely interrelated
questions, no matter how much or how little technical
musical training you happen to have had. Indeed I am

convinced that a clear understanding of what music can and should do for children is a teacher's greatest single resource in bringing it to them effectively.

You are, perhaps, a good musician. You may have studied music for many years. You may have been well taught. You can, perhaps, play the piano and even some other instrument. You can sing. You can read the musical notation. You understand the technical terminology of music, which seems so baffling to the uninitiated. I should probably make it clear at the onset that I do not intend to disparage such musicianship in this book or to cast aspersions on expert skill. If you are a good and well-trained musician, and also clearly understand what music can do for children and why they should have it, then you are splendidly equipped to bring it to them as it should be brought. You will find many uses for all the resources of musical skill and knowledge which you now possess. You will find also that your present resources will constantly expand as you use them. New horizons will continually open before you. Music will mean more and more to you as you become better and better able to make it mean what it should to your children. You will never cease to discover innumerable new, delightful, and rewarding ways of using your musicianship. But we shall see as we proceed that this very musicianship, if utilized wrongly, *can become an actual obstacle* to your effectiveness as a teacher.

But what of the contrary case? What if you are not a good musician? What if you are not a musician at all? What if you cannot play, cannot sing, cannot read music, and find yourself quite helpless in the presence of the *do-re-mi's*. This may very well be your situation, for it is true of a great many classroom teachers. Perhaps you are very humble about your musical equipment. Perhaps you are one of those teachers, of whom there are not a few, who are actually afraid of music and who shrink even from trying to do anything at all with it. Under such circumstances you may very well ask what good it does you to believe that music is valuable for your children, or to understand what specific benefits it can yield them. Are you relegated to wistful longing and frustrated helplessness? Are you defeated before you even start?

No, in fact you are not! And here is the reason. When you seriously tackle the question with which this chapter deals—the question *why*—you cannot long resist the conclusion that the reason for bringing music to children is not to teach them the musical techniques, but to help them become better and happier human beings, now and later on. Music can yield such human values, and they can be defined and particularized. Once a teacher clearly understands what they are, she quickly finds that she can work effectively for their achievement, even though she herself has little or no technical musical expertness. For what you have to do does not involve these techniques which you may or may not possess, but, instead, the organization of a range of convincing musical experiences—something that is certainly within your power.

Time and time again I have seen classroom teachers who were in no sense trained musicians do an excellent job of bringing music to their children. They did not understand the complexities of music; but they understood children, they had a keen sense of what was good for children, and they saw how music could help children as human beings. That was enough! They had a specific answer to the great question *why,* and that answer carried them through amazingly well. They found ways of getting where they wanted, primarily because they knew where they wanted to go, just as a group of young people with whom I am acquainted found a way of getting from New York to California, although they had hardly any money.

## II

In developing an answer to the question "Why music for your children?" I shall avoid all generalized arguments. Instead I shall try to point out what music actually does for children when it is effectively brought to them in class-room situations.

It is one of my responsibilities and privileges to visit many schools and many classrooms, to talk with many teachers, and to see many kinds of educational work in progress. If I could take you with me into certain class-rooms, you would have an answer to our question right before your eyes, in overwhelmingly convincing form. You would see teachers like yourself, bringing music to their children as something full of vital meaning and living appeal. You would sense, as I have often sensed, the instant, deep, and touching response of the children them-selves. And you would not need, any more than I need, to delve into educational theories in order to be quite sure that a good and even a wonderful thing was going on. And I would be surprised if there did not arise in your breast a wish to do likewise, and a conviction that you really could. Such human spectacles carry more persuasive power than a world of abstract argument, and answer our central question more decisively than any words.

But since we have no magic carpet which might make such expeditions possible, let us choose the next best al-ternative. Let me try to tell you what convictions have impressed themselves upon my mind as I have watched and talked and reflected, and also let me describe some of the actual situations out of which those convictions arose.

1. One universal impression that has come to me from visits to many classrooms is the simple but deep and strong enjoyment that children find in music when they experience it effectively. This response of sheer pleasure is unmistakable. I have seen it again and again. The following incident provides a good example, although it is only one of many I could describe.

Some months ago I was sitting in a second-grade room, watching the work. The room itself was quite a large one, in a fine modern school building, with movable seats and plenty of clear space. There were about twenty-five children in the group. Soon after my arrival, the teacher came to a terminal point in a lesson under way and proceeded to take up music. There was no shifting of places, no taking of "music seats," no reclassification into singers and non-singers. Music was quite evidently treated as a perfectly normal part of the day's doings. Indeed the teacher did not even make any announcement of what was going to happen. She just went to the phonograph, lifted the lid, adjusted the machine, and hunted a record—all without a word. But immediately a visible wave of anticipation ran through the room. There were smiles, soft hand clappings, bouncings up and down, and then attentive silence so as to discover what would come.

The music that came from the phonograph turned out to be "Golliwogg's Cakewalk," from the *Children's Corner* by Claude Debussy, played on the piano by Eugene List.* I was naturally surprised that the teacher gave no preliminary instructions or suggestions of any kind. Later I found that this was one of her self-invented techniques,

* The record used was "Golliwogg's Cakewalk," Young People's Record Club, 2001.

that she had accustomed the children to it, and in effect
built this situation all through the year. The children
looked inquiringly at one another and at the teacher, who
smiled back at them in silence. Then a very free response
began to manifest itself. Most, though not all of the children started to move about the room, interpreting the
music in bodily movement. A little boisterousness developed, but this was controlled at once by a quiet suggestion from the teacher that everyone listen so as to be
able to do "what the music said."

After this very free start, a certain amount of organizing
was done. Three or four children were asked to suggest
what might be done in expressing and interpreting the
music. The record was played several times, and modifications in the pattern of movement emerged. Watching the
children, one gained the impression that the mood and
content of the work were very well grasped by the majority,
for a genuine "realization" in terms of movement was
achieved. Most of the children were out of their seats,
but a few remained seated, most of them humming and
clapping, while one or two apparently did nothing but
listen attentively. The teacher, however, made no attempt
to force everybody to conform, or to "get into the game."
After a while the children all returned to their seats and
there was a little discussion. What kind of a piece was this?
How did it make them feel? There were plenty of answers.
Could they suggest a name for it? Here there was hesitation, but a few ideas for titles were put forward. Then the
teacher told them the actual title and also the name of the
composer of this piece of music.

Next, with a very smooth transition, she told them she
had found a new record which she liked and wondered if
they might like it too. It was quite evident that they were

more than willing to find out! The record was unfamiliar to me, but it turned out to be "Little Johnny Chicka-dee," sung by Rosemary Clooney.* The teacher played it through once. "Do you like it?" she asked. At once there were vigorous nods and "yeses," and not a few giggles at the charming and whimsical song. "Let's hear it again," she said, replaying the record. And now, with apparently no urging at all, quite a few of the children began to sing along with the performer. The teacher promptly picked up the opportunity, "Let's get so that we can really sing it." There were further repetitions. More and more children joined in. The record carried the singing along, and the song was learned like magic.

This verbal description cannot do justice to the actual scene. But one thing, I trust, is evident to you. This teacher was deliberately trying to give her children an ex-perience of musical enjoyment. She was shooting straight at this one goal. She subordinated everything to it and threw out anything that might have been irrelevant or dis-turbing. She might, for instance, have had them count out the beats of "Golliwogg's Cakewalk," as a preliminary to the study of time signatures later on, or picked out some tonal patterns from "Little Johnny Chickadee" and made a drill from them. But she did not. She aimed straight at enjoyment, and no one watching the children could doubt that she had hit the mark.

To arouse musical enjoyment or, perhaps even better, to let music be enjoyed by such simple and direct procedures as these—that surely is within the compass of a teacher whose musical skills are close to absolute zero. But was it worth doing? Was it the right thing to do? Were not many important factors completely lacking? Let us consider it

* Columbia MJV—73.

One can hardly deny that enjoyment is a good thing in itself, a good thing as far as it goes. But certain questions may still remain. Again and again I have heard teachers defend some procedure by saying that "the children love it." All too often this claim is made on behalf of some unusual and ingenious device more or less of a "trick" nature. For instance, a teacher once showed me with great pride a kind of little calculating machine which she had devised and constructed, evidently with much care and trouble, by which *do* could quickly be found and the key of a song established. She assured me that the children "loved" to work with it. Well, I was glad to know that they felt happy about it, but I confess to wondering whether the thing was really worth "loving." There, of course, is the point. Love, no doubt, is excellent. But there remains a question as to the value of what is being loved.

Let us raise this question in connection with the situation I have just described. What, in effect, were these children enjoying? An artificial device? A cleverly directed drill? Not at all. They were enjoying music! And who can deny that music is eminently worth enjoying, eminently worth loving? What one saw was an unmistakable spectacle of simple, childlike, human happiness, perhaps not so very profound. But when one thought about what it meant, and what might come from it in later years, one could not deny that it was a noble and fulfilling emotion. You may perhaps be inclined to say that the educational content was thin. Was it, really? There was the direct and simple realization of music, first through movement, then through song. Nothing more. No facts, no technicalities, no fundamentals, no voice placement—nothing of the kind. What, then, were these children learning? I will tell you in three words. They were learning *to enjoy music.*

That is a lesson with immediate values that are great and manifold, and with potential values that are lifelong. I think it was enough!

So we are beginning to get an answer to our question "Why music for your children?" Because they can find great enjoyment in it, and because it is worth enjoying. That is where we have arrived so far. And the practical moral? If, by the simplest and most direct of methods, you can give a group of children a real experience of musical pleasure, you have done a good job. That you can legitimately believe. Do not let gloomy thoughts about fundamentals, and quarter notes, and key signatures, and *do-re-mi's* shake your faith for a moment!

2. A second prevailing impression that I have received from many classroom contacts and experiences is that children find music a refreshing change in the course of the school day. The incident I have already described will serve to bring this home. There was enjoyment, to be sure, but also more than mere enjoyment. One had, very strongly and definitely, the sense that the children were responding eagerly to a new and different atmosphere, that they were entering into another *kind* of experience. I have noticed this repeatedly and unmistakably when children have been listening, perhaps quite quietly, while music filled the air, when they have been developing a setting for some simple piece with the use of easy-to-play instruments, when they have been realizing a composition in bodily movement, when some of the group have been playing flutophones* while others sang, and so on through many variations. One gets the definite impression that when music is brought to children directly and effectively,

* In case you do not know what a flutophone is, you will find it described on page 211.

they respond to something new, something different, something refreshing.

"But," you may say, "does this really amount to a great deal? The impression may be true enough, but surely the truth is rather superficial. Are you not saying that music serves as a sort of recess during the school day? Of course children welcome a change. But would not any kind of change do just as well?"

No! I do not believe that any kind of change would do as well, nor that the newness and refreshment that one senses in watching children experience music is superficial in the least. When you bring music to your children, you really are bringing them something new and different, something that has magic in it. *You are bringing them beauty.* And beauty is certainly not conspicuous in the rest of the curriculum. The bulk of this curriculum may be admirable. It may be well and wisely chosen. You may teach it with loving zeal. But there is no denying that its content is prevailingly intellectual to a really overwhelming degree. It deals with knowledge, with information, with ways of thinking, with techniques of understanding and analysis. Such matters are important, even essential. But our emphasis upon them is certainly lopsided and extreme. To use an expression that is today outmoded, but that still has some validity, the school sets itself to train the children's minds, but tends to neglect their emotions. And beauty has to do with the emotions, and the essence of music is beauty. Beauty is the new thing, the refreshing thing, that children find in music.

As you gain a human understanding of children, partly by observing them and working with them, partly by conjuring up your own childhood memories, you come to see that they are intensely sensitive to beauty. Children are natural poets. Sometimes this is hard for us older people to realize, because the cares of this world and perhaps the pressures of education have squeezed so much of the poetry out of us. I remember a little boy, on the last day of a greatly enjoyed country visit, saying that he wanted to wander all alone up the meadow, lie in the long grass, and take it all in. He was only a child and spoke with a child's simplicity. But in his words was unclouded and undistorted truth. He was longing for that refreshment of spirit which only beauty can give. He needed it, and he knew his own need. Your children, too, need this refreshment. Music can give it to them. That is why they ought to have music each school day.

Of course as I go on I shall try to point out at length the practical implications of the thinking we are developing in this chapter. But I cannot resist pausing here for a moment to remark how inevitably our answer to the question *why* leads us to cope with the question *how*. You propose to bring music to your children. Why? Because they need the refreshment of beauty. Very well! But unfortunately it is possible to teach music in such a way that there is no refreshment in it, and very little beauty. Indeed, some good people are inured to teaching it in this way. The study of the fundamentals, drill on the detail of the notation, memorizing of intricate terminology, anxious care over voice production—that is what music is too often made to mean to children. And some well-known music textbooks contain a great deal of material which has no beauty or appeal or poetic interest of its own, but which has been deliberately written for the sake of teaching the so-called fundamentals. You yourself feel that you cannot teach all these technical matters? Admirable! You should not even want to! But you can bring to your children varied, charming, appealing, poetic music; and you can enable them to experience it simply and directly. This, by all means, is the pathway to pursue.

3. Yet another striking impression I have gleaned is that music is something in which every child can happily and successfully participate. As we go on I shall refer to and describe many situations in which this possibility was realized. But one of the finest and most revealing examples I have ever seen was during a visit to a one-room, one-teacher, rural school.

There were about thirty-five pupils in the school, ranging all the way from the first to the eighth grade. Of the small number of older boys, at least three had changing voices. It was about as difficult a situation, musically, as could well be imagined. The young teacher was herself not much of a musician. Indeed she could not even play the piano. But she was determined to have music in her school and she solved her problem. She did it by distributing different responsibilities. One of the older boys had brought his accordion to school. He played a solo on it, and told the pupils something about the piece. Also he accompanied some of the songs, having rehearsed the accompaniments overnight. Two of the songs themselves had been chosen by a committee of pupils, who had tried to find pieces that would be enjoyed by all and had prepared short explanations of them. Other songs were selected then and there by acclamation, and still others were suggested by the teacher. An older girl accompanied two of them on the piano. Two girls and one boy took turns playing autoharp accompaniments on the five-bar autoharp which the teacher had personally purchased.* I was told that the instrument was in great demand during the lunch period.

* The autoharp is described on page 211.

It was a simple but quite varied musical program in which, so far as I could see, everyone had a sense of sharing. No one felt left out, and everyone had a good time. In spite of tremendous difficulties this young teacher had managed to organize a musically interested and responsive group.

This was a simple, straightforward, and sensible arrangement which worked very well in the situation described. It would not, however, apply in detail everywhere, for there might be no autoharp available, and nobody in the group might be able to play the accordion. But what we have here is an illustration of a very general principle. Music has a universal appeal, but there are many approaches to it, many ways of experiencing and dealing with it. It often happens that for certain children one particular approach will be more or less seriously blocked. Quite frequently children have trouble with singing, for instance. Very well, give such children opportunities to deal with music in other ways—by playing either simple or standard instruments, by realizing it in bodily movement, by listening, by creating. Children who have difficulty with singing can discover themselves musically in and through one or all of these other types of experience, and when this discovery has been made it often happens that their vocal inhibitions tend to disappear.

I know of a boy who thoroughly disliked music all the way up to the fourth grade. The approach was entirely through singing and he was unable to sing, or at least believed that he could not. The fourth-grade teacher, however, supplied him with a flutophone. He became fascinated. He took the instrument home with him and practiced assiduously. He found that he was able to take part in group musical undertakings at school and did so with great pleasure and satisfaction. His whole attitude was transformed; and by this simple, sensible, practical means the world of music was opened up before him.

For many years the Music Educators National Conference has carried at its masthead the motto "Music for every child. Every child for music." It is a good slogan, and quite realistic, so long as we are not wedded to one single approach. In most average families music, in actual effect, means piano study and nothing more; and in many elementary schools music means only singing. But what of those children who do not flourish either vocally or pianistically? If we accept such limitations, these children are automatically shut out. The universal slogan becomes nonsense, and the problem of individual differences is made insoluble.

What you should do, therefore, is to organize varieties of musical experience. This is musically sound, because you can still have coordinated group musical undertakings, although not everybody in the group need be doing the same thing at the same time. Educationally, too, it is admirable, because everyone has a chance to succeed authentically in the way that suits him best. One blessed thing about music is that, if you handle it properly, it gives you an opportunity to break away from the success-failure complex that dominates so much school work. Everyone can have the experience of success, because there are many different things that can be done with music, all of which are worth while and rewarding.

4. Another great value of music, which has impressed itself upon me in many contacts and observations, is that it can help children to attain better adjustments in general, and that it can lead them to reveal themselves in new ways, so that you can gain a fuller understanding of them, and guide them accordingly.

This point is made clear by the following story of Robert,

reported by a third-grade teacher. Throughout the year this teacher had encouraged and helped her children to carry on creative activities in music; or, to be more specific, she had guided them in composing music of their own. These activities culminated in the development of an Indian play, which was produced and also recorded. She writes as follows: "Educationally speaking, the most important result of our composing was the effect that it had upon individual children . . . For instance, Robert from the day school began in September was a problem. He did not like school and he insisted upon letting everybody know it. The first day of music class he told Miss Meyer that he hated music. He was belligerent, stubborn, and would not accept help with his academic work when it was offered. There seemed to be a wall between Robert and us which we were unable to break. Robert was the second child to volunteer to compose for our Indian play. He composed the Indian lullaby tune with the children helping him with the words. During the process of composition Robert began to show a feeling of pleasure and, in spite of himself, he was enjoying every moment of the experience. The children learned the song and Robert became, in the eyes of the group, one of the most important members. We were amazed at the complete change that has come over Robert since this experience. He is the child who is dancing the chant of the medicine man. Now Richard was a quiet, shy child who always gave the queerest answers to our questions and the most unpretentious suggestions for the solution of our problems. He does not have a good singing voice . . . Yet he has composed more songs than any of the other children." *

* From a report by Miss Esther Oehring and others on the recording of an Indian play, the report appearing in a non-copyright bulletin of

Recently I was watching a group of children realize a number of musical compositions in and through bodily movement. One of them was a Negro boy, much oversize for his grade. I was told his intelligence quotient was far below normal. The sensitiveness and discriminating insight he displayed as he interpreted in motion what he heard impressed me greatly and, when I was told that he had developed a passionate love for music, I could well believe it. I was told that he had overtaken the music supervisor and walked along with her on the way to school one day. "Mrs. ———," he had said, "you know, I just *love* music!" Academically speaking this boy would undoubtedly be classed as a failure. How easy it would be to say that he did not amount to much, and that the school had virtually nothing for him. But the moment musical opportunities were provided for him, something very different was revealed. And what of the future? Life for him would probably always be a humdrum affair of poorly paid and routine jobs. But the school had given him a precious possession which he could always cherish.

So I could go on, for there is an abundance of such instances. I think the reason why music can so often help children to achieve a better personal adjustment, and to reveal what is in them, is precisely that it comes to them as a new and refreshing realm of experience, a point I have already made. Here is a region in which they can be more completely themselves, where the inhibitions that often arise in connection with other aspects of their work are not present. But of course experiences of this kind do not come automatically or by chance. If we make music study equivalent to wrestling with an intellectual symbolism, if

the Laboratory School, Indiana State Teachers College, Terre Haute, Indiana.

we insist monopolistically upon the fetish of singing and therefore doom not a few children to more or less complete frustration, then such personal fulfillments and self-revelations become impossible in many cases. But if we make music what it ought to be for children—a many-sided experience of beauty—then these personal values can be achieved, along with all the rest.

5. Once again, music can exercise a powerful influence for the creation of happy and constructive relationships within your group. I know a third-grade teacher who always makes a point of organizing quite extensive musical experiences very early in the school year. She says that music acts "like magic" (to quote her very words) in pulling the group together and in making them at home with one another and with her. She has no one set formula which she always uses, but tries to adapt her procedures to what she knows of the backgrounds and tendencies of the children. Often she will particularly stress listening, closely associated with bodily movement. She may start off with a simple piece of recorded music, unfamiliar to them, and then suggest that they might like to express in movement what it "tells them to do." Often this comes as a new idea and there may be some hesitation. But within a couple of days the children open up. There are requests for this or that composition. Some of the children may bring favorite records to school. Initiative is stimulated. Natural leaders appear, who might otherwise be submerged for months. She avoids indiscriminate praise, so that the forth-putting children are not transformed into small prima donnas and the shy are not discouraged. Her aim is to see that everyone has a good time with music and to organize stimulating activities in which all can share. She uses music to start the school year off with the proper

spirit and continues to use music in order to maintain that spirit right through to the end.

I am sure I need not tell you, as a practical teacher, how very important is the happy and cooperative spirit of your group. It is valuable in itself, and it makes everything go better. There is no doubt that you can utilize music to create, maintain, and develop such a spirit. Music, indeed, is an agency ideally suited to this purpose. It has, in fact, been employed for just such ends from time immemorial. Music, in its very nature, is a social art. A musical under-taking can have an intrinsic significance and value and, besides this, sharing in it strongly tends to foster cohesive-ness and fellow-feeling among those who participate. Here is a very convincing reason for bringing music to your children. But once again it is well to remember that what should be brought to them is neither technical drill nor intellectual analysis, but music itself, intimately experi-enced and happily shared.

6. Going beyond your immediate group, music can do much to create a fine spirit and a good morale throughout the school. As an instance, consider the following rather ambitious schoolwide music project, which was developed in one of the elementary schools in the city of Baltimore.

Children's interest in musical instruments led to the con-ception and growth of a schoolwide music festival. Learning how to play rhythm band instruments, the tonette, song flute, autoharp and others, had made the children ask many ques-tions: Has man always made music? What kind of musical instruments did early man use? What was the first tune like? At this point the class was anxious to get to work to answer these and other questions.

Discussions followed to determine how to find the answers to these questions. Plans were made and groups were formed.

Soon many interesting reports were made from the intensive research done by these groups.

Some of these reports concerned Primitive Man and his music—the imitating of sounds made by wind and water, singing birds and insects. Interest in the oldest of all tunes led to the finding of one claimed by both Egypt and Arabia. It was adopted by the Crusaders, the Irish and many others. The most popular words to this ancient tune are "We won't go home till morning." This inspired the children to compose new words to this old tune and the introduction to the Music Festival, "A Greeting," was the result of their efforts.

A desire to make models of early musical instruments was born as the children acquired more and more knowledge of ancient and mediaeval instruments. These models included Pan's Pipes so loved by the early shepherds, the Alpenhorn of the mountaineers, and the dulcimer of Old Testament fame. A primitive lute and an old Egyptian harp joined the string group of models. An advantage of this activity was the development of the ability to recognize and place these various instruments and their descendants in their proper choirs.

From the beginning the project increased interest in the music lessons taught in the school. The violin class, the piano class and the class in other orchestral instruments began to attain their true stature. This new prestige led to more and better practices. A greater understanding and appreciation of the instruments were developed. A pride in playing could be detected quite easily when these young students played their "pieces" at appropriate spots in the program. Two of the high spots were the playing of "The Jolly Coppersmith" and "The Dancing Lesson" from *Hansel and Gretel,* by the Windsor Hills School Orchestra.

This keen musical interest that was aroused in one class soon spread throughout the entire school and quite naturally a Windsor Hills Music Festival came into being. Because of its nature, it developed rapidly and smoothly.

With music as the agent for this school project, continuity

was made possible and variety and interest could be maintained.

Tambourines and castanets accompanied songs and dances from Old Mexico and contributed much color and gaiety to the program.

The ever popular drum was represented by Dutch drummer boys setting the pace for some quaint Dutch songs and an original dance.

Bells and gongs, the most loved of all percussion instruments, added greatly to the charm and simplicity of a Chinese Temple Song and an interpretative dance depicting a busy street scene in China.

Colonial life in America was presented in a most effective manner by the use of instruments for accompaniment. The tonettes provided a fitting background for the oldest of all American tunes, "Yankee Doodle." Stephen Foster's "Oh, Susanna" was delightfully done to the tune of tinkling banjos. A dance to "Captain Jinks of the Horse Marines" gave an insight into the Colonial love for rhythm.

This music project was produced by the entire school and enjoyed by the entire school. From its inception, through its preparation, to its presentation, the keynote was enjoyment. Many factors were responsible for this mass pleasure. The fact that the appeal of music is universal presaged the success of the undertaking. With this firm foundation, numerous skillful teaching and learning processes arose that spread through the entire language-arts program. The periods of exploration and experimentation were fruitful with opportunities to develop the capacity to discriminate. The interchange of ideas, the acceptance or rejection of suggested changes produced very gratifying results in growth in the understanding of human relationships. Consciously and unconsciously, the children experienced living and working together in a truly democratic manner.

Growth along other lines was natural and inevitable. The desire to want to invent or create was given full expression.

The new ideas acquired produced many and varied reactions—some were inspired to write songs, others to compose, still others created new dance steps from the ideas and moods of the moment. Pride in achievement spurred these youthful composers and choreographers to greater efforts.

Modern life demands a refined listening attitude and the very nature of the activities involved insured the development of this attribute.

The musical knowledge to be derived from such a project is unlimited. Value, form, rhythm, etc., were learned in a pleasurable and understandable way.

Wholesale enjoyment, lasting benefit, broader understandings, keener appreciations—results of children's interests in musical instruments and melodies—what more could one expect of a single project?" *

This report quite rightly emphasizes the manifold and varied educational values which were realized in this undertaking. It is certainly important to consider such values. But the point I am stressing is this: Here was a highly significant and substantial educational enterprise which, in addition to combining rich content with dynamic enjoyment, certainly contributed also to the life of the school, because it involved all kinds of experiences in living and working together for a common goal. The school was undoubtedly a better and more effective school because the music was so imaginatively and constructively handled.

This project was, of course, an elaborate one. Quite probably you may feel unable to attempt anything so ambitious. I have quoted the description at length not for the sake of offering it as a model just as it stands, but for the reason that it contains many suggestions and ideas that

* Quoted from a mimeographed report from the Baltimore, Maryland Public Schools.

can be applied in more modest enterprises. Nor is it necessary to organize such elaborate and far-reaching schoolwide undertakings in order to use music for creating and fostering a good and healthy spirit in the institution. For instance, I know an elementary school, in an underprivileged district of one of our great cities, where music has functioned as such a constructive influence for many years, although the procedures are far simpler. Over a considerable period of time a very close relationship has been established between the musical activities in the classrooms and the assembly programs. There is a great deal of delightful singing. Much use is made of instruments of many types, both solo and in ensemble. From time to time the creative efforts of groups and individuals are presented in assembly programs. These programs often include creative and interpretative dancing, too. The place is known as a musical school, and many of the children who leave it continue to feel a very special loyalty and affection for it. During the last war many of the young soldiers who had gone through the grades there came back to the school while they were on leave, in order to sing and play with the children. Quite evidently, music has helped very appreciably to make this a good school—a school which children like to attend and of which they cherish happy memories.

To organize an all-school music festival may seem to you beyond your powers, for the time being at any rate, although the one in Baltimore was carried on chiefly by the classroom teachers. But it is by no means beyond your powers to work towards making your school a musical school; and, if you do so, you will be working for the benefit of the institution itself and of all the children in it.

7. Experience with music in school can have a beneficial effect upon children's lives out of school, can influence

them to make music part of their everyday living. Here we are face to face with a very large subject, and innumerable instances and suggestions could be put forward in connection with it. For the moment, however, only a few must suffice, although the topic will come up frequently as we proceed through this book.

Many classroom teachers make definite and often quite successful efforts to influence their children to listen to music on the radio at home. These teachers encourage children to tell of interesting music and interesting programs they have heard and enjoyed. They prepare for coming events on the radio by the use of records, pictures, stories, program notes, and so forth. In systems where there is a school broadcasting station, many teachers suggest that their children listen with some specific objective in mind, as for instance the comparison of their own performance with that of other groups in other schools. Some teachers find it valuable to use the radio during school time for a variety of purposes, one being to train the children in good listening etiquette. Bulletin boards, too, can often be used effectively to link music in and out of school. Teachers often encourage children to bring and post displays of pictures of musical organizations and personalities, also clippings of news stories about musical events and criticisms of concerts.

As an illustration, here is a specific incident showing how music can carry beyond the boundaries of the school. In a fifth-grade unit on early California, many Spanish songs were utilized. Numerous references to instruments in these songs aroused interest and a desire to include these instruments in the project. Castanets and tambourines were easy to include, but the children particularly wanted to use the guitar, since it was so much a part of life in the early days. One of the girls took private lessons in the guitar for two months, and the others found it a great delight to gather about her and sing while she played.

Once again, I know of a neighborhood music group of children who get together very informally at one another's homes to sing, to play, and to listen to the radio and the phonograph. The impulse for this group activity comes directly from the music that goes on at the local school.

Many music specialists have an uneasy feeling that their work ought to carry over into the out-of-school lives of the children much more extensively than it seems to do. They ask themselves why children do not sing their school songs at parties, on picnics, upon all sorts of informal occasions. It is perfectly true that such things ought to happen and equally true that they rarely occur. You, as a classroom teacher, may be in a better position than the specialist to explain this failure, because you know your children and can see the problem more directly in human terms. You will probably find that there are two reasons for this lack of carry-over. First, as to singing, the reason why many school songs are not used out of school is extremely obvious. It is due to lack of vitality both in the material and in the way it is handled. Consider one of the musical concoctions, made to order to exemplify a problem in notation, which is carefully executed in the schoolroom in a light head voice which the children are assured is beautiful. There is no intrinsic impulse to sing such a song in school and therefore no dynamic drive to carry it over into out-of-school living.

Then, in the second place, the influence of school music upon life out of school should certainly not be limited to the use of a certain repertoire of songs. It can be and should be a many-sided influence. The instances I have just presented were deliberately selected to illustrate this idea. To give children a repertoire of songs that they will sing because they like them is certainly desirable. Also it is attainable, if one has sense enough to go about it in the right way, which is the simple and direct way. But what you should be trying to do as well is to promote all kinds of musical interests, which can blossom out in innumerable directions for the immediate enrichment of children's lives. Make your children into singers when you can. This is a worthy goal, but only a part of what can be done, and you should not regard it as the ultimate end of your efforts. Seek rather to develop your children as musically interested young people—people, that is to say, who will turn naturally and happily to the refreshment of music in their daily lives, who will know where to find musical opportunities and how to use them when found, and who will actually create such opportunities when they are not present, ready-made.

8. Your children ought to have music as part of their school experiences because it can create constructive values for their future living, because it can yield them life-long benefits. Here we have a more speculative point than those presented so far, and one for which concrete illustrations cannot so readily be found. Yet it is so obviously valid that very little argument is needed to support it. Music is manifestly an asset in any person's life, even though one may not always be able to write a detailed bill of particulars in advance, showing exactly what it can do for him. Twenty years from now very few if any of your children will be professional musicians, nor is it likely that many of them will be excellent amateur performers, for it takes a great deal of hard work combined with ability and favorable opportunities to keep up this kind of amateur status. But twenty

years from now it can still mean a great deal to every one
of them to have had a variety of authentic musical experiences during their school years. A world of vital interest
and authentic values will be open to them, which otherwise
would probably be forever closed. Music for them will not
be a region of mystery, but a familiar and well-loved realm
—just a normal part of normal life, which is exactly what
it ought to be. They will be able to enjoy it, to understand
it, to talk about it, to think about it, to use it in many and
various ways. And although only a few of them may become amateur performers of high competence, many of
them will lack those deplorable inhibitions which prevent
so many grown-up people from experiencing the pleasure
of participating in music, as well as they can, when opportunity offers. Just possibly some of them may be classroom
teachers like yourself, and then their children too will
benefit from your endeavors! Such things as these really
can be brought to pass. Who can doubt that they are worth
while for you to attempt?

But here a question may arise in your mind. In the illustrations I have given and the comments that I have made
on them, virtually nothing has been said about the building of technical competence—about skills, and habits, and
knowledge. Above all, nothing has been said about music
reading. May not this mean that such work, while enjoyable and attractive for the moment, is devoid of all solid
and lasting values. May it not be yet another case of the
wheat which sprang up quickly overnight, but withered
swiftly away under the heat of the sun?

The answer is that the kind of musical activities and experiences which have been illustrated in this chapter—all
of them taken from the work of classroom teachers, all of
them exemplifying what is possible for you—are the kind

of activities and experiences that can be counted on both for the present and the future. It is a capital fallacy to think that one provides best for the musical future of a group of children by beginning with an assiduous grounding in the technical fundamentals. What should be done by all means is to sow living seed and to fertilize it, and *technical competence will take care of itself in its own good time.* It is infinitely more important, infinitely more promising for the future, that a child should have an orientation towards music, towards beauty, towards all that they can mean in life, than that he should know ten key signatures or be able to decipher a song in six-eight time. What I hope you will be able to see in all the illustrations I have presented is that they embodied *the initiation and fostering of a process of growth.* There is no better thing that anyone can do, and it is well within your power to accomplish this great good.

9. Finally, music can be a highly effective instrumentality for increasing and enriching the cultural contacts of your children. This is a possibility which is well illustrated in many of the instances already described. Consider how much in the way of historical and social understanding was involved in such an undertaking as the schoolwide music festival at Baltimore, or in the Indian play which had such beneficial effects upon some of the children who shared in creating it. Music is the very reverse of an isolated phenomenon, separated from the general concerns of mankind. On the contrary, it has always arisen under specific circumstances, and has expressed the values and meanings of the social environment in which it has been developed. There is something very intimate and convincing in coming into contact with the life of other times and other places, not merely through an intellectual description, but

by the actual and personal enjoyment of the art forms in general and the music in particular, which were projected out of that life. This makes the music itself more significant, and also it then becomes the vehicle of wider sympathies and more inclusive insights.

In the years before the war I visited a fourth-grade classroom where the children were carrying on a very simple but significant project making use of Czechoslovakian folk music. They explored the material with great interest, chose a list of songs which they particularly enjoyed, wrote them out with great care, and sent them with a jointly developed covering letter to a school in Czechoslovakia, the address of which they had managed to obtain. The children there responded in kind, and a most interesting correspondence was carried on for quite some time. For the American children, and also presumably for the foreign children as well, music itself became more meaningful and, through the agency of music, they gained a rich and very realistic contact with another culture and another way of life and became more cultivated human beings.

Clearly this suggests almost endless possibilities for the use of music. There is a wealth of folk music, both American and foreign, that is available both in printed and recorded form. Through such music children can be brought into intimate touch with many aspects of our own national life, and with life as it has been and is being lived among other peoples. Composed music, too, has of course expressed the values and meanings of the living environment out of which it arose. What is involved in practice is to enable children to understand something of the social and cultural background of the music that they use and, conversely, to introduce appropriate and relevant music freely in connection with units or topics in social studies, history, and so forth. Children can be brought to understand musical backgrounds by the simple method of telling them about such matters, by helping them to carry on research and to make discoveries of their own, or by organizing more ambitious projects such as dramatizations, exhibits, plays, and festivals. Such practices are musically sound, for the reason that music has always been very closely related to human living and becomes far more meaningful when these relationships are apprehended than when it is presented as a sort of disembodied voice arriving from nowhere in particular. And these practices also involve the further educational value of widening children's cultural horizons in a particularly effective and convincing way.

So we have here yet another point in answer to our question, "Why music for your children?" And as always, our answer to this question is full of practical implications and points straight to answers to the question *how*. Some of the more general of these implications I have already indicated, but there are two in particular that deserve special mention.

First it is evident, as I have already suggested, that music can be associated readily and fruitfully with many other subjects, or with the core curriculum or the general program. For instance, if children are studying the westward migration, something quite appreciable is added if they can sing some of the songs that the pioneers actually used. Many classroom teachers do, in fact, make much use of music interspersed incidentally throughout the day, as a comment or interpretation or enrichment of something that comes up in social studies, or reading, or science. When this is done, many of the other potential values of music are also realized. But while such incidental uses are desirable, music itself is quite sufficiently important to have its own rights and its own recognized and respected place in the daily schedule and the program as a whole.

The second implication to which I wish to call your attention is the extraordinary folly of packing the school music program with material manufactured simply to exemplify technical problems. This is like using material made to order to exemplify meter and structure when one proposes to bring poetry to children. A great wealth of music exists, abounding in cultural significance, effective precisely because of its emotional appeal, and excellently suited to the use and enjoyment of children. The time at your disposal is limited. Why choose anything but the best?

## III

So far we have dealt with the question "Why music for your children?" from the standpoint of the children. But the rewards, values, and satisfactions that come to the teacher are also important, as well as those that come to the pupils. So our discussion cannot be complete until we have at least briefly looked at our question from your own point of view and considered how it affects you.

Here at once two fundamental issues arise. Why should *you* take the responsibility for bringing music to your children? And what rewards can you expect, as a person and a teacher, in so doing?

1. It is likely that the first question has already arisen in your mind. Why should *you* be the one to bring music to your children? Is this really your responsibility? Is it not primarily the responsibility of the music specialist?

Let me say with great emphasis that you, rather than the music specialist, should certainly be the prime mover in bringing music to your children, although the specialist will still have an important and indeed essential part to play. This allocation of responsibility is directly implied in the viewpoint presented in this entire book and partly developed in the present chapter. So much will become more and more evident as we proceed; but here and now let me marshal some reasons for insisting that it is first and foremost your job to bring music to your children.

(a) The most obvious reason for this assertion is that the music specialist can make only occasional visits to your classroom. In some classrooms the only music work ever done occurs during these widely spaced visits. You would think this quite absurd in connection with any academic subject. It is just as absurd in connection with music, and perhaps even more so. If all the nine reasons we have developed for bringing music to your children are valid, then it is clear that they should have music as a stimulating and life-giving influence *every day*. It should not be confined even to one special period during the day. It can be continually brought into incidental but very helpful relationships with much that is going on outside the special music period. Musical opportunities, too, can be made available to the children outside school hours, during recess and lunch periods, for instance; and such opportunities are often exceedingly fruitful. No visiting specialist can accomplish all this. The implication of everything that has been said so far is that music is not being properly handled unless you make your classroom a musical classroom, not once a month, not merely sometimes, but always. You alone can do this.

(b) But what if the music specialist, instead of doing all the teaching, lays out work for you to cover until her next visit, indicating standards and suggesting procedures? Will you not have done your duty to your children by doing just as she says? By no means! You will still need to supplement her planning with planning of your own. If you will review the instances I have already cited of musical undertakings carried on by classroom teachers, you will be impressed by their variety and flexibility; and as you reflect upon the numerous additional instances I shall bring before you, this impression will be strengthened. There is no suggestion of a stated amount of ground to be covered in a given time, or of a standard procedure. Everything arises directly out of the human situation and is intimately adapted to it. It is this human situation itself, and the classroom teacher's understanding of it, that determines what is undertaken and how the undertaking is carried through. This is just as it should be, but it is something that the visiting specialist cannot manage. Inevitably she tends to think first of music as a subject, rather than thinking first of this particular group of children, of their needs and proclivities, and of what would be best for them. She sets up what seems a reasonable stint of work to be done and she shows you a standard procedure for doing it. Very likely she handles this procedure very well. Indeed you may find her competence within these limits somewhat dismaying, and feel that, for you, imitation would be hopeless. But the point to which you should cling is that this standard procedure is not oriented either towards your children or towards you. It arises out of certain preconceptions, not out of the immediate human situation. A belief that you ought to imitate it may inhibit you from bringing music to your children at all. But what you can do is to weave music into the fabric of human impulses, tendencies, and needs with which you are in contact every day. This is the proper and successful way of bringing music to your children; and, once again, you are the only one who can accomplish it.

(c) This brings me to the most fundamental and general of all reasons for insisting that music for your children is your responsibility. You are the person charged with their educational welfare—their welfare as human beings —while they are at school. This is directly implied by calling them *your* children. You want to use music to contribute to their welfare, which it certainly can. You want it to yield the nine types of human values which we have already enumerated. Just because you are so close to these children, you can see better than anyone else how music can be made fruitful in their lives in these ways. Music can bring great benefits to your children; and therefore it is your job to see that these benefits are realized, because this job can be done only through the light of your own wisdom, your own human sympathy and understanding.

Before leaving this subject let me remark that nothing I have said implies that the music specialist has no place in the scheme of things. I shall return to this issue again, although the present book is not written for music specialists. Very briefly, what is implied is that the music specialist, properly understood, is a service person or a "resource person." Her job should be to help you to better serve your children, not to tell you what to do on any basis of preconceived ideas.

2. And now we come to the second of our two issues. What rewards and satisfactions can you find, as a person and a teacher, in bringing music to your children? In general, the thing that can come to you from accepting your responsibility in regard to music is a new realization of the true significance of teaching. You will see, perhaps more clearly than you have before, that the effective teacher is not one who "gets across" a stated dose of subject matter in a given time, but rather one who constructively shapes and

moulds other lives. You will find yourself using music as a human influence, rather than an end in itself. You will find yourself bringing music to your children so that they may enjoy it, so that they may be refreshed by it, so that all of them may experience success with it, so that it helps them to a better personal adjustment, so that it helps to create a happy group spirit among them, so that it tends to permeate the whole school, so that it affects their living out of school, so that it influences their future living, so that it extends their cultural horizons. This does not in the least mean that your children will learn nothing of the substance and content or even the technical aspects of music from the undertakings you organize. Strange to say, subject matter is most surely grasped when it is presented in a human setting and in close touch with human needs, rather than systematically and entirely in its own right. You may be surprised to discover how much music your children actually can learn from undertakings organized primarily on a basis of human values. But the amount of music they acquire will not be the yardstick by which you measure your success. On the contrary, your success will be embodied in flesh and blood, and you will see the proof of it in this or that child who has received palpable benefit from the music you have brought to him. And there can be many such living proofs that your work has been worth doing.

Here, then, is the true significance of teaching; and you can come to perceive it very clearly and convincingly in bringing music to your children. Doing this can help you to be a better teacher in every area, and a person who is happier in all her work. For you can experience the thrill of giving something eagerly received and worth receiving, the thrill of new and charming relationships with your children, the thrill of discovering for yourself more and more of the world of beauty you are opening up for them, and possibly too the thrill of a new and well-founded self-confidence in your own powers.

# CHAPTER TWO

# The Right Approach

I

EVERYTHING, HOWEVER, DEPENDS ON THE
right approach. What, then, is the right approach in bringing music to children? This is a question of great practical importance, and one that troubles many a classroom
teacher greatly.

I remember visiting an elementary school where two of
the classroom teachers were trying to do something with
music. There was no music specialist employed by the
school system, so these two teachers were strictly on their
own. The general elementary supervisor told me about
them before we went to the school. She said that they were
doing what they could, but she seriously doubted whether
they were following the right line, and even wondered
whether their efforts amounted to much. So, apparently,
were they. It was quite evident that everybody concerned
was unnerved by my visit.

After I had watched these teachers in action and had an
opportunity to talk with them, the picture clarified itself
in my mind. They were carrying on what is often called
"rhythmics," but what I prefer to call the realization of
music through bodily movement. They made frequent
use of various singing games. There was also a good deal
of listening. These two teachers relied extensively on the
phonograph, because neither of them had more than an

elementary competence at the piano and were quite unsure of themselves when it came to singing. The account of what they were doing was spread before me with much diffidence and numerous apologies. They knew perfectly well that they were not following conventional procedures. Very humbly they pointed out that teaching the syllables and other technicalities of music was beyond their capacity. All they could do was to follow their best instincts. They hoped I might be kind, but they obviously expected me to form a poor opinion of their endeavors. The two teachers themselves and also the elementary supervisor were quite amazed when I waxed enthusiastic, praised their initiative, assured them that they were working in the right direction, and said that all they needed was to keep on following the line that they had taken with greater assurance and more extended resources.

For these two teachers the crucial practical issue was to understand the right approach. They had in their minds a conventional pattern for dealing with music, which is exemplified in many elementary schools all over the country. They lacked the skills necessary to work in this way, and this fact filled them with self-distrust. It was an eye-opener to them to be told that they were getting at music in the right way. I sincerely believe that they were. A good music supervisor could have given them a great deal of help, for they knew very little about materials, for instance, and there were all kinds of things that they could have done but had never thought of trying. But a supervisor who really knew her business—and that means a great deal more than simply possessing a fine repertoire of musical skills— would have confirmed them in the approach they were making on their own initiative.

You may very well feel a considerable sympathy for these

two teachers, for possibly you are in a similar position yourself. You may think your own musical equipment very meager, and feel many doubts about your ability to handle music properly. If this is the case an understanding of the right approach can be a life-saver; for it is not something abstruse and complicated, but a matter of straightforward common sense. Any teacher who does not let herself become bogged down by preconceptions can utilize this approach, for it is simple, direct, and above all, easy to follow. On the other hand, you may be musically very well equipped indeed. Even so, the question of the right approach is crucial, for your musicianship itself can lead you astray. Your danger is that of becoming complicated and technical, when you should be driving straight toward your goal.

## II

The right approach, then, is a crucial issue. But just what do we mean by "right approach"? Let us pause for a moment to make the matter clear.

If you want to go from wherever you happen to live to New York City, the "right approach" is the one that will get you there quickest. So too in teaching, the "right approach" is the one that gets you to your goal with a minimum of detours, wanderings around, and uncertainties. Very well, what goal or goals do you want to reach when you bring music to your children? In our previous chapter we formulated nine reasons why your children ought to have music as part of their school experience. We discovered nine types of benefits which they could gain from music. Obviously, then, these are your goals; these are the benefits which you hope will accrue from your efforts. So the "right approach" in dealing with music is the one that reaches these goals with a minimum of lost motion, and that assures these nine benefits to the largest possible number of children. It is as simple as that—a matter of straightforward common sense, as I have already said. The answer to our question about the nature of the right approach does not need to be dressed up in complicated educational jargon. It is something that any intelligent person can understand or, for the matter of that, figure out for himself if he stops to think about it.

In order to refresh your memory, let me list in brief and summary form the nine benefits that children can get from music. Here they are!

1. Through music children can discover possibilities for noble and rewarding enjoyment.
2. Through music children can experience the refreshing and renewing magic of beauty.
3. Through music children can be helped toward a better personal and emotional adjustment.
4. Through music children can have the stimulating and reassuring experience of significant success.
5. Through music children can be helped to achieve a happy and rewarding group spirit and feeling.
6. Through music the group morale of all the children in the school can be enhanced.
7. Through music children can discover rewarding interests and occupations in their out-of-school living.
8. Through music children can grow towards interests and occupations that will be rewarding in later life.
9. Through music children's cultural horizons can be broadened by means of exceedingly convincing and concrete experiences.

I will ask you to remember that this list of potential

musical benefits is not something laboriously worked out
on a basis of theory. It is not just a pretty educational pipe-
dream. I have seen every one of these benefits in process of
realization in many and many a classroom. They are practically feasible and right down to earth. Also let me call
your attention to one other thing about this list. All the
items on it are what I might call *human* benefits. Nothing
at all is said about musical attainments as such. What I
have tried to do is to summarize the specific and practical
ways in which music can help a child, or for that matter
an older person, to become a better and happier person
within himself and to live a better and more fruitful life.
Quite possibly you may be able to improve upon my list.
I hope you can! You may want to add to it, or to change
the emphasis here and there. But, in making changes, stick
to the same basis, the same criterion. Do not, for instance,
say that one of the great advantages of bringing music to
children is that it enables them to read the notation, or to
play the flute, or anything like that. If you add to my list,
be sure that any additions you make are further *human*
benefits—other contributions music can make for better
living, benefits which perhaps I have omitted.

Let me urge you to have this list of benefits or goals very
clearly and firmly in your mind. Never let it be very far
from your conscious thought, even in the utmost pressure
of your daily doings. It shows you the direction you must
always take. You cannot even begin to be intelligent about
the right approach to music unless you are very clear about
where you are going, any more than you can be intelligent
about the right road to New York unless you are very clear
in your wish to get to New York rather than to some other
place. But once you are clear about your goals, the question of the right approach is well on its way to an answer.

### III

Since the question of the right approach in bringing music to your children is a practical question, any answer that amounts to anything will have to be a concrete answer. I have already presented a number of instances of what classroom teachers are actually doing with music in order to show you why your children too should have music as part of their school experience. I propose to follow the same procedure in this chapter. Many of the instances we have already considered exemplify the right approach very specifically; we shall not forget them. But it seems well to present further evidence. What I propose to do is to gather together a fairly large handful of instances of music work conducted by classroom teachers, to present them *en bloc* without much comment, and then to ask what general guiding principles are exemplified in them. This ought to give us a notion of what the right approach really is, and help us to understand it in a concrete setting. Perhaps, for the sake of clarity and later reference, it may be well to number our illustrations.

1. My first instance is from a one-room, one-teacher, rural school. The teacher was unable to sing (or thought so). She could play the piano, but there was no piano or instrument of any kind in the school building. However there was a big, old-fashioned square piano in the house where the teacher was boarding, which was near the school. Each afternoon for the last period she took the children to her home. She taught many songs by playing them on the piano until the children were able to sing them. In this way a surprisingly large repertoire of songs was built up. These songs were used in the school building for a wide variety of purposes—for singing games, for programs ap-

propriate to seasons and holidays, and so on. In connection
with their health program, the children made up new
verses to familiar tunes. In the spring a festival was organized in the school yard. Parents and townspeople were
invited. The children played singing games, presented
spring songs. Some of them sang duets and solos. These
soloists were chosen by the children themselves, from their
own group. In a little play arising out of geography they
sang folk songs of the countries they were representing. It
was a musical school!

I cannot refrain from one comment before going on.
Common sense, ingenuity, and zeal *can* overcome poor
facilities and lack of musical skills!

2. Children in a first grade in a city elementary school
developed a little unit on community relationships, centering on the idea of getting to school in the morning. As the
sketch began, the child who played the part of "mother"
came out, wearing a long apron over her dress. She woke
her children and asked them to get ready for school. They
had chosen and learned a song telling of washing faces,
brushing teeth, etc., which was sung at this point. Then
they sang a safety song which they had learned, about
being careful of traffic on the way to school. A little traffic
cop with a borrowed badge held up his hands with huge
white cotton gloves to show when to cross the street. He
too sang a safety song. The children next enacted a stop at
a barber shop to enable a "brother" to get a haircut, all of
them singing of how he loved to feel the snip of the scissors.
The barber put a towel around the child's neck and pretended to cut his hair and put on brilliantine, as the child
sang about how much he loved the smell of it. The children went on their way, meeting the postman and the fire-
man and greeting each of them with an appropriate song.

The last stop before school was at the candy shop, which was also hailed in song, and the finale was the arrival at school. All this was planned and carried through under the guidance of the first-grade classroom teacher.

3. For a Lincoln's birthday program, children in the elementary grades dramatized a number of Negro spirituals, including "Deep River" and "Go Down Moses." This was a project which involved the cooperation of several grades and several teachers. In some cases the songs were learned from hearing them played at the piano, in other cases from records, and, in instances where the teacher in charge was able to sing, she taught the material by singing the songs for the children.

4. A Memorial Day program in a certain elementary school furnishes yet another instance of a project involving cooperation among several groups. A committee of pupils representing the groups involved was set up. After some discussion and reporting to and fro, this committee decided to use the topic "Our Defenders." The children collected stories and information about the various branches of the armed services and selected and arranged this material for presentation on the program. They also got information about the official songs of the various branches of the services, found these songs in various song books and in the form of records, where such were available, and learned them for use on the program.

5. A sixth-grade teacher bought a fine album of recordings of *The Nutcracker Suite* by Tchaikowsky and made the records available to her class. The children greatly enjoyed listening to the music, discussing it, and finding some background material bearing upon it. Then they thought it would be a good idea to make cardboard figures to illustrate the various selections in the suite, and to put

these figures around in their classroom. The figures were
made with great care, painted, and proudly displayed.

6. In a fifth grade the teacher asked the children to col-
lect and bring to school interesting information about
South America to supplement the material in their textbooks. As a result a very considerable amount of material
was brought together. There were story books dealing
with South America, records of South American music,
pictures of costumes worn there, descriptions and pictures
of South American dances, and South American songs
notated in various song books. The children undertook to
make a play depicting life in that continent. They wrote
the script by themselves, worked out dances by listening to
records, and learned a number of songs appropriate to the
action of their play.

7. The use of a set of bottles tuned to the scale has
proved exceedingly popular with second graders in another
school. The bottles are filled with varying amounts of
water to regulate their pitch, hung freely on a rack, and
tapped with a dowel stick or a tenpenny nail, or flipped
with the index finger. The children are encouraged to
make up tunes as they play this very simple instrument,
and the teacher jots these tunes down. In doing this she
does not use standard notation, but a simple number system, the bottles being numbered from one to eight in
ascending order of pitch. In the front of the room is an art
easel with thirty or forty sheets of newsprint paper on it.
When the children make up a tune, the teacher jots it
down on one of these sheets; then the children play it, sing
it, and perhaps revise it until it becomes a part of their
permanent "book of creative songs." This song is kept on
display on the easel with the rest of the collection. The
children are very proud of their work and are pleased to

display it to a visitor. At such times the teacher stands in front of the class and turns the newsprint sheets back and forth, while the children make selections for singing and playing.

8. The classroom teacher of this second grade was presenting the song "Bake a Pie." * She used dramatization to build up the impulse to sing freely and expressively. This being her purpose, she was wise enough to give the children a great deal of latitude in deciding on the simple dramatic action to go with the song; she confined herself to making suggestions and doing some steering. When the children sang the song, later, it was very instructive to notice how the interest and enthusiasm, and the sense of participation which the children developed in working out their dramatization, carried over into their singing.

9. In another second grade the song "Hickory-Dickory-Dock" was being used.** This time a little singing game was created by the children. The entire class stood, clasped their hands and let them hang down as indicated in the picture of the clock that illustrates the song in the book. Swinging right and left to the second phrase, they raised their arms to indicate "ran up the clock." With arms still raised, they clapped their hands to the words, "The clock struck one," and lowered their arms to show how "The mouse ran down." Then they returned to swinging the pendulum of the clock, using the motions with which they began the game.

10. A third grade developed quite an elaborate project in connection with *The Nutcracker Suite,* by Tchaikowsky. The teacher had brought the music to them in recorded

---

* *New Music Horizons,* Book 2, page 4. Silver Burdett Company, New York, N. Y.

** *Ibid.,* p. 61.

form shortly before Christmas. She told them one of the stories associated with this suite—that of the little girl who had been given a very funny nutcracker for Christmas, and dreamed that it had come to life and was leading all the other dolls and toys in a gay revel round the tree. The first suggestion made by the children after hearing this story was that they might make a play out of it, but, after starting on this undertaking, they found that they preferred to dance the music. Costumes and dramatizations were planned. With the cooperation of their parents, the children were able to make soldier suits and animal suits, the latter representing as many different kinds of animals as possible. A number of the girls were dressed as dolls from various countries.

All the children in costume were led in procession by Prince Nutcracker, to the music of the march from the suite. Then the girl who had been selected for the part pretended to be wafted off to Arabia, land of deserts, caravans, and camels, where she heard the "Danse Arabe" (another number from the suite). Then the little heroine went on an imaginary trip to China, listened to the "Danse Chinois," and saw strange figures dancing as before, led by Prince Nutcracker. After this she saw the toy flutes she had received on her Christmas tree dancing with the other toys led by Prince Nutcracker. The children thought fairy costumes were most suitable for this flute dance, as all the music here is high and quick. They made flutes which they played as they danced around the other toys to the music of "Mirlitons" (also from the suite). Just before the girl left fairyland, or Dreamland, she arrived at a place where there were many beautiful flowers, and danced with Prince Nutcracker to the "Dance of the Flowers."

From this orchestra recording the children also learned

the sound of the bassoon, the oboe, the clarinet, and the tambourine. Children who were studying some of these instruments brought them to class and demonstrated them.

11. A fifth grade, after attending a children's symphony concert, made two-inch cardboard figures of orchestra players, seated them in the proper order, including the conductor and the concertmaster. The group of small figures covered a table top three feet by four. Then the children gave a concert of the following recorded numbers: *Unfinished Symphony*, first movement (Schubert); *Surprise Symphony*, "Andante" (Haydn); *New World Symphony*, "Largo" (Dvorak).

12. In a Michigan rural school a group of children worked up a little musical program consisting of a piano solo or two, songs sung in unison and in two parts, and a number of folk dances, one of which was a square dance called by one of the children. This program was presented at a number of meetings of the Grange and various church groups, which paid the children for their services and enabled them to buy simple instruments for the use of the school. An interesting practice in some of these rural schools is that of inter-school visits. It may happen that in a school where the teacher is not very competent with music, the group does as much as it is able to do with certain numbers and then goes *en masse* to another school, where there is a teacher who is able to give additional help. These visits have many excellent results, one of them being the eye-opening experience which comes to certain children who had thought they did not like music until they found themselves participating in singing and folk dancing with another group which is musically enthusiastic.*

* I am indebted for this information to Miss Marie A. Adler, Asst. Professor of Music, Michigan State College.

## IV

These twelve instances, along with those previously presented, give us quite a substantial body of material to discuss. There will be many further examples of music work conducted by classroom teachers as we proceed. In what direction do all these described procedures point? Can one discover any *rationale*, any unifying ideas, running through them? Do they exemplify any definable approach to music, any doctrine about how it should be handled, which one can understand and apply? These are the questions to which we now turn.

1. The first thing to see is that all these procedures were organized with reference to the children themselves, and not with reference to any predetermined skills to be learned or items of knowledge to be acquired. The idea was to enlist a specific group of children in rewarding musical activities and experiences. One cannot find anywhere in these procedures even a tacit assumption that all children must learn to read the notation, or to "find their singing voices," or to play an instrument, or that they must memorize certain facts about music. One does, however, find an assumption of a broader kind, i.e., that all children will be helped and benefited if they really come into living contact with music. These procedures are all alike in their attempt to bring about such living contacts.

It may be interesting to check these procedures against the nine benefits, or values, which I have suggested that children may derive from music, and which were discussed at length in the preceding chapter and listed in summary form on page 41. One cannot, of course, bring procedures and values into a tidy one-to-one relationship, because any given good procedure can and will realize many values.

Conversely, too, any one given value may be effectively realized by a great many different teaching procedures. But it is often illuminating to look at a job of teaching and to ask oneself rather specifically just what good it does, what valuable outcomes are likely to arise from it, and what benefits it achieves on behalf of the learners. Let us review some of the instances now before us and ask ourselves these questions.

For a beginning let us take two of the simplest of our described procedures, the eighth and the ninth—the two singing games. One might very well ask whether they have any real importance, any educational significance at all. Are they not merely play-type activities, pleasant enough no doubt but quite trivial? Are they worth copying? Do they deserve serious consideration? The answer is that they aim straight at two, at least, of our basic musical values—enjoyment and group cooperativeness. The children were learning, first, that music is something to be enjoyed normally, naturally, wholeheartedly. This is a lesson well worth learning here and now, in school. There are specific musical reasons for such learning, also; children's willingness and ability to sing depends very much upon self-confidence and enjoyment. So even on quite narrow considerations, the enjoyment cultivated in these two undertakings was well worth cultivating; needless to say, musical enjoyment has far broader and more lasting influences than this. Then, secondly, these children certainly were learning to cooperate happily in a group enterprise. In both cases the teacher gave the children much latitude in choosing what to do. This was sound practice, musically and educationally, since, among other things, it made possible and promoted the experience of cooperation in a significant undertaking. The achievement of these two

values alone would be enough to justify these two undertakings and to make them significant. Further thought on
your part will uncover many other benefits that probably
came from them.

In example number one, that of the enterprising rural
school teacher, most and perhaps all of our nine values may
well have been realized. But the organization of musical
experiences outside school particularly suggests the seventh
value on our list. For it is reasonable to think that the
children were discovering music as something not confined
to school, but as having a real place in out-of-school living.

Instance number seven, again, in which tuned water
bottles were used for the creation of music, is a good example of a situation organized in such a way that many of
the children could experience success and the pride and
pleasure that come with it; and this, of course, is our fourth
value. The plan of inter-school visitation briefly described
in instance number twelve is a good application of the idea
of using music to build schoolwide morale and spirit. So
also the South American unit, described in instance number six, is a good example of the use of music for the
extension of cultural horizons, the ninth benefit in our list
of values.

I find it tempting to continue this discussion of the
relationship between procedures and values indefinitely,
which could easily be done. But I will leave you to fill out
the picture in as much detail as you wish. For I have
probably said enough to clarify the essential point. These
procedures were geared to human beings, human nature,
human values. They were intended to realize these values.
They were justified, educationally significant, and worthy
of all respect in so far as such realization took place. I do
not know, of course, what went on in the minds of the class-

room teachers who did these jobs of work, but it may very well have been something like this: "The shortest distance between two points is a straight line. I want to use music so that it will help my children to become better people and to live better lives. I will set up procedures with this and nothing else in view. This wish will be the controlling factor in my whole approach."

2. The second feature of all these described procedures to which I would like to call your attention is their remarkable variety. They range all the way from simple activities, lasting perhaps for fifteen minutes, to elaborate and highly developed projects running throughout most of the session. And they involve a great many different kinds of musical experiences and doings.

This extreme variety may quite possibly have been the first thing you noticed about them. You may very well have asked, as many teachers certainly would, whether they could all be good, or justifiable, or proper, or valid. And you may have wondered if it would not be necessary to say that this or that one among them was better or worse than others.

I do not think a comparative evaluation of this kind is either proper or possible. Once the unifying and central aim that we have just been discussing is adopted—the aim of using music to help children as human beings—we are immediately let in for an immense variety of procedure. Consider the very elaborate project described in instance number ten. Was this good or bad? To attempt to duplicate it under certain conditions might be very bad indeed. The teacher might not have the time or energy to do a good job. Physical resources might not be available. The people in the community might be uncooperative or even hostile. The children might set up resistances because they were totally unused to such doings. Under such circumstances the project would probably backfire and completely fail to realize any of its potential or intended values. But in the situation where it was actually carried through it was very good indeed, and realized those values excellently. Once again, the children who thrived musically in instance number ten might very well have been bored to death with the far less ambitious project described in instance number five, in which *The Nutcracker Suite* was also used. Or yet once again, the accordion playing described in Chapter One certainly would not be advisable everywhere, but in that particular situation it was a part of the solution of a most difficult problem.

What, then, is the conclusion? Shall we decide that "anything goes"? That anything and everything is all right? No, hardly that! Anything is all right *if it brings your children into fruitful contact with music.* There is the answer! It leads at once to four implications that are of the highest practical importance to you. (*a*) Never let anyone make you think that there is one and only one proper or ideal way of bringing music to children. Do not develop an inferiority complex about *your* way just because it is not stressed in all the textbooks or recommended by all the technicians. (*b*) You can learn a great deal from other teachers and their procedures, from a music specialist who really understands the needs of children, from textbooks that are well organized to help you drive toward the proper goals. You can get ideas, suggestions, hints, some of which you can use now, others of which you may be able to use later. But beware of trying to copy other teachers and other people's procedures in detail. Fine teaching is an extremely personal matter and one teacher's meat may be another teacher's poison. (*c*) The only way of defining a proper procedure is to be sure that it has the proper aim—the aim of using music to help children as human beings. Outside of that, everything depends on such circumstances as the resources of the teacher, the resources, physical and otherwise, of the situation, the proclivities of the children, and so on. (*d*) You may not be able to organize elaborate projects and puts on "big shows." You may not be able to teach the technical aspects of music in a systematic fashion. *But there will always be something you can do musically for your children,* and that something will be worth while both for them and for you. That, perhaps, is the most important of all implications to be drawn from the tremendous variety of the procedures we have been considering.

3. The third distinctive feature of all these undertakings is their essential simplicity and directness. At first sight this may seem like a startling remark. What about instance number ten, the ambitious project based on *The Nutcracker Suite?* What about the schoolwide music festival described in the preceding chapter? Can one call enterprises of this caliber simple and direct? Surely there is a contradiction here.

If any such doubts and questionings assail you, let me remind you that I spoke of the *essential* simplicity of these undertakings. In a certain sense the two instances just mentioned are complicated, elaborate, ambitious, and hard to organize and manage. But essentially—that is to say, with reference to the aims to be achieved—they are simple and direct. Perhaps I can best make this clear by presenting a comparison. I have before me a course of study in music prepared by the music staff of a medium-sized city. The people who developed it started off with a general statement of aims or objectives. These aims and objectives are, at least in part, not dissimilar to those discussed in our

previous chapter and briefly listed in this one, although
they are a good deal less specific. There are some important divergences. For instance, the makers of the course
of study thought that music should be used to train children's minds, a proposition about which I would have
very grave misgivings. In the main, however, the emphasis
was consistent with that advocated here, namely that music
should contribute to personal fulfillment and to better
living. Such, then, was the goal which these workers said
they were contemplating. But when one passes on from the
statement of objectives to the body of the document, one
finds that everything is centered upon and subordinated to
the systematic teaching of musical notation. Now this is
what I would call a complicated and indirect approach to
the goal that was contemplated in this course of study. It
is not altogether impossible that a few children might
reach that goal by following such a road. After several
years of effort—and several years of effort were definitely
indicated in the course of study—a small proportion of
them might acquire a really effective reading skill, which
is no doubt a useful possession although not a very common one, even among professional musicians. This reading skill might be the means of opening up music as something to be enjoyed and fruitfully used for these fortunate
few. But even they would have taken a very long way
round to get there, and the great majority would certainly
have fallen by the wayside.

This probably shows you what I mean by simplicity
and directness. If you want children to enjoy music, enable
them to enjoy it here and now. If you want music to be
a means of refreshment to them, make it refreshing immediately. If you want it to contribute to their personal
adjustment, to their group spirit, to their out-of-school liv-

ing, arrange matters so that these things happen right away. So also for all the values we have considered. Do not go on the assumption that children must spend years on a round of rather arid experiences before it is possible for them to have others that are rich and repaying. The time for rich and repaying musical experiences for your children is now, not some time in the future. I should say that the makers of this course of study were like people trying to get from Chicago to New York by heading for Point Barrow. They were certainly choosing a roundabout route. They would certainly run into a great many serious and needless obstacles. And it is at least doubtful whether any of those whom they were guiding would ever reach the goal at all.

All the undertakings we have been considering as illustrations differ in principle and in kind from the course of study I have mentioned, and from many other courses of study in music I have seen. In these undertakings the children were being given rich and repaying musical experiences, directly and obviously embodying the contemplated objectives. The assumption in all of them is that nothing else really matters, and it is a correct assumption, so far as I can see. One can give children a rich and repaying musical experience by having them sing around a square piano. One can do the same by enabling them to work out an elaborate choreography for the "Danse Arabe" in *The Nutcracker Suite*. One is a very unassuming enterprise, whereas the other is very ambitious. But both are essentially direct and simple, because they both drive straight towards the contemplated goals by the shortest possible route.

All this has much practical reassurance for you as a classroom teacher. You may feel that you cannot do the com-

plicated things, the technical things, that are recommended
in numerous courses of study in music. All you can do is
to have children enjoy music, experience its refreshment,
fulfill themselves through its use, find and reveal themselves by means of it. All you can do, in effect, are simple
things. Well, the simple things are the right things, the
important things, the vital things. And these are within
your own capacity.

4. Another important feature of these undertakings is
that they tended to be organized experience-wise rather than
lesson-wise. They were organized, that is to say, not to
impart a stated and predetermined body of content, but to
bring to the children a fruitful and repaying musical experience. This does not mean that they were haphazard, or
slipshod, or extemporized on the spur of the moment. On
the contrary, it must be perfectly evident to every practical
teacher that they all required careful planning, that some
of them called for a great deal of planning, and also that
without such planning they could not have succeeded. But
the way that one plans depends entirely on what one wants
to accomplish. This is, perhaps, a rather obvious statement, but it deserves mention because to many teachers the
very word planning immediately suggests the making of
lesson plans of the conventional and well-known kind. To
be sure, that is how one goes to work if there is a definite
item of content which one wishes to impart. In music such
a definite item might be the dotted quarter note, or the
three-four time signature, or the scale-wise tonal pattern,
or what not. If, on the contrary, one wishes to bring a
convincing and valuable musical experience to one's children, one goes to work quite differently. To provide such
musical experiences was clearly the intention in all these
undertakings; and anyone who reads between the lines can

see that they were carefully and skillfully organized to accomplish this end.

Would it then be true to say that no intrinsic musical content was learned, no musical skills developed, no substantial knowledge acquired? Very evidently the answer is in the negative. Consider, for instance, our third instance in which Negro spirituals were dramatized for a Lincoln's birthday program, or our fourth instance, in which a project was built around the topic "Our Defenders." The primary intention indubitably was to organize convincing and inspiring musical experiences, rather than to teach stated skills or stated knowledge. But those experiences were rich in content. They carried considerable knowledge along with them. And they involved at least the beginnings of vocal skill, for the proper start in all singing is the experience of singing meaningful and expressive words and music with the consciousness that they are meaningful and expressive. Or consider our seventh instance, in which creative work was done largely with the aid of an array of tuned water bottles. Here again the story is the same. The vital element in the situation was the musical experience itself, and it was put in its proper and central place. But the children could hardly help learning a good deal about music, almost unconsciously, because it was necessary to see that the bottles were in tune and that they were arranged on the rack in scalewise order. The fact that these bottles were identified by means of numbers, which was of course a practical device, also pointed directly towards the start of an understanding of musical relationships. So one might go on with a discussion of all the instances that were presented, but enough has been said to make the matter clear. Almost any rich musical experience will lead children to learn something of

the subject-matter content of music. One does not organize
the experience for the sake of the content, but for the sake
of the children. But one does bring in the content as a
normal and natural element in the experience.

5. Yet another point to which attention should be called
is the musical quality of the experiences around which
these undertakings were organized. In almost every case
it is clear that the music used was *good music*. (One might
have a slight misgiving about the safety songs mentioned in
instance number two.)

The statement that good music was used in these undertakings may strike you as suspiciously like metaphysics.
What is "good music," you may very well ask? How does it
differ from "bad music"? Does not the concept "good
music" inevitably plunge us into dubious theorizing which
can have no possible practical point? Not in the least! By
"good music" I simply mean expressive music, poetic music
—music with a charm and a life of its own. In one of these
undertakings we found the children using the little song
"Bake a Pie," and in another they used the Mother Goose
song, "Hickory-Dickory-Dock." In one of the undertakings
described in the preceding chapter, the children learned to
sing "Little Johnny Chickadee." No one can call these examples of great music. But they are all good because they
are expressive, because they have a real charm of their
own, because they "say something." Many cowboy songs,
many folk songs (but by no means all, for many of them
are deadly), many Negro spirituals deserve to be called
"good music," for the simple reason that they have the
spirit of life authentically in them. Music created by children is often good in this genuine sense. As to the relationship of "good music" to what would be considered "great
music," it is this: Mankind has produced an enormous

amount of music which is genuinely and authentically
good. One might think of it as grassroots music. Out of it,
as from a seed-bed, have arisen the great masterpieces. The
difference between grassroots music and the great masterpieces is simply one of degree or intensity, not of kind.
One might say that the masterpiece is music which is very
*very* good. All music which is good in the sense I have
explained is suitable for the educational and human purposes we have been discussing, and this includes music
ranging from the simple song to the supreme masterpiece.

Bad music, on the other hand, is music manufactured for
a specific purpose instead of being created to express a
poetic feeling. We have so-called music which is made
for the sake of advertising commercial products, or helping people to remember facts, or teaching specific lessons
about safety and health and things to do around the home.
The trouble is that such music is not expressive, not significant artistically. The same is true of musical material
constructed to give drill on technical problems, or on the
so-called fundamentals, or on note-reading, and so forth.
Such material is in the nature of an exercise, and should
be so considered. In and of itself it has no direct artistic
value, and is not the kind of stuff to use in activities designed to illuminate the lives of children with the light
of beauty.

Why then do we find "good" (i.e., genuinely expressive)
music constantly used, and "bad" (i.e., uninspired) music
eschewed in the undertakings we have been considering?
Surely the reason is obvious. Only good music can provide
convincing, inspiring, and fruitful musical experiences.
Bad music cannot be used to achieve the contemplated
goals. No one can enjoy it, because it is not enjoyable.
No one can be refreshed by it, because it is not refreshing.

It is not likely to enable all children to have the experience of success, because it does not inspire anyone to succeed with it. It does not help children towards a better personal adjustment, because it lacks "pull" and "lift." It cannot do much to promote group spirit, because there is not much spirit about it. It cannot permeate the life of the school, because it has no life of its own. It will not be used out of school, because nobody wants to use it. It will not tend to make future living more musical, because the quicker it is forgotten the better. And although it may contain a cultural content, it contains it in a peculiarly dull and lesson-wise carapace.

These are excellent reasons for avoiding bad, manufactured music. There are two reasons why it is rather widely used. The first reason is that it is well suited to a lesson-wise organization, though thoroughly unsuited to an experience-wise organization. A song (really a disguised exercise) designed to teach the dotted quarter note, or some fact about vitamins in milk, may seem a very happy choice if you want to teach the dotted quarter note or the vitamin content of milk. The use of jingles for such purposes is a centuries-old pedagogical practice. In these latter days it has come to light once again in the singing commercial, which is also very bad music and very bad poetry. Many teachers are afraid of experience, because one cannot always pin down the valuable outcomes which are derived from it. So they cling to the lesson-wise organization. Hence the wide use of much bad music. The second reason for the extensive use of such music in our schools is that for the most part it is very easy. Music concocted for special purposes may seem to be very easy, but there is plenty of charming music that is also easy. In one real sense, indeed, good and appealing music tends to be

easier than made-to-order stuff, because it carries within
itself an incentive to achieve.

How can you tell good music from bad music? This is
a real poser, and, to be frank, I cannot present you with
any neat formula. I assure you, however, that you most
certainly can tell the difference. If you went to a piano
recital and heard nothing but Czerny studies, you would
probably not be very much pleased. You would find it dull,
stupid, boring, no matter how amazing the acrobatics of
the performer. That is just about the answer to our question. You have to rely upon your own emotional reaction
to a piece of music. Also you can learn a great deal from
the reactions of other people, and especially those of your
children. You will not make a right judgment every time;
but after all one makes mistakes sometimes even in arithmetic. You may not always be able to explain the reasons
for your choice in philosophic terms. But to say that you
cannot in general pretty well tell the difference between
good and bad music is simply silly. For the distinction I
have drawn comes down to simply this: Good music is
music that a person can love; bad music no one can love.

A great deal more could be said about the choice of
suitable music for your children. Involved in this, also, is
the problem of jazz, of swing, of popular music, of classical
music. I shall return to this subject later on, after we have
discussed a number of other matters. For the time being
I leave it as it now stands.

6. It is important to realize that in all these instances
of music work conducted by classroom teachers which I
have presented, the teachers involved had persisted in the
right approach for a considerable time. This is shown
quite clearly in the first example cited in our opening
chapter, where the children responded to music without

any instruction or directions of any kind from the teacher.
They had become accustomed to so doing. It had become
the tradition of the classroom to show initiative, responsiveness, and freedom. What I saw there, with some surprise, was the outcome of a process of growth that had
been going on for several months.

This build-up, this process of steady growth, this increasingly sure and effective adjustment is altogether necessary. So much should be very obvious. You cannot possibly
expect the ideal approach to reveal all its values and potentialities in a day or a week. You yourself need to accumu-
late confidence and "know-how." The children need to
achieve an accommodation. At first some of them may
hesitate to express themselves in song or in rhythmic
movement; they may be shy about trying out simple
instruments; invitations to listen may be awkwardly received; suggestions to create may produce only a blank
look. Attitudes have to be established and this takes time.
I shall return to this problem when we discuss the fulfillment of your musical purposes to have your children
realize music in movement, listen to it, sing it, play it,
and create it. For the moment I mention it only to put
you on your guard against premature disappointment. Do
not expect too much too soon. In the nature of things,
any goal becomes more visible as one gets closer to it. And
if you commit yourself to the right approach, you will
find that it goes steadily better and better as both you and
your children discover how to deal with it.

## V

The right approach in bringing music to your children
is to aim always at human values, to vary your procedures
in accordance with your situation and to be confident in

so doing, to be quite sure that your procedures are directly and simply associated with your aims, to think and plan in terms of musical experiences rather than of music lessons, to be sensitive to the intrinsic musical quality of those experiences, and to persist in spite of early difficulties and partial frustrations.

Now let us contrast this with the wrong approach— an approach, however, which is widely recommended and frequently accepted as "standard" and proper. This contrast can be drawn quite briefly.

1. The standard but wrong approach centers chiefly upon musical notation and upon music reading, although there is usually some fine talk about musical values and human values. Nothing realistic, however, is done to promote and achieve such values. This is a radical falsification at the start.

2. The standard but wrong approach sets up a sequence of notational problems as the essential content. This essential content is usually interlarded with some listening experiences, usually spoken of as "appreciation lessons." Such a use of the word "appreciation" is highly significant. Apparently the essential content has nothing to do with appreciation. Usually this is all too true. What is called "creative music" is recommended primarily because it helps to teach the notation, which is a perversion of the first magnitude. Song material is chosen for the sake of exemplifying notational problems and therefore tends to be very deadly. Much is made of certain devices for the teaching of notational concepts, the best known being the famous syllables. Devotees of this approach sometimes get into quite violent quarrels about whether to use syllables, numbers, or some other device. Here is an admirable instance of a completely futile educational wrangle. The point is

that one ought to center everything on authentic and repaying musical experience, so that the choice between these
various devices becomes almost meaningless.

3. Devotees of the standard but wrong approach undertake to teach a selected set of so-called "tonal patterns"
which are supposed to constitute a basic "musical vocabulary." Songs are selected because they embody these "tonal
patterns," and children are not to be allowed to "create"
until they have acquired a sufficient "musical vocabulary."
Again we have a travesty of what the creative process really
means. This wrong approach assumes that children who
have been hearing music almost since the day they were
born have no "musical vocabulary" at all by the time they
are six years old, and must be painfully taught music like
a new language before they can be permitted to try to
speak in musical terms.

4. This standard but wrong approach makes a fetish
of singing, particularly of unaccompanied singing and,
more particularly still, of unaccompanied singing unaided
by the teacher. Thus there is created a refractory and indeed
insoluble "problem of individual differences." It is as
though a carpenter should make a number of holes all of
the same size for dowel pins of different sizes, and then
rant about the annoying "individual differences" of the
pins. What this extreme vocal fetish actually does is to kill
all chance of success and of happy self-expression for a great
many children. When time for music comes, the children
take special seats with the good singers in the back of the
room and the poor singers in front, in order to spread the
group tone. Children cease to be children and become
canaries, blackbirds, and those blackest of all blackbirds,
monotones. The child who cannot sing is classified as unmusical. This pattern of human and educational outrages

is due entirely to the inveterate worship of unaccompanied, unaided group singing. Strange to say, however, this worship of singing is quite inconsistent with the emphasis upon the notation, for musical notation is far more easily learned on an instrument than by means of the voice.

5. This standard but wrong approach is the source and fount of many disasters. Its prevalence is the chief reason why grade-school music in this country is very far from what it ought to be and might be. Let me here mention five major evils that flow from it.

(a) It does not and cannot promote either musical values or human values, in spite of much fine talk. Musical values cannot be achieved without the consistent use of good music. The human values which music is capable of realizing cannot be achieved unless children have direct and simple experiences with good music, in the sense in which I have defined that term.

(b) The standard but wrong approach does not even approximately achieve its own stated purpose, the teaching of music reading. Exceedingly few sixth-grade children in this country are in fact able to read music, in spite of the efforts made to teach them to do so. We have here one of the most abysmal and complete failures in American education. Surely it is time to change our course!

(c) The standard but wrong approach involves a perverse and extremely narrow use of the musical equipment of the music specialist. Instead of enabling her to devote all her energy and imagination to bringing music, in all its richness, simply and directly to children, she functions as a technician—in effect, an expert do-finder.

(d) The standard but wrong approach inevitably undermines the confidence of the average classroom teacher, because she has not spent years of her life acquiring the narrow and sterile skills it requires. This spells certain disaster, for music can never flourish in the elementary school unless it is carried on by the classroom teachers. The right approach, on the contrary, builds up the confidence of the classroom teacher, because when she adopts it she can see that there are always fruitful things for her to do with music.

(e) The standard but wrong approach continually suggests that music is a holy mystery, a subject apart, something too fine for human nature's daily food, to be understood and handled only by initiates. This is a good way to inflict upon it a ghastly if not a mortal wound, and it happens to be preposterous. The implication of the right approach is that music is a normal part of education and of living, and that the right way to deal with it is also the right way to deal with everything in the school program.

CHAPTER THREE

# Your Musical Resources

I

WHAT IS INVOLVED IN BRINGING MUSIC TO
your children is now becoming reasonably clear. Your children should experience music through expressive bodily movement and dramatization, through listening, through singing, through playing instruments of various kinds, and through creative activities. These five types of experience have been inherent in the numerous instances of procedure which we have already discussed, and we shall find them again and again, in many and various settings, as we go on. These are the five ways, and the only five ways, in which human beings have always dealt with music. Bringing music to your children can only mean organizing for them some or all of these five types of opportunity.

But can you organize them? Have you yourself the musical resources which make this possible? That is the question which we must now consider. In the five chapters following this one I shall deal at some length and in some detail with each of these five types or avenues of musical experience and activity in turn—with expressive bodily movement and dramatization, listening, singing, instrument playing, and creative activities. I shall try to show how you can and should go about promoting and organizing them; and this discussion will naturally bring up the question of what equipment and abilities you will need.

But before embarking on any of these specific discussions it seems well to look at the problem of your musical resources in general, and to make a quick survey of what resources you now have or can readily develop, always with reference to the things you ought to do in bringing music to your children.

I know very well that when I mention expressive bodily movement, listening, singing, instrument playing, and creating, a good many classroom teachers will be inclined to say that it is impossible for them even to attempt to organize some of these five types of opportunity. Some teachers tend to feel at once that they lack the necessary resources. Expressive bodily movement (sometimes called "rhythmics") and listening they believe that they might be able to manage. But how can they teach children to sing when they cannot sing themselves? How can they teach children to play an instrument when they themselves play none? And as for creative work, how can this be handled when they are unable to write down the music that children might suggest? Such questions and doubts are perfectly natural, and at first sight the obstacles they indicate seem to be very formidable. In later chapters I shall hope to show that there are many practical ways of dealing with these obstacles and that in fact all classroom teachers can do far more in promoting these five types of musical experience than they often think possible. But first there is a more general consideration to which I wish to call your attention. This consideration is of the utmost importance. *If you have the right point of view, the right approach in bringing music to your children, then many seeming impossibilities are at once and amazingly transformed into possibilities.*

We saw in the preceding chapter that the great essential

always is to organize rich, convincing, stimulating musical experiences "tailor made" to fit your children's needs and proclivities as human beings. That, and nothing more! How, then, does this bear upon the problem of promoting expressive bodily movement, listening, singing, instrumental playing, and creating? For the moment let us narrow the question down to singing and instrument playing, for these are the activities that cause many classroom teachers to feel the gravest misgivings. As to singing, when you adopt the viewpoint I have indicated, you see at once that what you ought to do is not primarily to teach children to use their voices properly, to develop proper tone and placement, and so forth, though you can do something about even such matters. Instead, the thing you should drive at above all else is to give them the rich experiences that come from singing beautiful and expressive songs, and of doing so with enjoyment. *How* you get them to sing matters far less than the fact that they *do* sing, and that they like to sing; there are plenty of ways of dealing with the problem *how*. Again, mention of instrument playing should not for a moment suggest to your mind anything like giving piano lessons, or flute lessons, or violin lessons. What it does indicate is that your children should have rich and varied experiences with the making of music by mechanical means. There are plenty of pitch-producing mechanisms which are exceedingly easy to master, and yet whose use can be very repaying to children and indeed to many grown-ups as well.

To sum up, the point is that the performance of music by voice or instrument can be a very simple, accessible, direct affair, with technical difficulties reduced to the vanishing point. And yet it can be exceedingly worth while. Men have made music by voice and instrument, and have loved making it and benefited from making it, for countless ages before the concert artist with his impressive technical equipment appeared on the human scene. Musical performance should mean, first and foremost, not technical expertness but musical experience. That is what it ought to mean and can mean for your children.

With your mind at ease regarding singing and instrumental playing, the remaining three of our five types of musical activity should not seem so very alarming or difficult. Perhaps the thought of organizing creative work in music may give you a moment's pause if you cannot handle the notation; but as I shall point out before long, there is an entirely feasible solution to that problem. What you should always remember is that in bringing music to your children you should not begin with its technical aspects. You should concentrate on bringing music to them as an experience. It is entirely possible to organize musical experiences in which technical considerations are subordinated, but which are nevertheless significant, rich, convincing, and full of promise for future fruitfulness. This, beyond all question, is the proper policy to adopt in bringing music to your children. This is what you should do when you organize musical experiences through expressive bodily movement, listening, singing, instrument playing, and creation.

These five types or varieties of musical experience, looked at from the point of view just indicated, are in no sense separate specialties, carried on in watertight compartments. This point will be emphasized again and again, as we proceed. Listening, for instance, tends to flow over into expressive movement, and it also provides some of the best of all impulsions to sing. When a song is being sung, there is no reason in the world why some of the children should not accompany it on simple instruments, or why others of them should not dance. And as for creative activity, it can and should mean the composition of melodies, but also beyond this it can and should influence everything you do with music and with children. Expressive bodily movement, listening, singing, instrument playing, and creation are not to be considered and taught as ends in themselves. Instead they should be viewed as five means of achieving one great end—the organizing of convincing musical experiences which will benefit your children as human beings.

I am sure you will immediately see how everything that I have been saying transforms the problem of your musical resources. If you have some musical skills you can put them to good uses, although mere possession of them does not guarantee that you will know what to do with them. But, incomparably, the most important musical resources for doing the kind of work we are contemplating are not in the nature of musical skills at all. For the direct teaching of musical techniques, skills are necessary. But the organizing of musical experiences requires something very different. Some of the resources for this kind of work you already possess, although you may not recognize these resources for what they are. Other resources are directly present in your immediate situation, and all you need to do is to open your eyes and see them there. Still others are very easily available and can be found very readily, once you know where to look. None of the resources necessary for bringing music to your children are inaccessible. The undertaking is within your power.

There are two types of musical resources to be considered in our survey—human resources that can be drawn on and material resources that can be acquired. Let us deal with human resources first.

## II

Among the human resources available to you, in bringing music to your children, are those that exist or can be developed in your situation, and those that exist or can be developed in yourself.

1. A teacher who wishes to do what she can with music is often able to find people both capable of helping her and glad to do so, among her pupils and also among the parents and friends of the school in the community. For instance, I know of several rural school teachers who have enlisted the aid of parents who were able to play the piano or some other instrument, or to sing. These parents did not actually take over the teaching of all music in the school. Instead, the teacher had certain projects and undertakings in mind which she talked over with the interested parent, often gaining some valuable suggestions. The parent then came to school to contribute her musical skill, perhaps as accompanist, or song leader, or by furnishing solo music. As you can readily see, many values can be achieved through such happy arrangements. A cooperative relationship is established with the parent concerned, who gains a better idea of what the teacher is trying to do. And the children are led to feel the importance, and the out-of-school ramifications, of their musical activities when parents lend a hand with these undertakings.

Again, I know of many instances in which classroom teachers have organized the cooperation of individual pupils who were taking music lessons, or who were for one reason or another specially interested in music and in a special position to help with it. A certain fourth-grade teacher who could sing a little, but could not play the piano, got together a small group of accompanists from among her class. She worked with them out of school hours, talked over her plans with them. She aided them and they aided her. For everyone concerned, these were valuable experiences. The children were provided with musical opportunities which come all too rarely to those taking private music lessons, and they definitely developed a feeling of service and responsibility. The same values were involved in an arrangement set up in a rural school where, at the teacher's suggestion, the children elected a music committee. This committee cooperated very actively with the teacher in planning and arranging programs, and in finding suitable materials. Members also assumed considerable leadership from time to time in preparing and rehearsing work that was to be presented at meetings of the Parent Teachers Association and the local Grange.

An enterprising teacher can often enlist the interest and cooperation of local musicians, with very fortunate results. For example, a third-grade teacher talked over her work and plans with the organist of her local church. This gentleman invited her to bring her group to the church, where the children grouped themselves about the console while he explained and demonstrated the working of the organ, answered questions, and played a few selections. They were allowed to manipulate the stops and pistons and to touch the keys. It was a rich and stimulating experience, both in its musical and human values, and produced a profound and lasting impression. In fact there were so many favorable repercussions, and the organist himself enjoyed it all so much, that this visit has become an annual event that is eagerly anticipated.

The widespread interest in recorded music that exists

among children can be a gold mine to any teacher who
wishes to exploit the human resources of her situation.
Considerable embarrassment resulted in an instance I know
of, in which these possibilities were entirely missed. A
boy entered junior high school with a notation on his
cumulative record card to the effect that he was unmusical
and uninterested in music. The notation had been made
by three of his elementary school teachers. But his junior
high school homeroom teacher discovered that he was
an enthusiastic and remarkably discriminating record col-
lector who had a familiarity with music quite amazing
for one his age!

A classroom teacher will find it profitable to discover,
by judicious questions and leading suggestions, whether
any of her children are specially interested in records, and
whether they have collections at home. If so, numerous
opportunities are likely to suggest themselves. Such children can be encouraged to bring favorite records to school
and to demonstrate and explain them. They can be asked
to think of records that might be used for this or that
special occasion, or in connection with this or that topic.
If the question of purchasing records for the classroom or
the school arises, these children can take the lead in discussing it. All such experiences can be very valuable, both
in a musical and a human sense, as you will clearly see if
you stop for a moment to think of the numerous and
many-sided benefits which can come from them. They
excellently exemplify just the kind of thing that bringing
music to children ought to mean and can mean. The only
people who would doubt their far-reaching educational
significance are those who are so completely wedded to a
technical approach to music that nothing else seems to
them substantial or worth while doing in the classroom.

When one thinks of records and recorded music, all sorts of further opportunities for using and exploiting human resources come to mind. For instance, there may be a question of purchasing a phonograph for the classroom or the school. Here is a fine chance to do some very vital and functional music teaching. What kind of phonograph should it be? What should be its acoustical characteristics? What are some of the uses to which it should be put? Very often all the decisions about the phonograph are turned over to some expert, or are made out of hand by some well-meaning committee of donors. Most of these people would be interested in recommendations submitted to them by a class of children, however; particularly if they are led to understand why this was done. Such a procedure opens up all kinds of possibilities for discussing music, musical values, and the music program, both with the clientele of the school and with the children themselves who are directly concerned.

In a considerable and increasing number of schools, nowadays, opportunities for informal listening out of regularly scheduled hours are being provided. One often finds turntables equipped with ear phones in the school library, where children can listen to records without disturbing others. My experience has been that classroom teachers and librarians are much more likely to take the initiative in securing such equipment than are the music specialists, and that principals, classroom teachers, and librarians are much more likely to be aware of its values. This tends to make one wonder a little . . .

If you want to exploit and develop to the full the human resources of your situation, it is very important for you to be willing to *learn along with your children*. Here is one striking instance of what came of such a willingness.

A fifth-grade teacher, with the help both of her children and of the music specialist, developed a far-reaching unit which was finally given the title "The Romance of Bells." This unit suggested itself to the teacher when she saw one of the boys tapping a set of Chinese bells. It got under way before she was able to make any adequate study or preparation of her own, but she learned along with the class. Much background material was found in the book entitled *Bells, Their History, Legends, Making and Uses,* by Satis N. Coleman (Rand McNally Company, Chicago, 1928).

From this and other suggested sources teacher and children learned together that the Chinese were the first to cast bells and that the Chinese and the Japanese held bells in sacred awe. They assembled much interesting material about the christening of bells during the Middle Ages and why mission bells were brought to California. A bell collection was started and many items were borrowed for an exhibit, including a lava bell from Mexico, a real Chinese gong bell, Chinese wind bells, Japanese tea bells, Mission bells, a replica of the Liberty Bell, dinner bells, school bells, cow bells, etc. Bottles, pots, and glasses were assembled, and were found useful in construction work. Poems and books with stories about bells, drums, and percussion instruments were put on the exhibit table. Maps and pictures of countries where bells were used were displayed. Then children began experimenting with all kinds of sound-producing materials,—wood, tin, iron, brass, copper, glass. They noted that the sounds produced by some kinds of material were more pleasing than those from others, and wondered why. They started to make their own bells and in so doing collected and used all sorts of material, including bamboo, flowerpots, bottles of various sorts, glasses, bowls, nail kegs, tin cans, oatmeal boxes, and other kinds.

A new and keener interest arose in rhythm bands, in the school orchestra and the municipal band. Teacher and children together worked out a dramatization of the story "Why The Chimes Rang." In connection with this they were anxious to get a set of chimes, and were for a while at a loss. But the father of one of the children, who was an oil field worker, heard what was going on and brought them some lengths of steel pipe. The children had already discovered the relationship of length to pitch. The pipes were carefully measured and cut. Some of the boys made a wooden frame in the school shop, and one of the girls was able to get some rawhide strips for hanging the pipes. Thus the problem of chimes was solved.

From all this there developed, quite incidentally, a great deal in the way of aural discrimination. This in turn led to an interest in why and how various peoples had their own characteristic types of music, often very different from our own. In connection with some experimentation with glasses, the group found three which produced a minor chord, and on these glasses they composed their first melody. By means of a careful selection of glasses, bottles, and flowerpots they were able to produce the complete major scale. They filled glasses and bottles with water, noting how the character of the container and the depth of the water affected both the pitch and the quality of the tone produced. They listed their observations and conclusions as follows:

1. The size and thickness of a glass or bottle affect its pitch and tone quality.

2. The pitch can be regulated by the amount of water in the glasses or bottles.

3. Pitch is lowered by adding water to the glass or bottle and raised by decreasing the amount of water.

4. Some glasses and bottles will not tune lower, no matter how much water is added.

5. When corks are placed in the bottles, the water does not evaporate and the pitch remains the same.

6. A better tone is given when the glass is struck lightly just below the neck.

7. Tones are softened when the glasses and bottles are placed in soft paper. Felt-covered mallets also produce soft tones.

8. Stickers placed on the glass, at a level even with the water's edge, indicate the point at which the original pitch may be found in case the water evaporates, and help when the glass is refilled. The notes of the scale (*do-re-mi-fa-so-la-ti-do*) or their corresponding numbers (1-2-3-4-5-6-7-8) can be written on the stickers. These can also be placed on the bottom of the glass face upward, as they show through the water. Similar stickers can be placed on the bottles.

Many melodies were played on the bottles, all transposed into the key of C, to which the bottles were tuned, and an original "bottle song" was written. The children tested flowerpots, matching them against the tuning fork, and found one which gave the tone of C.

Later these children all learned that the flute and the organ are outgrowths of the Panpipes. This led to an interest in the woodwind instruments. Members of the school orchestra came to the classroom to play upon and demonstrate instruments of this type. The children made Panpipes out of bamboo and tested them, pitch by pitch, at the piano. Some of them made marimbas in the shop out of redwood, finding that the longer the bar the deeper the tone, that hollowing the underside of the bar deepens the tone still more, and that the tone is softer and more resonant if the wood is shellacked. They also discovered that for best results the bar should be attached to its support at the point of least vibration, and that this could be found by scattering sawdust on the bar, since the sawdust collects at the ends when the bar is tapped, thus indicating the nodal point.*

Here is a striking example of what can happen when a teacher, instead of centralizing everything in her own hands, becomes herself a learner, and behaves like the leader and organizer of a group of learners. The probability that any classroom teacher would be a "ready-made" expert on bells, so to speak, completely primed to develop the original hint out of which this unit grew, is, to put it mildly, quite remote. But an exceedingly interesting and repaying undertaking became possible because this teacher capitalized on the great range of human resources which became available to her when she was willing and glad to learn along with her children.

Such far-reaching, elaborate, and ambitious projects are certainly not feasible in any and every situation. To carry them through, a teacher must have much freedom in controlling the allocation of time, and much understanding cooperation from the school authorities and people in the community, not to speak of plenty of energy and initiative of her own. But the principle of being willing to learn along with one's children, which is involved in extensive undertakings like that just described, is also applicable everywhere, and can be just as fruitfully exemplified in far less spectacular doings.

For instance, while a third-grade teacher was discussing radio programs with her group, the subject of cowboy songs came up. Several of the children had recently been listen-

* This unit is reported in *Music in the Elementary School*, California State Department of Education, Sacramento, California, 1939.

ing to programs of this kind and spoke of them with much interest and enthusiasm. The teacher certainly knew very little about cowboys, their life, or their music, and indeed had never even tried to teach the children to sing, this being an ability in which she thought herself wholly deficient. However, she was willing to follow the trend of discussion wherever it might lead; so when one of the boys revealed, by a casual comment, that he owned a collection of recorded cowboy songs, and when it was suggested that he might bring some of them to school, she encouraged him to do so. The records were brought, played, and enjoyed. Some questions arose about various expressions and references they contained. Neither the teacher nor anyone else knew the answers, but everyone wondered how they might be found. Under the teacher's guidance the group decided to make a search. Books and stories about Western life were referred to. Somebody knew of the record album, *Lore of the West,** which was brought to school also. Much information was discovered in the illustrated booklet which goes with the album. In the course of all these events, the children wanted to learn to sing some of these songs. The teacher, as I say, considered herself strictly a "non-singer," but she was willing to try anything once, and thought that no great harm could be done if the group tried to sing along with the records. The recorded presentation was not ideally suitable for this purpose; but here, as so often happens, the proverb "where there's a will there's a way" was well illustrated, and a number of the songs were learned. As a result of this whole undertaking, everybody, both children and teacher, found out some very interesting things about the West in general and cowboys in particular, and the teacher made the notable discovery

* Victor Y 388: two ten inch records.

that getting her group to sing was by no means the flat impossibility that she had previously supposed.

By way of yet another illustration, a sixth-grade teacher had been using the song "Botany Bay" * with her group. The song had been learned, but the teacher wished to carry forward with a dramatization. She called attention to the picture which appears along with the song in the textbook. The boys in the room "hit the deck" as the picture suggests. One of the biggest boys in the room, who was an accordion player, became a central figure. He sat on a chair with the other boys around him, pushing in and pulling out on his instrument in time to the waltz swing of the song. The whole response was spontaneous and uninhibited, and a very fine interpretation was achieved. The teacher was, in this case, able to sing; but something strikingly valuable was accomplished because she was willing to turn over initiative and leadership to someone able to do something beyond her own capacity.

Consider how much would have been lost if the teachers in the instances I have described had behaved as though they and they alone were the sources of all wisdom and all knowledge, and had refused to venture a single step beyond territories already thoroughly familiar to them. Many exceedingly repaying musical possibilities would have gone by the board. Chances to promote and foster human values in and through musical undertakings would have been missed. And the teachers concerned would never have had experiences certain to enhance their own self-confidence and to give them a new vision of the possibilities and meanings of their work. More and better music, a richer realization of human values, an enhancement of

* *New Music Horizons,* Silver Burdett Company, New York: Book 6. page 8.

your own professional capacities—all these things you can gain by utilizing the human resources of your situation through a willingness to *learn along with your children*.

2. Now let us turn to a consideration of the human resources for the management and organization of music which already exist in you, yourself, or which you can readily develop.

Although technical musical skills are certainly not to be discounted, I would put first of all *imagination in dealing practically with the problem of bringing music to your children*. You know just what you want to do. You want to organize rich, repaying, many-sided musical experiences for and with the children with whom you are dealing, the children whom you know as human beings. You want these experiences to be convincing and stimulating to them. There is not just one way of achieving such a goal; the way that might suit another teacher and another group of children might be quite unsuited to you and your children. There is not just one best way even for you and your own group. There are many good ways and, if you keep your purpose clear and your eyes open and use your imagination, you will keep on discovering them.

It is perfectly possible for you to cultivate imagination about your work, to develop in yourself the ability of thinking of things to do. The chief reason why I have filled this book with so many concrete illustrations is that they tend to stimulate the imagination. I do not present them as examples to be copied, but as suggestions which can start you off on the business of thinking and exploring. This I believe is your most important personal resource as a teacher. So, in effect, a great deal of the material in these pages has to do with the development of an imaginative attack upon the problem of bringing music to your children. But since at this point we are discussing the subject directly, one or two specially selected examples may be both illuminating and helpful.

By way of a start, consider the piano. To the ordinary view a piano is just an instrument on which many people take lessons, and which some people manage to play. I know plenty of good and well-meaning professional musicians whose chief idea in helping classroom teachers with music is to enable them to use the piano as an instrument upon which to play. Now I have not one word to say against piano-playing ability. It can be a very useful resource in bringing music to your children, though with a great many teachers it is nothing of the kind. By all means develop the ability to play the piano if you can. But besides and beyond this, develop the ability to look at the piano with an imaginative eye.

If you do look at it in this way, what are the things you see? Here are some of them, at least. The piano has insides, and these insides are interesting. Your children will probably find them intriguing. They can learn a great deal about music from these insides. There are strings of different lengths and thicknesses. Why? The strings are arranged in three's, two's, and one's. Again why? Hammers jump up and hit the strings and then fall back. The hammers are felt-covered. What happens if the felt gets hard? What happens if we hit a string with a fingernail instead of pressing the key that sets a hammer in motion? What happens if we sweep the strings with a fingernail? If we pluck or hit a stretched piece of wire, does it make a sound like the piano? Why not? What happens inside a piano when the two pedals are used? The piano needs tuning and adjustment from time to time. What can be learned from watching the tuner at his work? What about the keys, both black and white? Surely they suggest a good deal more than technical problems. Is it not possible to use them for experimenting with different pitches? Can one match the tones they produce by singing, or by means of pitches produced by a water glass? Can one make up tunes on the black keys alone, or on the white keys alone? Can you identify the white keys by numbers? Can one write down one's tune by using such numbers, so that another person could play it? Can one discover interesting things that happen when several keys are struck at once? How softly can one play a note? How loudly?

I shall do nothing more than raise these questions, because my purpose is not to describe an array of specific teaching procedures, but to suggest ways of using the piano imaginatively as a means of helping children towards better musical discrimination and musical understanding. If you are interested in such possibilities, you might get hold of the record *Said the Piano to the Harpsichord* * and, after listening to it, put together everything I have said and consider the teaching possibilities presented.

Or again, what of the music that you hear at a motion picture theatre or perhaps at a restaurant which has music "piped in" by Musak? Are there not attractive and feasible possibilities here? Some of your children will have had opportunities to listen to such music. Attention can be called to it. It can be discussed. What effect did it have? Was it suitable or unsuitable? Was it music selected from the standard repertoire? If so, could it be identified and named? Was it specially composed for the film? If so, by whom? Has the composer written any other music? Could any of it be obtained in recorded form, so that you and your children could listen to it and talk about it in school,

* Young People's Record Club 411.

and thus come to understand and appreciate it more fully? Without imagination, "occasional" music (movie music, dinner music, and the like) is no more than one of the frequent experiences of everyday life. But imagination can transform it into a rich and serviceable agency for accomplishing those aims which should be continually before you as you bring music to your children.

The use of imagination as a resource in organizing rewarding and significant musical experiences is an inexhaustible subject, but perhaps these few illustrations, chosen quite haphazardly, may suffice to suggest to you its importance and possibilities, particularly as they are supplemented throughout this book. The imaginative and resourceful teacher can find innumerable musical leads and hints in her daily contacts, in the books she reads, in the other subjects she teaches, in the questions and reactions of her children. Of all the influences which may prevent her from discovering and following such leads, the two most serious are the belief that there is only one set standard, only one "good" plan for the teaching of music, and the belief that no one can handle music fruitfully unless he is possessed of very considerable technical skill.

While an enterprising imagination is by far the most important of your personal resources in bringing music to your children, there is one item of technical or semi-technical equipment which can be very useful to you, and which, fortunately, is easily acquired. This is the ability to write down or "notate" a simple piece of music. For instance, if your children are composing a song of their own, or if they are working out a setting of a familiar song or piece with the use of simple instruments, it can be important to get the results down on paper. Unquestionably the best way of putting music on paper is by means of the regular musical notation. No other system can convey musical intentions so completely and precisely. But much can be done by means of far easier substitutes. In fact, you can accomplish just about all that is really necessary for your own purposes if you notate music by a readily learned number system.*

For the substance of what I am going to suggest I am indebted to the presentation in *The Psaltery Book,* by Satis N. Coleman.** As you might expect, the notational system presented by Mrs. Coleman was created for the instrument about which the book is written, the psaltery, which is a zither-type instrument. However, this method and the symbols it employs can be used quite generally and found practical for classroom use, since the pitches produced by the psaltery correspond exactly to the range of the average singer's voice. The essential idea is to assign numbers as names to the fifteen strings of the psaltery. Thus the scale of C, which begins with middle C on the piano, is called by numbers 1 to 8. The pitches above this central octave are indicated by repeating numbers and underlining them, the pitches below have lines above the numbers.

$$\underline{1}\ \underline{2}\ \underline{3}\ \underline{4}\ \underline{5}$$
$$1\ 2\ 3\ 4\ 5\ 6\ 7\ 8$$
$$5\ 6\ \overline{7}\ \overline{8}$$
$$G\ A\ B\ C\ D\ E\ F\ G\ A\ B\ C\ D\ E\ F\ C$$

* In case this bold and cavalier treatment of that sacred cow, the standard notation, causes you any misgivings, you may be interested to know that many great composers have used their own homemade system of symbols in the preliminary stages of their work.

** *The Psaltery Book* is published as Volume IV of *The Creative Music Series,* John Day Company, New York, 1930, and is also published separately by the Creative Music Studio, 15 Claremont Avenue, New York 27, N.Y., 1928.

This method gives us a symbol or name for each separate note or tone or pitch that children are likely to use. You can, for instance, employ this system for writing down all the notes of the well-known song "Lightly Row." Here are the numerical note-names of the four lines of this song.

```
5 3 3    4 2 2    1 2 3 4 5 5 5
5 3 3    4 2 2    1 3 5 5 3
2 2 2 2 2 3 4    3 3 3 3 3 4 5
5 3 3    4 2 2    1 3 5 5 1
```

If you experiment a little with this plan, you will find that a great deal can be done with it, and that you can use it to make a written record of the notes of many simple songs and pieces.

But you will also find that there are certain important things about the music of even very simple songs and melodies which the system as described up to this point cannot record. One of these important things is what might be called the "swing" of the music. Here is the way in which Mrs. Coleman deals with this factor.

"Different tunes have different ways of swinging," she says.* Once a tune is learned, it is important to get the proper "swing." She advises us that we can tell what kind of "swing" a piece of music has, by listening for the heavy or *accented* notes. It will soon be ascertained that there are both light notes and heavy notes, and that these come at regular places. "Sometimes it is heavy-light, heavy-light, with every other beat accented. Sometimes it is heavy-light-light, with every third beat accented; and sometimes it is heavy-light-light-light, with every fourth beat accented." One must be sure to place the accent in the right

* *The Psaltery Book,* page 13.

place, for it is this accent that tells us what the "pulse" of
the music is. When the accent comes on every other beat,
we know the tune is in "one-two pulse." When it comes on
every third beat, we know the tune is in "one-two-three
pulse," because the beats "go with a one-two-three, one-two-
three swing." Mrs. Coleman suggests trying out these
pulses on one string of the psaltery, but you can do it just
as well by tapping, or perhaps even by singing one note.

Now the question is how to indicate, or write down,
these various types of patterns of pulses. This is done by
introducing vertical lines between the numbers. Thus the
song "Lightly Row," with the pulse-pattern indicated,
would look like this:

```
| 5 3 3 –  | 4 2 2 –  | 1 2 3 4 | 5 5 5 – |
| 5 3 3 –  | 4 2 2    | 1 3 5 5 | 3 – – – |
| 2 2 2 2  | 2 3 4 –  | 3 3 3 3 | 3 4 5 – |
| 5 3 3 –  | 4 2 2 –  | 1 3 5 5 | 1 – – – |
```

The pulse-pattern in this song is "heavy-light-light-light,"
with an accent coming every fourth time, as you can tell
if you sing, hum, or tap it. So, by placing a vertical line
before each accent, to give the eye warning that it is coming, we automatically divide the song into measures, each
with an equal number of pulses, the first accented, the other
three unaccented. One more point needs explaining here.
If you sing or even say the words of the first line, you will
notice that there is an accent on the first syllable of
"lightly" each time it occurs. It goes like this,

Light-ly row, light-ly row!

But in these two measures, or groups of notes or beats,

there are only three and not four separate elements. However, as Mrs. Coleman puts it, there is a rule of music that all measures in a piece have the same number of beats, or else the regular swing would be broken up. But a wait may count as a beat, just as a note may count as a beat. Therefore, in the first two measures or groups of beats in our song, we have drawn a line to indicate that there is a wait which accounts for the fourth element.

These "waits" occur because the notes in most pieces differ not only in pitch, but also in length, and some notes are held for more than one beat. On the other hand sometimes there are two notes to be sung to one beat. This is indicated by putting a circle around the notes to be included in one beat. This has been done with the song "Hush thee, my baby"; the notes which you would encircle, when writing the song, are shown in parentheses, as follows:

```
| 3 (3 2) | 1 1 |  2 2  | (3 2)   1 |
| 5 (5 4) | 3 3 | (2 1)   (2 3) | 1 -
| 3 (3 4) | 5 5 |  6 6  | (5 4)   3 |
| 3 (3 4) | 5 5 |  6 6  |  5 -  |
| 3 (3 2) | 1 1 |  2 2  | (3 2)   1 |
| 5 (5 4) | 3 3 | (2 1)   (2 3) | 1 - |
```

Yet another musical element can be indicated in this notation. To cite Mrs. Coleman once again: "Have you ever sung songs in which an occasional note seemed to come with a kind of jerk? In the first line of 'My country, 'tis of thee,' the two words ' 'tis' and 'of' are a little different in their swing, and do not fill the regular beats as evenly as the other notes do. This break in the regular swing is caused by holding one note longer than usual, and then making up for the lost time by letting the next note pay for it. There is also another place in the first line of this song where this borrowing occurs. In the word 'liberty' the first syllable has more than its regular share of time, and the second syllable has less. In order that this borrowed time may not interfere with the beauty of the rhythm, the first note is allowed to borrow *exactly half* a beat from the next note. This makes the first note a beat-and-a-half long and the next one only half a beat. The way we show this in written music is to put a dot after the first note, and this dot shows that the note is once-and-a-half as long as it would be without the dot. Since the borrowed part (represented by the dot) and the quick note that follows it together make one beat, we will put a circle round the dot and the note, just as we put a circle around two quick notes." * This is how Mrs. Coleman writes the tune that goes with the words "My country! 'tis of thee, Sweet land of liberty."

| 1 1 2 | 7̄ (.1) 2 | 3 3 4 | 3 (.2) 1 |

This notational scheme has its limitations. But for many of your purposes it is quite practical. Indeed, as I shall point out later on, its very limitations offer certain very interesting teaching possibilities and opportunities.

## III

We now turn to consider material resources that are available to you in bringing music to your children. First among such material resources are books of various types, many of which can be very helpful to you. A considerable number of useful and practical books are listed in the selected bibliography, see page 281. But since the array

* *The Psaltery Book,* page 47.

there presented may prove bewildering, I shall call your attention to a few of the items on which you might well make a start, although everything listed in the bibliography is of practical value in one way or another.

1. There are a number of books about music and musicians. Many of them have interest and value for you, and also can be fruitfully used by children in working out units, projects, correlations, dramatizations, and so forth, and in doing research on matters of interest to them.

Consider, for instance, the long list of books written by Opal Wheeler, either as sole author, or in collaboration with Sybil Deucher. Or, to be specific, glance through *Robert Schumann and Mascot Ziff,* by these two authors. This is one of a very successful series of such titles. All of them are well written for children and at the same time offer good, sound content. They lend themselves to the development of plays and dramatizations centering around the personalities of various composers, to the preparation of program notes for class concerts and assembly presentations, and other such purposes.

I should also mention *History Sings,* by Hazel G. Kinscella. This book deals with and presents folk music, popular music, and "standard" music associated with events and epochs in American history. It is illustrated and rich and interesting in content. You may perhaps feel that it is written primarily for you rather than for the children, although the older ones can use and enjoy it. It is obviously valuable in suggesting units, projects, dramatizations, correlations, backgrounds for music, and incidental music in connection with topics in history or social studies.

Or once more, consider such a book as *How Man Made Music* by Fannie R. Buchannan. This is a concrete account of the evolution of music and contains much information about music making in earlier ages. Its treatment makes it suitable for children, but there is much in it for you also.

These, of course, are only scattered suggestions from a very "live" list of titles. I make them simply for the sake of getting you started, and encouraging you to explore.

2. You will find quite a few collections of songs listed in the bibliography. Song books are extremely numerous, and I have not even tried to include all the good ones. But you will do well to familiarize yourself with some of them. This can be a pleasant and revealing experience for you personally, and it will almost certainly lead you to discover excellent teaching material.

Perhaps you have available one of the regular series of school music textbooks. The best of these series can rightly be numbered among the successes of American educational publishing. You should, however, learn to use them with due discrimination. For your purposes the best of these series are those which contain the widest choice of intrinsically interesting and genuinely expressive music—music of true poetic value, which for this reason may be called "good" in the sense explained earlier in these pages. The obvious defect of a great many textbooks is that they are not easily adapted to the approach that we have been recommending here, since they are centered rather exclusively on the aim of teaching children to read. Accordingly such series tend to include a good deal of material which has little or no authentic musical appeal—material "made to order" primarily to exemplify problems connected with the notation. Sometimes, too, they are loaded with material manufactured to fit into units in the social studies or the core program. Such material, as we have already seen, is not well suited to realize the values that you ought to contemplate in bringing music to your children. If you have on hand a set of school music books seriously open to these criticisms, do not let these books dominate your teaching. Do not follow them slavishly. Use them as a source collection for the fulfillment of purposes and plans of your own, made always for the benefit of the children with whom you are dealing. Feel no misgivings about picking out what is really good and appealing, and rely upon your own taste and judgment rather than upon those of an editor who, in the nature of things, can know little or nothing of the needs and proclivities of your particular group of children.

Good textbooks will offer you much good music and also many good ideas. The best of them should be supplemented. You should be familiar with other sources of song material. One of the very best is *American Folk Songs for Children,* by Ruth Crawford Seeger. This is an excellent collection, attractive in format, profusely illustrated. It furnishes interesting discussions of American folk music and its backgrounds and many very helpful and practical suggestions for using such music. The accompaniment problem is very well handled, for the songs can be accompanied on the guitar, the autoharp, the mandolin, the banjo, the accordion, or the harmonica, or by very free and easy chording on the piano. Incidentally, the indexes provided will help you to make the best possible use of the book. A great many of the songs in it are available in recorded form.

Two other good song books, especially suited to the primary grades, are *Songs to Grow On,* by Janet E. Tobitt, and *Sing Mother Goose,* by Opal Wheeler. For the upper grades, there are *Christmas Carols* by Hendrik W. Van Loon and Grace Castagnetta, *Sing for America,* by Opal Wheeler, and *Treasure Chest of World Wide Songs.*

The song books and collections I have just mentioned are by no manner of means the only good ones. But if you will examine these books you will learn something about music and something about teaching, as well as finding the experience enjoyable. You will see at once that the people who edited them had a very simple purpose—to bring together good live songs which would induce the act of singing, and to arrange them so that they could be handled by a person with a very modest technical equipment. This, of course, puts them right in line with your own purposes and situations.

3. Again, if you are interested in enabling your children to experience music through expressive bodily movement and dramatization, you will find much in the bibliography that can be very helpful.

Consider, for instance, *Mother Goose Dances,* by Edith de Nancrede and Gertrude M. Smith. The book contains twenty-four "Mother Goose Dances" and is arranged with the simplest ones first. They are designed to combine singing, dancing, and dramatic expression. Various dance steps are introduced. Costuming with "slight suggestions" as to character is indicated. Easy piano accompaniments are provided. The book is illustrated, and the authors provide good, workable directions.

Yet another such book is *Rhythms and Dances for Elementary School, Grades One to Eight,* by Dorothy LaSalle. It is a large collection of rhythm and dance material, set up grade-wise (although you need not feel it your sacred duty to stick to the indicated grade classification!). Fairly easy piano accompaniments, and good instructions and references are provided.

A book of a somewhat different type is *Sing and Dance; Folk Songs and Dances including American Play-Party*

*Games,* by Beatrice Hunt, with music by Harry R. Wilson. This book contains thirty-eight folk dances and singing games, using much familiar music, a good deal of which is available on records. It is illustrated and contains practical instructions. It is not designed especially for children, but you can benefit by examining it, for much of the material and many suggestions can be adapted, and the book will give you plenty of good ideas.

If you ever wish to do serious research on rhythmics, folk dances, singing games, and the like, by far your best source is *An Index to Folk Dances and Singing Games,* and *An Index to Folk Dances and Singing Games: Supplement.* The former is published by the Minneapolis Public Library and the latter by the American Library Association. Considering that these two items together run to about three hundred pages, you may infer that there is no lack of material on this subject.

One or two comments need to be made about all the publications in this group. In the first place, do not feel bound to follow any of the instructions in detail or to abide by any indicated gradewise order or classification. At first you may feel happier if you stick to the book. But you have not really learned to handle expressive bodily movement properly until you can evoke the movement-patterns from your own children's impulses and responses to the music. Good books can give you ideas in plenty, and ideas are very useful. But do not let even the best book dictate either to you or to your children. Then secondly, remember that you are not teaching graceful, or cute, or spectacular, or skillful bodily movement as such. What you are aiming at is a peculiarly convincing type of musical experience, a peculiarly intimate and potent musical response. This is why such books as *Rhythms for Children,* by Mary S. Shafer, or *Creative Rhythms,* by Rhoda R. Sutton, are definitely limited in value and can even be dangerous, although both contain good suggestions. These two books both present various patterns of rhythmic response to music specially composed for the purpose. But this at once puts the cart before the horse, so far as your work is concerned at least. In your classroom the movement should be for the sake of the music, and it would be a fundamental mistake to supply music for a given pattern of movement.

4. If you are interested in simple musical instruments, their making, playing, uses and potential values, your two best sources are *Creative Music for Children,* by Satis N. Coleman, and *Music in the New School,* by Beatrice Perham. The former book has become somewhat of a classic. It is largely devoted to the making in school and at home of a wide variety of easy-to-play instruments, and this subject is dealt with in a practical and stimulating fashion. The latter book treats, rather intensively, the selection and use of simple instruments, both ready-made and home-made. Both the titles are a trifle misleading, since they suggest something both more extensive and more remote from actual practical school possibilities than is actually presented. Both of them are full of good, concrete, usable ideas, and both embody the viewpoint and approach here recommended.

5. There is an extreme scarcity of so-called professional books on music (i.e. books addressed to teachers on what to do and why and how to do it) which are likely to be helpful to classroom teachers. Almost all such books are directed towards the interests and needs of music specialists, and most of them more or less assume a viewpoint with which classroom teachers may not be in sympathy, and

which few of them can apply in action. For your purposes, perhaps the best of the professional books is *There's Music in Children,* by Emma D. Sheehy. Its content and method of presentation are as charming as its very suggestive title. It is full of insight, wisdom, and practical advice. It offers no cut-and-dried method, but there is much in it to stimulate your own imaginative planning.

## IV

Phonograph records constitute the second major material resource available to you in bringing music to your children. You may perhaps think of records primarily in terms of listening, but they can also serve a great many other purposes. They can encourage singing, stimulate creative activities, provide music for expressive bodily movement and dramatization, in addition to making possible a wide variety of types of listening. In the following chapters I shall have much to say about the use of phonograph records in connection with all such experiences and activities. But here I am presenting a preliminary introductory survey of this very valuable and practical resource, which you cannot afford to ignore.

A noteworthy development in this field has been the extensive commercial production of phonograph records specially designed for children. Such records have achieved a truly striking popularity. Much of the material put out is sheer trash, on the level of comic books at their worst; but a considerable amount of it is excellent. Some of the concerns producing what are, on the whole, superior children's recordings are the Children's Record Guild, the Young People's Record Club, Decca, Allegro, Columbia, and RCA Victor. A selected list of such records, with the addresses of the issuing firms, appears on pages 293-299.

Due in part to the influence of these commercial releases, the publishers of most of the recent school music series have been putting out recordings of the material contained in their books. There are, for instance, record albums to go along with *Our Singing World, The American Singer, Our Singing School,* and *New Music Horizons.*\* Also there is at least one important release of records especially designed for school use, but not associated with any set of books. This is the *RCA Basic Record Library for Elementary Schools.* It consists of twenty-one albums containing eighty-five records, and three hundred and seventy compositions, many of them greatly abbreviated. It is intended for use in listening and singing, and for singing games and rhythm band activities. Included are albums of Christmas songs, Indian songs, and patriotic songs.

In discussing records which you might find useful I have made numerous references in these pages to this *RCA Basic Record Library for Elementary Schools* because it is widely distributed, which means that you may very likely find it available. It is in many ways an excellent collection of materials, but by no means the only good one. Some of the recent school music series have brought out record collections which you will find extremely helpful, and I shall refer to them from time to time; and of course there are many suitable records issued by commercial concerns separately. The point is not specially to recommend one particular set, but simply to give you a definite starting point in exploring this great and valuable resource—something you will find both interesting and repaying not only professionally, but also in terms of your own enjoyment.

\* These are all recent school music series. They are listed, together with publishers and editors, in the bibliography.

The advent of this great and growing body of new material clearly means that new and very practical devices have become available to all teachers, and more particularly for classroom teachers who wish to bring music to their children, but who find themselves deficient in musical skills. But it has a far wider significance than this. Records do not lend themselves to the conventional technical approach to the presentation and organization of music, centering largely upon the notation. They strongly favor an emphasis upon free, enjoyable, significant and varied musical experience, with much group and individual participation of various kinds, and wide contacts with music of authentic expressive appeal. Not all music specialists seem to have realized this as yet. However, one may say with great confidence that, with so much new wine pouring in, the old bottles are in the process of being burst. It is discouraging to note that the recordings of songs of one school music series are accompanied, in one album, by remarkably stilted and pedantic teaching suggestions, which stick as closely as possible to the familiar formula of tonal pattern study. Yet, on the other hand, another of the more recent of these school music record sets presents music carefully chosen to provide a basis for expressive bodily movement, creative and rhythm band activities, and correlation with other subjects of the curriculum, as well as listening and singing with the record. The accompanying teachers handbooks contain detailed suggestions for using all these records in many, fruitful ways. Thus we see some progress.

I suggest that you proceed to make a study of the new resource offered you by records. It might be well to confine yourself to so-called children's records, and to commercial releases only, at least as a beginning. The reasons for these two suggested limitations are purely practical. It is certainly true that you can find good uses for innumerable standard records not specially intended for children. But an examination of some good children's records will give you many ideas about how to choose standard records, and what to do with them.

First try "Hymns for Children," sung by Floyd Sherman with organ accompaniment.* This is a long-playing record. That is to say, it has to be used with a special pick-up, on a turntable revolving 33 times a minute instead of the standard 78 times a minutes. This latter mechanical feature may be a problem for you if you do not have the proper equipment. But long-playing records are here to stay, and if you are going to use this resource, you might as well familiarize yourself with this type of record from the start. Note how well this record lends itself to singing and the direct learning of the hymns which it presents.

Next try "Grandfather's Farm," ** which is a set of songs appropriate to the title, with an interesting and amusing story continuity. It can certainly be used as a "singalong" record, but I introduce it here to suggest other purposes. One of the songs, "Down on Grandfather's Farm" recounts a number of things to be found there—a big gray horse, a woolly sheep, a waddling duck, a red rooster. This sort of song readily suggests the creation of a number of additional stanzas, along with appropriate sound and instrumental effects.*** Also this record introduces a round, using the

* Columbia MJV—65.
** Children's Record Guild CRG 5004.
*** Time and again songs have been used for this purpose by people who were indifferent to the notational problems beloved by educators, but who considered music as something to be freely enjoyed. For instance, in the old West, the famous song "Goodbye Old Paint" was used as the closing music at dances, and the dance went on as long as anyone could think of any more stanzas.

song "Sweetly Sings the Donkey." It is good for listening, and also for imitation. You and your children can develop rounds and sing in parts, and enjoy doing so, if only you refuse to be tripped up by your own fears, but simply go right ahead and do it!

By way of another contrast, try *The Concertina That Crossed the Country.** It consists of authentic songs of early American life, with a continuity dealing with the gold rush days. The songs can be sung, dramatized, accompanied with settings of simple instruments. The material obviously suggests possible correlations.

The record, "Singing Games" ** also will repay your attention. It consists of a number of game songs well sung by Donald Dane, with instructions and suggestions on the envelope (which need not be slavishly followed).

The fourth album of the *New Music Horizons Records**** also features American singing games, including "John the Rabbit," "Pawpaw Patch," and "Tideo." Dance directions are furnished in the manual that accompanies these records, but the manual also suggests how the children can be led to listen to what the music tells them to do and invent dramatizations and games of their own. Similarly, "Let's Play and Sing," **** one of the records in the first album, presents songs about the postman and the ice cream man, giving the children opportunity to dramatize these important persons in their real-life setting and invent their own games. The manual suggests exploring the possibilities of various instruments to discover one suitable for the ice cream man's bell; also a trip into the com-

* Young People's Record Club 414.
** MGM—56.
*** Columbia—Set MJV-79.
**** Columbia—Set MJV-76.

munity to visit the shoemaker and other community helpers as a background for another of the songs in the album, "The Little Shoemaker." On the reverse of this record is "The Little Dustman," a song written by Brahms especially for children, and suited for quiet listening.

The record "Jazz Band" * is also worthy of notice. It is a superior recording giving the history of jazz, and using real New Orleans jazz.

This is a fair scattering of instances, although it by no means exhausts all the available types of good children's records. But it should suffice to get you well started. You can see what kind of material there is, and some of the things that you can do with it. And you can make a beginning in establishing your own criteria for judgment and selection. To repeat, there are many standard records, not specifically for children, which you can certainly use to advantage. Also many of the records which go along with the various series are excellent and suitable for your purposes.

I bring this discussion of records to a close with a few general comments and cautions. It is exceedingly desirable to have at least a fairly good phonograph. Many of the phonographs one hears in classrooms are sadly inadequate, with very small loudspeakers and crude pickups. Many of the children will have far better instruments in their homes. An adequate instrument would probably cost between fifty and a hundred dollars, but it is money well spent, for poor instruments produce a poor sound, no matter how good the record is. It is by all means desirable to train the children in the use and care of the phonograph, including the changing of needles at frequent intervals. The advent of long-playing records, to which I have already

* Young People's Record Club 410.

referred, creates somewhat of a problem. This needed equipment is now on the market at a wide range of prices. But one difficulty in using these records is that it is often almost impossible to bring the needle down at a given point or passage, at times when you do not wish to play the entire record. Also you should be warned that in dealing with records there is often a most annoying problem of availability. The major recording companies, with their strong commercial bias, have not yet developed much feeling of responsibility for seeing that records highly suitable for educational purposes are actually on hand, even when they are listed in the catalog.

CHAPTER FOUR

# Expressive Bodily Movement

I

NOT LONG AGO I SAW A THIRD-GRADE
teacher make a very charming and rewarding use of the
piece called *Country Gardens,* by Percy Grainger. She
introduced the music to the children by saying that she
had a record that she was sure they would all enjoy, after
which she put it on the phonograph and played it. Even
while the children were still in their seats, most of them
began to move in response to the swing and lilt of the
piece; heads and bodies swayed and there were gentle
movements of arms and hands. After playing the record
through once, the teacher said, "I can see that the music
is telling us lots of things to do. Wouldn't you all like to
get up and show just what it says?"

Evidently this was a signal which was well understood,
for the children immediately left their seats and grouped
themselves expectantly in the large open space at one side
of the room. Then the music began again and everyone
got into the swing. Some children were rather inhibited
and did not catch the rhythm very well. Others "realized"
the music more perfectly and completely. It was manifest,
however, that everyone felt free to do what he could. The
teacher made no obvious criticisms and gave no obvious
instructions, but gently and subtly pulled everything
together. "The music is telling us some pretty things to

do with our arms, isn't it?" she would say. Or again, "It
shows us just how to move our feet." The record was
played through three times while the children moved
to it and, while not everyone reached the same level of
achievement, it was unmistakably evident that a better
and fuller musical response was emerging throughout the
group. "I guess you liked that piece, didn't you?" asked the
teacher in conclusion, to which question there was an enthusiastic response. "Maybe it would be a good idea to
come back to it again before too long?" she continued with
a rising inflection, again eliciting nods and yeses. Then she
went on to something else.

This teacher was doing what every teacher ought to do.
She was bringing music to her children *through the experience of expressive bodily movement.* Quite probably,
like many other classroom teachers, you feel that here, at
least, is something that you really can do with music.
Creating opportunities for children to realize music
through bodily movement is quite a popular choice with
many teachers, and a good deal of it goes on in the schools.
In fact it may be your first idea of what to do if you wish
to bring music to your children. For this there are two
reasons.

First of all, you may tell yourself that the creation of
such opportunities calls for no technical musical skill, so
that it is within your own capacities. Secondly, experience
and observation may have taught you that children find
great pleasure and refreshment in moving freely to music,
and that it comes to them as a delightful and beneficial
change after sitting still for quite a while. Many teachers
find these two reasons very convincing, and there is no
doubt that they are excellent reasons as far as they go.

But you may also have the belief, perhaps not fully explicit, that experiences of expressive bodily movement, enjoyable though they may be, are not so very significant. After all, you may be inclined to wonder if there is anything much that the children are learning. Are there not far more important types of musical activity and experience? If you could teach your children how music is put together, or how it is notated, or how to sing with properly produced voices, would you not be doing a far more solid and valuable job? To organize opportunities for free and expressive bodily response to music is something you feel able to do. It is worth doing because it is enjoyable. But surely it does not amount to so very much. Such may quite possibly be your feeling about it.

Let me say emphatically that such humility and self-disparagement are entirely needless. In the first place, it is certainly within your powers to bring to your children a wide and varied range of musical experiences. I have already insisted on this point in general, and I shall hope to give positive proof of it, in a specific way, and with practical applications, in the four chapters that follow this one.

In the second place, experiencing music in and through expressive bodily movement is very far from trivial or insignificant. On the contrary, it is profoundly important and full of rich and far-reaching possibilities. When such experiences are very meager and restricted, or perhaps entirely absent—and this is the state of affairs in many school situations—the whole music program lacks a very vital element. For the matter of that, there are innumerable expert professional musicians who have highly developed technical skills, but whose musicianship is restricted, limited, and warped, simply because they have never known what it is to realize music through free movement. Of course we are not concerned in our classrooms with the preliminary training of professional musicians; but I bring up the point here to show you that when you give your children opportunities to experience music through bodily movement you are doing something that is the reverse of trivial—something that is profoundly important and profoundly right—something that can have a lasting influence upon your children throughout all their lives. So do not think that your preference for this type of activity is but a reflection of your own limitations. It is a type of activity which can be lightly regarded only by people who are musically and emotionally purblind, and who are hide-bound in conventional ideas and ways. It is an activity full of rich and varied potential values. Of this you can rest assured.

But if the experience of realizing music through expressive bodily movement is in fact to yield its rich and varied potential values, you must first know what these values are and, secondly, you must organize the experience itself in such a way that they will accrue. Here we come to the main business of this chapter—the definition of the values and the description and discussion of procedures through which they can be achieved. But before plunging in, there is a question of terminology which is very important, and which ought to be clarified. This question needs to be briefly discussed for two reasons. First, there are a number of terms which have come to be quite widely used in connection with this whole matter of experiencing music through bodily movement. If you do not know what they mean, they may easily cause you needless confusion. Second, it is quite important to avoid wrong or unfortunate terminology and to choose and stick to right terminology, because the wrong words readily suggest doing the wrong things, while the right words tend to suggest doing the right things and doing them in the right fashion. Response to music in and through bodily movement, when it is organized and carried on in a teaching situation, is often called *rhythmics*. This term is not bad, but it is also not so very good. The trouble with it lies in its limited suggestiveness. Bodily movement can express or realize much more in music than what is ordinarily called rhythm. For instance, one can catch and sense the up-and-down movement of melody in particular, or of a musical passage in general, in and through a pattern of bodily motion. Or again, the pattern of response can make the structure clear. For example, one often finds a piece of music put together in what is called an ABA form—that is, there is a beginning section, then a sharply contrasting section, and then a return to the beginning section, perhaps with some modifications. Such a musical structure can be conveyed and felt in bodily movement through effecting a change in the direction or type of movement when the middle section appears, and then by shifting back to the movement-pattern of the opening section when it reappears. Nor is this ABA pattern by any manner of means the only type of musical structure that lends itself to realization in motion. Once again, there can be an expression of mood. Music which is heavy or dull-colored, so to speak, like a dirge, would be felt and expressed by one type of movement, whereas brilliant, brightly colored music, such as a jig or a lively march, would be felt and expressed by another type. Music embodies many such nuances and differences of color or quality, which can certainly be conveyed and experienced in appropriate movement-patterns. Bodily movement can thus embody the mood, an extremely important element of music. Often, too, music may suggest a story or a scene, and obviously this can be projected more or less completely in and through movement. So the term *rhythmics* is much too limited to convey properly what we ought to have in mind.

Again, you may hear the term *eurhythmics* used in connection with bodily movement to music. This word has taken on quite a special meaning. It refers to the specific and highly developed plan devised by Émile Jaques-Dalcroze and taught by him, for many years, at Hellerau in Switzerland. Work in eurhythmics has been introduced into this country and promoted by the Dalcroze School of Music in New York. It is, as I say, quite elaborate and technical and calls for a good deal of special training. When well managed it is splendid and repaying and can yield very remarkable results. But it has never been successfully adapted for use in our American schools on any large scale.

Yet another term, less well known but sometimes used, is *creative dance*. This word is employed by Mrs. Louise Humphreys as a designation for her work in the public schools of Passaic, New Jersey. This work consists of a remarkable sequential plan, running all through the first six grades and beyond, for the realization of music through very free, though organized, bodily movement. What is actually done is admirable. But the term *creative dance* may seem to you somewhat formidable. It may seem to suggest that you have to teach the dance, which of course has many skills and techniques of its own. This is not what Mrs. Humphreys means, nor is it what she does. But the suggestion is implicit in her terminology, nevertheless.

The best term to use in our thinking and planning is *response to, or experience of, music through expressive bodily movement*. It is somewhat long and clumsy, which is a disadvantage. I will not guarantee to use it consistently and exclusively on all occasions. But it conveys precisely what we ought to have in mind, it covers the ground, and it suggests the proper emphasis.

It is possible to set up a fourfold classification of such responses, all of which embody the fundamental tenet of our approach, "Doing what the music tells us to do." There can be *free creative activity*, such as that described in the illustration used to open this chapter. There can be *impersonation* and its more elaborate counterpart, *dramatization*, with responses ranging from very simple extemporized activities, in which a child becomes a policeman, a pony, a leaping deer, or a puffing train, all the way to carefully prepared and elaborate presentations. There is also the use of *fundamental movements*, that is, allowing the children to decide whether the music is best adapted to running, skipping, jumping, or some other pattern of movement common to everyday life. The action of the legs, arms, and trunk, in performing their natural functions, are called fundamental movements.

In addition to these important four responses, there are singing games, folk dances, and square dances, which are special types. These types overlap, sometimes it is impossible to say into which category your classroom activity fits best. But the terms or classifications are not important. What should be stressed is that all these forms have many uses and can achieve many values. However, in considering the values of the whole field of *response to music through expressive bodily movement*, it must be noted that the last-mentioned types place the emphasis upon a more or less stereotyped pattern of movement rather than upon the actual realization of the music, and are thus less useful than the four described first, for building an understanding of what the music says, and what it means.

## II

Experiencing music through expressive bodily move-ment is immensely valuable and important for the follow-ing reasons.

1. Movement is basic in music. Indeed one can even say that music *is movement* embodied and conveyed in the medium of sound. This is an idea which has been empha-sized again and again, and repeated in many forms by many students of the arts.

You can readily convince yourself of the force and truth of this general statement. Select a record and listen to it. Any piece of music will do, though it is best to choose one which you immediately enjoy. Play it to yourself when you are all alone and not likely to be disturbed for some time. Go over it again and again, so that you come more and more to realize just what constitutes the pattern of sound that flows into your ears. Has movement anything to do with what you are hearing? Indeed it has! You will become very sure of this as you proceed. First, perhaps, you notice a recurrent beat, which is apt to start you to swing-ing your foot or tapping your finger. Indeed, since you are all alone with no one to embarrass you, there will prob-ably be a tendency for you to make much larger movements than these as you respond to the beat. But in addition to the beat you will notice that the music constantly rises and falls, sometimes abruptly, sometimes smoothly and gradually. How natural it is to catch this rise and fall with corresponding movements of the limbs and body. Some-times the music moves slowly, sometimes it moves fast, and sometimes its tempo changes. Often you will notice moments when the onward flow of the sound seems to come to a momentary point of rest, after which it resumes again. Sometimes you will notice what can only be called a change in the direction of the flow. Sometimes the music is loud, which seems to call for vigorous and energetic movement. Sometimes it is soft, demanding movement which is gentle and restrained. Sometimes it swells out, sometimes it dies down. So you will come to see that music, in a strange but genuine sense, is the projection of movement in the real sense of the word.

Moreover you will notice that all these patterns of movement, which you come to grasp more and more completely as you go on listening and attending, and which are so naturally associated with actual movements of your own limbs and body, have the effect of establishing a mood. There is the slow beat and heavy motion of a funeral march, the circling sway of a Strauss waltz such as *The Beautiful Blue Danube,* the sharp angular darting motions of some jazz, the upward sweep and downward pleading of a love song. You will find that mood and movement are associated in music and that they are conveyed in endless fascinating variations. It may be that, as you listen to certain pieces of music, scenes or stories will suggest themselves, although with many people this hardly happens at all. If such scenes and stories do arise in your mind, they are almost certain to involve motion—swaying trees, flowing water, drifting clouds, swooping birds, dancing figures, and so forth. And all this imaginary motion will be in keeping with the mood of the music itself.

These things have been noticed from time immemorial. They have been given a place of central importance in the thinking of students who have endeavored to explain the art of music, or at least to analyze the effects it produces on human beings and the reasons for its appeal. You can convince yourself of all this by nothing more elaborate

than quiet, uninhibited, reflective listening. Such thoughtful listening can amount to a very significant and revealing
music lesson, for it can show you the fundamental truth
of the statement that music is the embodiment of movement in the medium of tone.

What I have said points immediately to some very crucial
practical conclusions. In general, responding to music
through expressive bodily movement should be regarded
and treated as a very repaying form of musical participation. The slogan "no appreciation without participation"
is a familiar one, and there is much truth in it. What is
usually meant by participating in music, however, is performance on some standard instrument or with the voice.
But here technical barriers exist. Children and young
people must tread a long and weary road before they can
experience much music through their own playing of the
piano or the violin, or their own solo singing—or so, at
least, it is supposed. And even comparatively advanced
students are so taken up with technical problems that they
often get very little of what could reasonably be called
musical appreciation from their work with any of these
performing media. But in expressive bodily response
purely technical problems almost vanish, and there is a
very direct and intimate contact with the music itself.
Experiences of this kind enable children, and for that
matter adults as well, to enter directly into the music, for
the body itself becomes an expressive instrument.

If this is borne in mind, you can see how opportunities
for the realization of music through bodily movement
ought to be organized and conducted. The controlling
factor in the situation should always be the music itself.
Children should be encouraged and helped to attend to
the music, and to do what it tells them to do in the way

of movement. It is a mistake to dictate stereotyped patterns of action. It is a mistake for the teacher to allow the children to rely primarily on directions or even suggestions from her, although she may often find this a temptation. It is a mistake to pick out one or two children who are doing very well and to use them as models for the others to imitate. This does not mean that the teacher should avoid giving any kind of help. But the help she offers should be for the sake of focusing their attention on the music. It would, for instance, be unfortunate to say, "Notice what Mary does when she comes to those fast notes at the end of the piece." But it would be perfectly legitimate to say, "There were some fast notes at the end of this piece. A few children heard them, and that was nice." * In the one case, attention is drawn to Mary, and in the other to the music.

There are some elements in music's patterns which evoke expressive bodily movement more easily and obviously than others. Most children will respond readily, though with varying degrees of precision, to the mood and to the swing or beat. The problem then becomes one of helping them to recognize subtler elements in the music which are very important, and which contribute so much to its beauty. This can be done by suggestions and well-timed questions, always centering on the music itself. Can we notice places where the music goes faster, where it goes slower, where it climbs up, where it slides down, where it repeats, where something quite different comes in, where it almost stops and then goes on again? "Some of the children are hearing these things, and that's fine!" If you simply tell the chil-

* I owe this illustration to Mrs. Louise Humphreys, who refers to the problem in her pamphlet *Music Contributing to the Education of Children*, Passaic Public Schools, Passaic, N.J., 1948.

dren what to do, they will try to do what you say. But what you should want is for them to do what *the music* says.

They will not all do the same things, but this is just as it should be. Some of them will go much further than others in recognizing and responding to musical subtleties. Indeed, there may well be some in your group who will be able to reveal to you beauties in the music which you yourself have failed to perceive. By all means give such children the fullest possible opportunities for expressive action, by choosing music from time to time which offers delicacies and refinements that can be an inspiration and a challenge to them. (*Clair de lune,* by Claude Debussy, might be an example.) But beware lest the achievement of the few may become the discouragement and frustration of the others. Use plenty of music which all can enjoy and to which all can successfully respond. And do not introduce a star system, in which a few children are held up as models for the emulation, probably hopeless, of all the rest.

You will readily see that it is consistent with this whole point of view to return quite often to music which has been experienced and realized in and through expressive bodily movement. The children listen to it again. By a question or a suggestion you help them to see things in it which were previously unperceived. They penetrate further into its beauties. Their participation becomes more and more discriminating, and their appreciation deeper.

Thus expressive bodily movement can be an extremely fruitful medium for effective contact with music. Those who quite wrongly imagine that a sensitive and discriminating response to musical values and relationships can be achieved only through intellectual analysis, and thus is the special province of only relatively mature and advanced

students, will be astonished to find how far simple and
direct experiences of expressive movement can take children in

> Untwisting all the chains that tie
> The hidden soul of harmony.

2. Because expressive bodily movement is such a natural,
easy, and direct medium for coming into contact with and
participating in music, it has very close affiliations with
listening, singing, and playing.

To begin with listening, contrast the following two
lessons. I once observed a conventional lesson in "music
appreciation" on the *Minute Waltz* of Chopin, as given
to a tenth-grade group. The teacher began by naming the
composer, putting the dates of his birth and death on the
blackboard, and explaining something of his life and his
musical characteristics. Then the waltz was played through,
following which there was an analysis dealing with its
broad ABA structure, its key and chief key changes, its
rhythm, and other matters which one would certainly call
semi-technical at least. There was then a narration of the
story or legend to the effect that this piece is supposed
to portray Mme. George Sand's little dog chasing its tail;
this without much emphasis, however. There were some
questions back and forth. A few illustrative excerpts were
picked out and played. Finally the piece as a whole was
presented once again. I had no certain way of discovering
how effective this lesson may have been, but from the
attitude of the class I judged that most of them did not
get a great deal out of it. But whether or no the lesson was
well suited for a tenth-grade group, it would undoubtedly
have been wide of the mark for young children.

Yet I have seen this very piece presented in a third grade,

where the children had been accustomed for some time past to realize music in and through expressive bodily movement. This was the means by which they took hold of the *Minute Waltz*. One could not for a moment doubt that most if not all of them greatly enjoyed the experience. And it certainly seemed as though a goodly proportion of them responded discriminatingly to every point in the music which had been emphasized in the appreciation lesson, and which may or may not have been grasped by the tenth-graders. Yet the third-graders were given not one word of abstract technical analysis. All they had was the experience of realizing the music in movement, but this was enough to enable them to discover the essential things about it.

It is indubitably true that the association between listening and bodily movement is a natural and fruitful one, particularly for children.* For this is an excellent reason, which is well worth understanding. Listening to music is not done with the ears alone, but with the whole body, or better still, with the whole personality, both mental and physical. So when children can move expressively in the way the music tells them to, their bodies are often being made more aptly responsive to music. Under such circumstances, children can achieve an intuitive understanding out of which technical and intellectual understandings can be developed later on.

In the same way, expressive bodily movement interweaves naturally with singing and playing. Watch children singing spontaneously. They hold no set pose. They do

---

* Here, perhaps, I should anticipate a point to be developed in the following chapter. It would be quite wrong to conclude that children should *always* be expected or urged to move their bodies whenever they listen to music. There are many good ways of listening.

not consciously control their breathing. They make no attempts at correct vocal placement. All such things are later sophistications. Children associate spontaneous singing with movement, with such things as clapping, skipping, walking, bouncing up and down. What we want to do is to guide and refine this natural association between song and movement and to direct it towards musical ends without losing its vitality. Let those who wish to do so sing while they move. Let those who wish to do so simply sit and sing while others move. Do not be disturbed if, while some pattern of movement-realization is going on, some of your group prefer to be quiet onlookers, for the time-being. Try to create situations in which the music can take hold of the child through expressive bodily movement and come out simply and naturally by way of his voice. This at once overcomes some of the chief difficulties connected with singing in school, difficulties which are caused very largely by an inhibiting and formal setting.

To associate the playing of even simple instruments with free and expressive bodily movement obviously involves certain difficulties which are not present with singing. But still there are possibilities too valuable to be ignored. There is no reason why all the children in a group engaged in making music with easy-to-play instruments such as tambourines, rattles, rhythm sticks, triangles, or for that matter recorders or flutophones, should always follow the conventions of the symphony orchestra by remaining glued to their seats. One recalls certain Greek friezes which show such instruments being enthusiastically played by enthusiastic dancers. Surely the marching band need not be the only exemplification in the school system of a peripatetic musicianship!

3. The realization of music through expressive bodily

movement is a medium of musical participation in which
all, or very nearly all, of your children can have the experience of authentic success. As we have already seen, one of
the important reasons for bringing music to your children
is that it can give them the invigorating and encouraging
sense of succeeding, and there is no doubt that success can
come to them through this type of participation. But it
will not come to them automatically or by magic. Situations and opportunities must be properly organized, activities must be rightly guided if this value is to be achieved.
So there are some practical considerations to be discussed.

If you have had any experience at all in organizing
response to music through movement, a certain question
may arise in your mind when I say that such activities
can spell success for the great majority of your children,
if not for all of them. For it will be quite obvious to you
that not all of the children do equally well. Some of them
will be capable of subtle and beautiful realizations, but
they will grade down from this high level through lesser
degrees of completeness and precision; and you will notice
some who have trouble even in keeping time to the beat.
Individual differences are by no means obliterated and
there is no use shirking the fact. What conclusions are we
to draw? In particular, is it realistic to believe that even
those whose bodily responses seem very inadequate are
still gaining anything that can be called an experience of
success? This question deserves a careful and honest
answer. In dealing with it, the following points are relevant to our discussion.

(a) When you watch some child who is unable even
to keep time precisely to the beat of the music, do not
jump to the conclusion that he is getting nothing at all
from his responses. There is still another factor in the

music which he may be sensing. This is its mood, or feeling, or emotional content. Perhaps he does not catch it as adequately as the child whose bodily responses are beautiful, subtle, and complete, although you cannot be too sure even of this. You can see that he does *not* keep time to the beat; but you cannot be sure that his heart is not responding to the appeal. If he is responding to it, he is having an experience of authentic success, for the appeal of music is its very essence. Do not, therefore, be in any hurry to write him off as a failure.

(b) Remember that you should always be encouraging and helping children to respond *to the music,* each in his own way. You are not requiring them to follow your instructions, in doing which they may obviously succeed or fail. You are not trying to get them to copy other children as models, in doing which once more they may clearly succeed or fail. You wish them to become absorbed in the music, to be carried along by it, to listen to it, to do what it tells them to do. You choose a variety of pieces, some of them easy for everyone to realize more or less completely, others to challenge those children who are able to respond to fine nuance. But even with the latter type of piece, you encourage everybody to do what he can and to feel adequate in so doing. Even so, it is always possible that some will completely fail. But evidently the chances of failure, of a complete breakdown and frustration of response, are greatly reduced.

(c) You should be very careful of the sense in which you use the words "success" and "failure," particularly in your own thinking. You are not trying to get children to succeed in the sense of putting on a show, or making themselves conspicuous, or capturing the admiration of others. The success at which you are aiming is something that goes on inside the child. What a child does may seem awkward, clumsy, poorly timed, and very inadequate. But if he is keenly feeling and deeply enjoying the music which he senses through the free movements of his body, the experience is one of success in the most authentic sense. In talking about such a child teachers will often say that he succeeds "in his own way," or that what he is doing is successful "for him." In so far as this implies a limitation, I would object even to such an interpretation. Such a child may be achieving a true and genuine musical success, which may have the happiest effects both on his immediate adjustment and his later development. Remember that what goes on is a transaction between the child and the music and, if the music is yielding its values, then he is getting what you should want him to get, no matter how awkwardly he moves.

(d) Far and away the most prolific cause of failure in responding to music through expressive bodily movement is inhibition, embarrassment, and the feeling of looking foolish. This feeling may be caused by influences outside the school, by physical awkwardness, and by the self-consciousness that develops as children grow older. In organizing activities in your classroom it is most important to avoid anything that might give rise to inhibition, and to do everything possible to overcome it in children in whom it is present. An important part of solving this difficulty is to steadily encourage children to respond to the music and to do what it tells them to do, each in his own way. Never try to force a hesitating or uncooperating child. Never subject him to humiliation, even by implication, for this is bad for him and bad for everybody else in the room. The response of a group of children to music through expressive bodily movement generates a strong appeal which acts potently on all its members, even those who are hesitant and withdrawn. Let this appeal exercise its influence, which is stronger than any that can be generated by direct instructions from you, although, if you are tactful and understanding, you can often point it up by a word, or a smile, or by getting into the game yourself.

Remember, also, that there is such a factor as psychological momentum. As children become accustomed, over a period of time, to realizing music through expressive movement, inhibitions tend to dissolve and responses become more assured, more adequate, more repaying. In starting these activities with children who are not adjusted to them, it may be wise to begin with somewhat stylized and well-defined patterns of action, such as organized singing games. With older children, organized folk dances or square dances have been found helpful. Indeed such stereotypes need never be abandoned. But do not be wholly satisfied with them. Use them as ways and means of getting the ball rolling. Work steadily towards freedom and individuality in expressive response, for you are not teaching dancing but promoting the realization of music through the medium of the body.

4. Responding to music through expressive bodily movement can do much to foster constructive and desirable relationships within a group of children, because it offers excellent opportunities for winning group appreciation for individuals within the group. While the primary aim should be always a realization of the music, this does not mean that individuals should never be singled out for the attention of the group. In fact it may often be a very fortunate move to give certain children opportunities for demonstrating, as soloists, what the music says to them and how they react to it. Of course the danger is that this may

result in attempts at imitation. Thus it would be a mistake to pick out an individual whose realizations in the medium of movement were outstandingly excellent, to use him as a model, and to intimate directly or indirectly that everyone else should try to do exactly what he does. But a child who is projecting his own musical insights and feelings with manifest enthusiasm and pleasure can be a source of inspiration, encouragement, and suggestion. The rest of the children will glimpse things that can be done. This makes them think of things they themselves might do. Without such stimulus these ideas might never have occurred to them. Moreover an opportunity for solo response can be valuable also for the individual concerned. Such an opportunity can come as a challenge, a stimulus, a recognition that builds self-confidence, and thus be healthy and beneficial. This is particularly true of children who otherwise play a rather obscure and mediocre part in the group, who do not shine elsewhere, and who perhaps feel themselves to be nonentities.

Of course you will not want to turn your soloists into self-conceited stars, or to make anyone else feel hopeless when he compares himself to them. But these misfortunes should be, in large measure, avoidable. When you select children for solo responses, do not intimate that they are doing very much better than others. Simply call on an individual and ask if he would like to show what the music tells him to do while the rest stand or sit and watch. Do not select individuals simply on the basis of their performance. Always consider the personality as a whole. Of course you will not select as soloists children who are so awkward and limited in their responses that they are likely to look foolish in front of the others. But on the other hand, you should not choose simply on the basis of superior grace, or precision, or adequacy of movement displayed. It is well from time to time to let children volunteer for solo responses. By and large one would say that if a child wants to have such an opportunity, if he finds genuine pleasure in it, this is a reason for giving it to him—not a final or decisive reason, to be sure, for there may be other considerations, but a genuine one nevertheless. If you watch carefully you can find out a good deal about your children by noticing who volunteers and who does not. Here, as always, you need to control the situation with tact and insight. Do not let the privileges and pleasures of solo response be monopolized by a few voluble hand-brandishers; and be particularly on the lookout for children who seem to wish for such chances but who are a little slow and backward about pressing their claims.

When it comes to dramatizations, singing games, and the like, rather more in the way of definite organization becomes possible and there can be many opportunities for leadership, followership, and cooperation. Individual children can be given opportunities to work out their own ideas or to choose others to work along with them. In some cases such individuals or small groups can organize a game or a dramatization in which the whole class will participate, although you will usually need to keep in pretty close touch with what goes on, to see that proposals are feasible and clear; otherwise they might lead to general frustration within the group.

What is the general outcome of all this? I hope that the four points I have presented have led you to the conviction that response to music through the medium of expressive bodily movement, far from being a triviality, can be a highly significant experience, rich in both human and musical values. Indeed it is interesting to notice that both human and musical benefits are closely intertwined. Teachers are sometimes brought up against the question "Should we teach children, or should we teach music?" The answer is very clear. We should teach both, and at the same time. We cannot teach music well except in a setting of human fulfillment; and when we teach music as it should be taught, namely in terms of direct, simple and yet convincing experience, then by that very act we make it an instrumentality for human fulfillment. The fundamental objection to the conventional scheme of musical instruction as it appears in many an elementary school classroom is precisely that it establishes a dualism between music as a subject and the child as a human being. When this happens, neither music nor children are well served. But when musical participation through expressive bodily movement is organized and guided as it can and should be, this dualism disappears. Children are led both to self-fulfillment and musical fulfillment in one unitary process. Surely, then, you need feel no misgivings or the need for any apologies when you bring music to your children through such experiences. You need have no sense that, while this may be all that you can do for them, it does not amount to so very much.

### III

Now for a detailed consideration of procedures in organizing response to music through expressive bodily movement. The approach can be through *free creative activity,* through *impersonation,* through *dramatization,* and through the use of *fundamental movements,* as we have seen. These four types of procedure are by no means mutually exclusive. They can be combined, elements of one can be used in another. You do not have to stick to any one of them all the time. Which one of them is best will depend upon the situation and the children, for, like all teaching procedures, they are nothing but tools or instrumentalities for achieving certain goals and realizing certain values.

While good teaching can never be reduced to a routine or a formula, the following rather specific suggestions may give you some practical ideas about what to do in connection with each of these lines of approach.*

1. *Approach by the organization of creative responses.* For the sake of concreteness we will have in mind primarily a first-grade situation, although adaptations can readily be made for other levels. A record very well suited for use in connection with expressive bodily movement in the first grade is the third record in Volume I, "The Rhythm Program," of the *RCA Victor Basic Record Library for Elementary Schools.* This record contains several abbreviated musical selections. We will use it for illustrative purposes.

The first consideration in dealing with the children is the setting of the stage. This can be done by telling them that music is like magic, and that if we listen to it carefully it might tell us to walk, or march, or run, or skip, or even go to sleep. Then announce that you are going to play several short selections, so that the children can listen and decide what activity each different piece might suggest. Impress upon them the need to listen quietly. Then play just enough of each selection on the record so that the children will be able to discover differences in mood and tempo. This should lead to a brief discussion of these

* For the material here presented I am indebted largely to the type-script pamphlet "Fun With Rhythm," prepared by the Division of Music Education of the Philadelphia Public Schools.

pieces and their musical characteristics and differences.

Now play the "Military March." The children listen and are encouraged to begin to move hands, arms, and bodies spontaneously, in time with the rhythm, which in this case is quite easy for them. If the physical conditions of the room make it possible, ask all the children who would like to do what the music tells them to do to find a space in which to dance, so that each child will have enough room to move freely. Then play the selection over and let them respond. Although the music is a march, do not be surprised if some of the children skip instead of walking, or otherwise depart from your expectations. It will probably be a good idea to repeat the selection at least once more, asking everybody to listen carefully and to think whether they can find any new or different things it seems to tell them to do. Still further repetitions may be desirable if the children remain interested. Otherwise shift to the next selection on the record.

If physical conditions make it impossible for all the children who want to participate to do so simultaneously, take a group at a time; but avoid forcing or constraining timid individuals. Those who remain seated may clap out the rhythm, or they may enjoy pretending to play various band instruments, or if rhythm instruments are available these can be used. Perhaps a few of the children might like to take turns as leader of the band, but in choosing them you need to have in mind the considerations previously discussed. It may also be desirable to pick out one or two children to dance for the class. This can help timid and hesitating individuals to see how easy and enjoyable it is to move as the music tells them to move. Take a positive attitude in all your comments and suggestions, in trying to get the children to attend to the music, in helping them to think of things to do, and in building their self-confidence. If some noisiness or rowdyism tends to develop, remind them that everybody needs to be able to hear the music properly.

When you have finished with the "Military March," take up the second selection on the same record, which is "Skipping Theme." Play the selection to them and discuss it with them, asking, for instance, whether they think it is lively or dreamy, fast or slow, and so forth. Proceed with this selection as before. This time you will probably find more self-confidence, easier enjoyment, and a greater variety of free response, since everybody is getting used to the situation.

Another selection on the record is called "Flying Birds." Do not tell the children the title at first. Play the music to them, discuss it with them, and ask if it makes them think of any stories, or whether anybody can suggest a good name for it. You are likely to get quite a variety of ideas here, but there will probably be a good deal of consistency in these ideas. Not all the children may think of birds, but most of them will think of other flying, swooping, swaying or moving things. It may prove interesting to have individuals or groups who have worked out an interpretation present it for the rest to see.

Finally it may be desirable to play all three selections one right after another, with hardly any comment, letting as many children as possible respond. This makes for alertness to changes of mood and tempo. Children enjoy the stimulating challenge of such transitions. You must judge whether this final recapitulation should follow immediately after the third selection, or be postponed until next day.

The realization of music through expressive movement

can often be made more stimulating and interesting for children by the use of a few simple physical properties. Balloons, for instance, supply both color and movement. When attached to a string they can be waved to and fro; when allowed to float freely they can be guided and manipulated by light touches. The use of variously colored scarves, again, makes possible many beautiful extemporized movement-patterns. The scarves can fly freely, float, flutter, whirl, ripple, flap, and trail. In one classroom the children were observed rolling them up like cocoons while the teacher played a drum-roll. Such properties can be exceedingly appealing and often have a striking effect on unresponsive or hesitant children.

Always you should be particularly solicitous of the timid and hesitating child. Do not try to force him to participate. Simply allowing him to watch the other children without embarrassment will often draw him into the activity. Sometimes if you take him quietly by the hand and dance with him, he will gain the self-confidence he needs. Or if you have on hand some simple rhythm instruments, he may eagerly accept the chance to play on one of them and do so with abandon and self-forgetfulness. If this happens, you might perhaps suggest that he become the "leader of the band." What is needed is tact and patience in overcoming his inhibitions, so that he can share in an activity which can do much to help him find himself both personally and musically.

2. *Approach by impersonation.* This does not differ either in intention or in essential emphasis from the foregoing. It simply brings in an added factor, that of "pretending to be" something or somebody. There are many different ways in which impersonation can be organized and guided by the teacher who is sensitive to music.

For instance, you may play a piece of music and ask the children to listen and to decide what animal or thing the music suggests. To be specific, let us take "Nice Doggy! Nice Kitty!" Album II, *New Music Horizons Records,* Columbia MJV-77. The record presents the story of a dog and a cat. Ask the children what this music suggests, of course without telling them the title in advance. Choose a group to demonstrate their idea of how the cat acts and how the dog acts as the song progresses. If possible, arrange matters so that the others will have to guess which animal the performers are pretending to be. Repeat the selection as often as seems desirable, with other presentations by other groups.

An impersonation can be directly suggested by the teacher. You might say, "Let's pretend we're animals at the zoo," or "Let's be animals on the farm." Play a musical selection which seems characteristic of the animal they are going to imitate. Thus you might use "The Elephant," found on the above-mentioned record, asking the children to listen for the elephants in the music and to notice how this music describes their slow, heavy, lumbering walk. The children then pretend they are elephants and move to this music.

In choosing music for bodily response, it is important that the tempo be one that the children can follow without difficulty. If you are able to play the piano, of course, this problem can readily be solved. Avoid the use of records with elaborate instrumentation, which is apt to be distracting for young children.

3. *Dramatization.* There is no sharp dividing line between impersonation and dramatization; the only difference is that in the latter the story element becomes more prominent. Dramatization can be used very effec-

tively in connection with a great many songs. Let the children listen to the song on the record (if it is so presented), and encourage them to sing alone quite freely just as they wish. When they have gained some impression of it, suggest that they might like to act it out. One of numerous ways to handle the situation from that point on would be for the children to choose the characters mentioned in the song, and to sing it while these characters dramatize the story. Or you yourself might tell a story to the class and get the children to select individuals to represent the various characters. Then you might get them to select appropriate music to go with these characters, something that they are likely to enjoy doing, after which the story is acted out while the music is played. Or the children themselves might make up a story to be treated in the way just described.

Dramatization, too, can be used in connection with instrumental music. Tell the children that composers often have a story in mind when they write music. Play the selection "Praeludium," by Jarnefelt, record 3, Volume II, "The Rhythm Program," *RCA Victor Basic Record Library for Elementary Schools*. Ask the children to listen for the story in the music. Develop the story, as heard in the music, with the class. For this you will find suggestions in the front of this album, where the "program" of this piece is explained. Choose children to represent the characters, run through the story first without the music, and then dramatize it with the music.

4. *Utilizing fundamental movements*. Sometimes, in dealing with slow and unresponsive groups, a teacher may find it advisable to emphasize what are often called "fundamental movements," i.e., walking, running, skipping, jumping. (There is no definitive list of such movements.) If

this approach is adopted, the purpose should primarily be to get matters started, and you should work towards more initiative and greater freedom of choice and expression as time goes on.

One way to utilize fundamental movements is for the teacher to have the children walk quietly round the room. When they are seated again she says, "When you were walking, I heard your feet tapping out a rhythm like this," upon which she beats out the rhythm of walking on a tom-tom. Then the children are asked to walk round the room to the tom-tom rhythm. While walking, they may also clap out the rhythm, and it may be possible to have a child play the tom-tom during the activity. Then the teacher asks the children to listen to "some walking music" that she is going to play. A suitable selection is "Amaryllis," by Ghys, which may be found in Volume IV of "The Rhythm Program." After the children have listened to the music, it should be played again while they walk around the room in time to the rhythm. It should be made clear to the children that they must start and stop with the music, and that they must step lightly so that the music can be heard. The activity can be carried further by the use of rhythm instruments, which the children play while they are walking. Finally, certain individuals can be selected to demonstrate as soloists, which may furnish a starting point for more variation and freedom of response among the other members of the class.

Or one can take a piece of music such as the "Military March," already mentioned, play it to the children, and ask them whether it tells them to walk, march, skip, hop, jump, and so forth. When this has been discussed and decided, it may be well to repeat the piece while the children clap, so that it becomes more or less familiar. Then it is repeated, while the children move quietly around the room, using the type of movement that has been indicated.

## IV

It will, no doubt, be quite evident that singing games, folk dances, and square dances can very appropriately be used to provide experience in responding to music through bodily movement. You will find a good deal of material bearing on these topics in the bibliography on page 283, with full instructions about how to proceed. These activities are often greatly enjoyed, and can do much to overcome inhibitions and build self-confidence. Thus they unquestionably have a place in your work. You should, however, remember that since they can lead away from the kind of response with which you should be chiefly concerned, because they tend to place the emphasis upon a more or less stereotyped pattern of movement rather than upon the actual realization of the music, they need to be used with some discrimination, and for intelligently envisaged purposes, and hardly as staple fare in promoting musical participation through the medium of expressive bodily movement.

One way of dealing with this problem is to guide and encourage children in developing singing games of their own, instead of following standard instructions. This was done by a third grade teacher who used the "Weaving Song," which appears on page 97 of Book 3, *New Music Horizons*. The game that was created used the idea of throwing the bobbin shuttle left and right, and the children worked it out with two swings to each measure.

Or again, dance forms can be developed and utilized in the setting of wider projects, dealing for instance with frontier life, or historical episodes, or Indian life. One such undertaking grew up in a third grade as a result of the children's interest in Indians. After they had discovered and read the legend of the Rain Dance, one of them suggested that they might dramatize it. The idea was taken up by the class and, as matters went on, they decided to work towards a final performance to which their parents would be invited. Various dance interpretations were made on composed Indian music, such as "From the Land of the Sky-Blue Water," by Cadman, "By the Waters of Minnetonka," by Lieurance, "From an Indian Lodge," by MacDowell, and from material found in *The Book of Indian Crafts and Indian Lore,* by Julius H. Salomon. Finally they worked out the ceremony of the Rain Dance, with the dancers carrying green boughs in their left hands and rain rattles in their right hands, with which they beat out the rhythm and made rain sounds. The group then transformed itself into an orchestra, using tom-toms and a water drum, all self-made, the only costume being a headdress of paper, colored as a war bonnet. Together they chanted the self-composed chant:

> Send the rain; send the rain;
> Great Spirit, hear our cry.
>   Save our crops; save our crops;
> Rain Gods, oh hear our call;
> Send us the rain! Send us the rain!

# CHAPTER FIVE

# Listening

LET US BEGIN BY LOOKING AT WHAT HAP-
pened in a California classroom:

"Come, boys and girls," said Miss M., the first-grade teacher.
"You have been working hard; let us sit up close together, rest,
and enjoy some music."

The little folk in that "busy bee-hive" room ran to get their
chairs and gather round the teacher. How lovely the music
was! How many happy, funny things it said to them!

The phonograph began to play. Ah, that was familiar.
"Rock-a-bye Baby (RCA Victor record number 22617, also
Basic Record Library E-77). Soon each child was lost in interpreting the music as he saw fit. Some rocked an imaginary
cradle; some played they were trees, and their arms became
the cradles, while others put their cheeks on their hands and
swayed gently back and forth. The music stopped. Johnny
said, very softly, "My baby isn't asleep yet, may we sing the
song?" There was a nod of assent. Then they sang:

"Rock-a-bye baby, on the tree top,
When the wind blows the cradle will rock,
When the bough breaks the cradle will fall,
Down will come baby, cradle, and all."

As the song ended, the tones came more and more softly,
until, at the end, all were sure that the baby was really asleep.

But listen! Other music was being played. As the children

knew, they had freedom to live the music, it was only a moment until the room had a company of stiff-jointed imaginary tin soldiers stepping about to the "March of the Tin Soldiers" (RCA Victor record, number 20399) by Tchaikowsky. (Also E-73, Basic Record Library.)

The music ended and thirty little tin soldiers became boys and girls again, running quietly to their seats.

Miss M. said, "I want you to listen very carefully to see if the next music is about soldiers, church, or fairies." Then came the strains of "The First Noel," quiet and happy but not like marching or dancing. All agreed that it was church music except one child who said that he had never been to church, so did not know. Then they listened to the music once more, sitting up very straight, with their hands on their laps, making believe they were in church.

But what was this picture being shown them? What queer-looking little men! Trolls? Goblins? Brownies? These were the peculiar kind of fairy folk who live underground and often play tricks on people. Miss M. said, "I think our next music will tell you about these little men. If you feel like playing you are trolls or goblins, you may act as the music tells you." "In the Hall of the Mountain King," *Peer Gynt Suite* was heard. Soon most of the children were dancing all kinds of fantastic positions. And how they did enjoy it!

When the music stopped the teacher said, "We should learn how to act when we attend a concert, so I am going to let you listen quietly and courteously to a beautiful piece of music. We must not talk, for the composer is trying to tell us a story through his music. Beethoven's *Minuet in G* (RCA Victor record number 1434) was the selection.

When this was finished Miss M. said, "Now it is almost time for us to go home. Shall we let Janet choose our last piece for today?" Janet said, "I like to play I'm a fairy; may we have the fairy piece?" Miss M. smiled her assent.

The *Fairies' Scherzo,* by Schubert (RCA Victor Basic Record Library E-71) was played. No other sound could be heard.

If the children had been real fairies the room could hardly have been more quiet, and, as the music ended, the "fairies" danced to their seats, happy and alert, with music having become, during that period, so much a part of them, that the impressions received will never be erased throughout all the years to come.*

Many things are conveyed and suggested by this account of an admirably planned and organized musical experience. The first and most obvious of them is the general importance of listening as a fruitful contact with music. When you bring music to your children you wish it to be a source of pleasure and refreshment, an instrumentality which will help towards a better emotional adjustment as individuals, which will tend to create a happy and beneficial morale in your group, which will be an influence for good in their out-of-school living both here and now and later on, and provide a means of enlarging their cultural horizons. One cannot but feel that all these values were tangibly achieved in the organized experience just described. They were brought about primarily by the skillful use of listening. So the first conclusion to be drawn is this: *When you bring music to your children, see that they have varied and fruitful opportunities to listen.*

The second noteworthy point is that a teacher can organize exceedingly rewarding listening experiences without possessing an elaborate equipment of musical skills. This is certainly true. Of course the activities just described took place in the first grade; but comparable activities in the same vein, and with the same general intention, can be conducted also at higher levels by teachers who have

---

* *Music Education in the Elementary School.* California State Department of Education, Sacramento, California, 1939, pp. 80-81.

LISTENING 141

very little specific musical training. Listening opportunities are easy to organize in the specific sense that no formidable technical obstacles stand in the way.

In another sense, however, the organization of fruitful
listening opportunities is a very challenging job, requiring
skill, resourcefulness, and above all an understanding of
children and a recognition of what music can and should do
for them. This is the third point to which attention should
be called, and it is very well exemplified in our described
pattern of classroom activity. It is very clear that this
teacher had no fixed or standard scheme for presenting
what is sometimes called a "listening lesson," or an "appreciation lesson." But equally clearly she had in mind certain purposes, and wanted to bring her children certain
benefits. She wished to give them pleasure. She wished
to give them a refreshing change. She wished to pull them
together as a group. She wished to reveal to them something of the meaning of music as an expressive cultural
medium. She wished to influence their out-of-school behavior. With tact, subtlety, and imagination she adapted
her procedures to these ends, and listening to music was
the primary means that she used. If you ask whether she
was really teaching music, the only possible answer is that
she was indeed teaching it, and in the best possible way;
for in the light of her sympathetic understanding of her
children, she was using music, and more particularly listening to music, to achieve certain clearly envisaged
human values.

So the central question which you or any teacher must
face if you are to organize listening experiences intelligently, and to make them fruitful, is this: "What do you
want your children to get from these experiences?" This
question is highly practical. Indeed it is crucial. This is

because there is no one "proper" procedure, no correct or standard plan of organizing listening experiences. Listening to music can serve a great variety of purposes, and the way in which you organize any listening experience will depend entirely on what purposes you wish to achieve.

At first sight this may seem to make things quite difficult for you. Many teachers are very much pleased to be handed a definite scheme of procedure, laid out step by step, and often feel unhappy or even at a loss when no such scheme is forthcoming. They want to be told just what to do and how and when to do it, partly, perhaps, because of timidity, but also because they are anxious to serve their children as well as possible. This self-distrust is particularly likely to arise in connection with music, which is supposed to be formidable and mysterious. As a matter of fact, however, working in accordance with some fixed scheme never makes for the best and most effective teaching. A teacher should always, first and foremost, be clear in her own mind what she wants to achieve and then consider how best she can achieve it in her own way and with reference to the particular group of children with whom she is dealing. This working principle is true in general, and it applies very directly and beautifully to the organizing of listening experiences for your children. For the truth is that if you are clear about what you want them to get from listening —if, that is to say, you have a good understanding of the *why* of listening—the problem of how to organize and manage listening experiences is much more than half solved for you.

So my main business in this chapter is to deal with the question "What should your children get from listening to music?" and, in the light of whatever answers we can find, to consider what you can do to help them get it. But before we come to this, there are two points with which it is most important to deal explicitly and emphatically, although much that has already been said bears on them.

First, *do not think of listening to music in terms of music appreciation.* This is a very common way of thinking, but also a very bad one. There are three fatal objections to it. (*a*) If we are going to talk about music appreciation at all (and it is a far more dubious concept than people ordinarily realize), then obviously people can and should "appreciate" music in many ways—through singing, through playing, through expressive bodily movement, through creation. There is no reason at all to limit appreciation to listening. (*b*) If we implicitly or explicitly limit appreciation to listening, this carries with it the assumption that singing and playing are primarily technical activities and that any study of the notation we may undertake involves primarily intellectual and technical rather than musical values. No greater or more destructive error is possible, and the fact that it is all too often embodied in practice does not make it a whit less disastrous and indefensible. (*c*) But what of the concept of music appreciation itself? Is it justifiable? Does it properly define our controlling aim? This is the most crucial of the three points I am here raising. If by aiming at music appreciation you mean trying to get your children to like music just for the sake of liking music, then the purpose is misconceived and the concept is invalid. The far deeper goal you should be trying to achieve is to get your children to accept and enjoy music as a beneficial influence in their lives. If this is what you mean by promoting music appreciation, then the aim is correct. And as to listening, it is only one among many means by which you may hope to achieve your purpose in bringing music to children.

Second, *do not think of organizing listening experiences in terms of conducting "appreciation lessons."* There is a fairly well-defined standard scheme for handling so-called "appreciation lessons," which is presented in many books and manuals on the teaching of music and in many courses of study. The emphasis is placed upon the historical setting of the composition, facts about the composer, recognition and explanation of the instruments used, analysis of the structure of the music, and so forth. That is to say, the conventional appreciation lesson is a procedure for teaching a body of content without any realistic consideration of just what good the particular group of children concerned will get out of it as human beings. But for you this latter issue must always be paramount.

You propose to have your children listen to a particular piece of music and to do so in a particular way and with a deliberately selected emphasis. Why? Just what will it do for them? Exactly what good do you hope will come of it? If you cannot answer these questions specifically, if you cannot point to any human values that you have in mind, if all you can say is that the piece is a well-recognized musical composition about which it is important for them to know something, then you will not make listening a vital or a fruitful influence, or indeed an experience worth organizing at all. Yet thousands of teachers present thousands of standard appreciation lessons without even asking themselves these questions, let alone having good and concrete answers to them.

What you have to try to do is to organize music in general, and listening in particular, in a way that aims straight at certain goals and contemplates certain beneficial changes in your children's lives, both now and later on. In aiming at these goals, in seeking to achieve these human values through the instrumentality of listening, you will not be obliged to ignore or reject the kind of material commonly found in conventional appreciation lessons. Historical backgrounds, biographical facts, explanations of instrumental effects and structural characteristics—all such things can be used to serve your purposes. But whereas in the conventional content lesson all this material is like stone in a quarry, you propose to take out this stone and build out of it an edifice in which human life may be better and fuller. You must use material. So much, surely, is superlatively obvious. But you use it, not for its own sake, but for the sake of your children. You use it to inspire, to enlighten, to influence, to reveal.

Now that we have noted these cautions and qualifications, we are ready to proceed with our central question, "What things should your children get from listening to music, and how can you see that they get them?" In a peculiar and special sense this is a baffling question, not because there is so little to say about it, but because there is so much. The values that can come from listening are so numerous and so varied that any attempt at classification is very risky. One is exceedingly apt to leave out considerations of the first importance. We must make the attempt, however, although very likely you will be able to supplement the suggestions I shall put forward.

## II

In the first place you should do everything you can to help your children *discover listening itself*. We are surrounded on all sides by many ready-made, easily available opportunities to experience the pleasure, the refreshment, the manifold potential values of listening to music. With a little energy and initiative, additional opportunities can be created. But a great many people go through the world almost completely unaware of all this. The opportunities are there, but they do not avail themselves of them. I suggest, therefore, that one of the most important things for you to have in mind is to open your children's eyes to the possibilities and rewards of listening, that you should consider this to be one of your principal aims, and that you should direct your procedures straight at it.

To say that you should do everything you can to interest your children in listening is surely a simple, straightforward, sensible proposition. But also it is a very important one. Many people find and always have found listening to music an exceedingly significant, stimulating, and valuable experience. It can bring any person a great wealth of personal pleasure throughout the whole course of his life. It can make the phonograph and the radio valuable instrumentalities for refreshment and enrichment. It can open up many avenues of interest and achievement. For instance, I know plenty of people who have found new friendships and new associations through their enthusiasm for recorded music and the collecting of records. I know children who have taught themselves an amazing amount about the art of music, about acoustics and electronics, about the lives and work of composers, about the background of our American folk songs—all these achievements being touched off by their interest in record collecting. In some of our larger cities one or more of the broadcasting stations specialize in the presentation of fine and varied musical programs, about which they issue booklets and information, as promotional material. Unquestionably these broadcasts exercise a great deal of influence and have impelled many people toward an eager love for music which has literally changed the pattern of all their lives.

I mention all this because it so often happens that listening is not taken very seriously. It tends to be treated as one of the extras, rather than one of the essentials in a substantial program of musical instruction. To be able to find *do,* to be able to read, to know the key signature of F-sharp minor, or the fingering of the clarinet or the transposition of the French horn—these are the kind of things that amount to something. But listening? Its effects do not reveal themselves in any obviously tangible form. One cannot very well mark children on it. One cannot use it for winning contests or putting on shows. It is merely something that people seem to like to do and therefore must be counted among the educational trivialities.

Any such tolerant but supercilious disparagement of listening is in the highest degree fallacious and unrealistic. It turns upon the assumption that no teacher is doing right by a child unless she is trying to cram blocks of content into his head, and marking him on the extent to which they stick there. On the contrary, the teacher's primary business is to use the materials of culture to help the child to better and more complete fulfillment as a person. It follows, therefore, that when you enable a child to discover listening you are doing something which is the reverse of trivial, something of a pre-eminent educational soundness and importance; for that discovery may very well influence the whole of his life for the better.

Your first purpose, then, will be to help your children to discover listening itself. How can this be done? How must you shape up the listening experiences which you organize for your children in order to achieve this aim?

1. First you will shape up and organize listening experiences in your classroom in such a way as to reveal to your children *opportunities for listening.* You will not set

up an orderly sequence of cut-and-dried "appreciation lessons," which always carry with them the subtle but disastrous implication that they are undertakings confined strictly to the school. On the contrary, your thought will be that while the listening experiences going on in your classroom should be valuable and inspiring in themselves as enjoyed in the classroom setting, they should constantly tend to incite and inspire children to explore music outside the classroom and outside the school, and should be designed to show them in a practical way how to go about this business of exploration. Moreover you will not vaguely hope that the music going on in your classroom may have this influence beyond its walls. You will deliberately and consciously plan matters so that the influence you desire is actually brought to bear.

Consider, for instance, how this concerns the use of records for listening. Certainly recorded music should be chosen and presented so as to be enjoyable, stimulating, interesting, significant. But along with all this, it can be handled in such a way that the suggestion is constantly made to the children that they themselves might enjoy it on their own initiative. What records do you use? Do they come from a school collection? Well then, do the children know about it? Are they aware of what it contains and what it lacks? Do they ever have a chance to explore in it? When you have played a record and it has been unusually enjoyed by the children, do you ever think to tell them what company releases it, how much it costs, where they might buy or borrow it? Do you ever bring items to school from your own record collection, if you have one? If so, do you let the children know what you are doing? If a school recording is very bad, and you possess the same recording in very good condition, have you ever played them both to reveal the difference? Might this not have an effect on discrimination and influence choice? Have you any record collectors among the children of your group? If so, have you ever given them a chance to talk about and display their treasures, to tell about what they have and would like to have? Enthusiasm is catching, you know! Do your children have any chances to use the school records and reproducing equipment out of hours? Have you ever tried to persuade the authorities to install listening equipment in the library? Could you get together a group of record enthusiasts among your children and give them responsibility for maintaining a regular feature on the bulletin board, dealing, let us say, with current releases? Might it ever be feasible to take your children on a visit to the local music store for a demonstration of fine phonographs? Are there any possibilities for teaching material in the advertising copy of the phonograph manufacturers?

Or again, what about radio programs? If you are going to organize vital and functional listening experiences, surely it would be just as well not to go on the apparent assumption that this is a world in which the radio does not exist. Might it not be worth while to have a calendar list of good musical programs which will be forthcoming on accessible stations? If you know of some work that is going to be played over the air, why not give your children a preview, or sample, in recorded form? This, incidentally, is at least one small contribution to the great and vexing question of what kind of music to use. In the present instance you choose a piece of music, not for its own sake, but because you want to get the children to listen to a good radio program, which means that your choice is "functional"! Can you encourage any individuals in your group to discover enjoyable radio programs for themselves and to tell the rest about them? Might it not be a good idea to talk about a radio program that a number of the children had heard? Might not this incite those who had not heard it to listen to the next one? Can you use your bulletin board to feature prospective programs?

Once more, what about "live performance"? Have you any friends who are musical amateurs? Would they perhaps enjoy coming to play or sing to the children? Might it be a good idea to get them to tell the children something about themselves and about music—what music they were studying, how long they had been working at it, what other music they had in mind to work on, how long they practiced, how they first got started, how they liked it, why they kept it up? Can you not imagine such a friendly, personal musicale and chat having a profound effect on some individuals in your group? Could you ever cajole a professional artist into doing something of the sort? A little impudence, you know, can be justified in a good cause! What about the school band or orchestra or choir? Would it be possible to have your children visit a rehearsal? Would some of the performers visit your room for a demonstration? What about concerts in the school, in the community, in accessible communities elsewhere? Do you make any attempt to feature them? Can you get advance copies of programs or program notes and play and talk about some of the music with your children?

Motion picture music, too, is worth more than a passing thought. Can you find out anything about the musical scores of current or coming films? Would it be possible for any of your children who happen to be movie fans to find out about this and report to the group? Is any of the music familiar? Can some of it be played and discussed in your classroom either before the film comes to town or

afterwards? Can you ever get a discussion going about particularly striking or interesting music that has been used
along with a film?

Then there are a great many interesting and attractive
books about music. Could you manage to have one or more
of them on display once in a while? Why not talk about
them casually, tell of some of the interesting things in
them, discuss them, recommend them, tell the children
where to get hold of them? What, you may ask, has this to
do with listening? My answer is very simple. I have known
quite a few cases in which children have been inspired
with an ardent desire to hear certain music by reading
about it in a book. Also, as I surely need not remind you,
there are plenty of articles about music and also critical
reviews. Many of them make fine bulletin board material
and lend themselves to interesting and fertile discussions,
which in turn can lead straight to listening both in and out
of school.

We have here, as you will see, quite a large array of suggestions; and I have no doubt that many more will occur
to you as you think over the problem of helping your
children to discover opportunities for listening. You will
notice at once that these suggestions make the management
of listening in your classroom very different from the setting up of a stereotyped sequence of appreciation lessons.
You are not trying to teach a predetermined body of content, but to influence behavior along constructive and
fruitful lines; and your choice and use of material and resources are realistically directed towards this end.

2. In the second place, you will shape up and organize
listening experiences in order to help your children to discover *different ways of listening.* If you will refer back to
the lesson described at the beginning of this chapter, you

will see that this was done very well indeed by the teacher concerned. Sometimes the children listened to music in a setting of very active physical response; sometimes they listened very quietly; sometimes they sat decorously after the fashion of a well-behaved concert audience. These are all different ways of listening, and there are a great many more. It is worth while, also, to notice how the teacher got the children to respond in these varied ways. There was a happy combination of suggestion and active leadership from her, and freedom and choice on the part of the group. Here you will find something that will repay a little thought.

It is often strongly urged that children, and particularly young children, should definitely be encouraged to respond very freely while they are listening to music—that they should be allowed to hum, sing, clap, move about the room, comment, and ask questions. There is no doubt whatever that such freedom can very often add much to the pleasure and effectiveness of the listening experience. You can prove this to yourself by noting your own reactions when you are listening to music in solitude and without inhibitions. You will frequently find yourself inclined to rise from your chair, to walk about, to make various motions which you might not like anyone else to observe, and to exclaim and talk to yourself. Since, as we have seen, music is intrinsically associated with movement, there is an excellent reason why freedom to move about can enhance enjoyment. Certainly the stereotype of the well-behaved concert auditor, who must consider the convenience of others, not to mention their opinions, does not exemplify the sole and only mode of response of a listener. And if such motor and verbal freedom has palpable values for an adult like yourself, those values are still greater in the case of young children. Moreover, if your children are led to discover that it is not always necessarily the proper thing to sit still and keep quiet when music is being played, if they learn in the classroom the invigorating and enhancing effects of free response, the same freedom of reaction will tend to carry over to what solitary listening they do out of school.

But it would be a great mistake to make an issue of always *forcing* children to move about, to hum, to extemporize an impersonation, and so forth, whenever they listen to music. Mrs. Emma Sheehy tells of a child of pre-school age whose parents practically compelled her to engage in dramatic play in response to a new record which they had bought for her, and which strongly suggested such an activity. The child was reluctant, but the parents had been told that this was the proper way for her to behave and they virtually insisted. She consented somewhat unwillingly and for the moment all seemed well. But after that day she would have absolutely nothing to do with the new record, which happened to be an unusually attractive one. Thus it is quite proper to suggest or encourage free motor and verbal responses. But to insist upon them under all circumstances, or to be disturbed when they do not appear, would be extremely unwise.

With even quite young children quiet listening, perhaps with closed eyes, can result in really profound enjoyment. A very sensitive and intelligent teacher told me of an incident that occurred when she suggested this type of listening in a first grade. The composition being played was an abbreviation of Debussy's *Clair de lune*. It was received in complete silence and stillness and, when it was over, the little boy next to her opened his eyes and whispered, as if to himself, "Beautiful!"

Once again, there are significant differences in psychological effect between shared listening and solitary listening, and you should do what you can to help your children to discover both types. To share enjoyment with a group of others can often enhance one's own pleasure, for the corporate attitude of the group tends to convey itself to its members. Also, when the music stops, there can be discussion, and various children can tell what they most liked, after which all can listen to it again. Then, too, there can be a very genuine pleasure in bringing some favorite composition or record to school, telling the group about it, and playing it to them. All these are forms or types of sharing which tend to enhance and, as it were, to focalize enjoyment, and there are many more besides. Solitary listening, in the nature of things, can only be organized to a rather limited extent in school. Still, something can be done by making equipment available in the classroom and by having listening equipment with ear phones installed in the library. But you can usually do a great deal to encourage and help children to listen to music by themselves at home. Showing an interest in what they have heard, asking questions, giving hints, offering suggestions, all these are some of the ways and means by which children can be influenced to discover and use opportunities for the solitary enjoyment of music.

3. Finally, if you stick with consistency to your purpose of helping your children to discover listening, you will regard the listening experiences which you organize in your classroom essentially as a *series of inducements*. Ground-covering, in particular, you will consider entirely irrelevant. Teachers tend to be greatly oppressed by the tyranny of the standard stint—a certain amount of material to be handled, a certain number of pages to be assigned, a certain number of topics to be presented, a certain number of

problems to be worked out, or, in music, a certain list of
compositions to be heard. This bondage is quite without a
rational foundation. Why just this particular list of records? What would happen if different ones were substi-
tuted or if all that were listed were not presented? These
are questions to which no sensible answer is possible. So if
you try to orient your teaching to the covering of a stated
amount of ground, you deprive yourself of every vestige of
an intelligible criterion. But if you tell yourself that you
propose to help your children to discover listening, then
you have an aim which is both realistic and feasible, and
which, for that reason, can be translated into practice quite
readily, and the results observed.

Your procedures will, in principle, resemble those of the
advertising manager of a department store who is arranging a window display. You will not try to show everything. From among your wares you will choose those most
likely to please and intrigue your customers. You will
show them under circumstances best calculated to reveal
and enhance their attractiveness. For your initial purpose
will simply be to start your customers buying, after which
you can get them to keep right on buying.

### III

In the second place, you will wish to help your children
*to discover what to listen to.* You will wish to begin opening up for them the immense and varied world of music,
so that they can at least make a start in finding out what
there is in it. This matter of discovering music is, of
course, closely associated with the discovery of listening
itself; but there is enough distinction to justify separate
discussion of this matter.

Here once more, as so often happens, many baffling practical problems and controversial issues are immediately solved when you set your sights on a realistic and sensible aim, when you know just what it is that you are trying to do for your children. Let us consider some of these issues.

1. What kind of music should you choose in organizing listening experiences for your children? This is a question which has aroused plenty of argument. Some people have insisted that jazz should be avoided because it is supposed to have a harmful effect on character; others say it ought to be included because it has an important place in modern life. Some people express doubts about popular music, such as selections from successful musical shows like *South Pacific;* others feel strongly that popular music ought to be used in the school. On this level, however, the debate gets nowhere, because there is no proper basis for decision.

Your children themselves are always the determining factor. You must consider so far as you can their whole life backgrounds and their level of maturity, remembering that, among other things, you are trying to reveal to them what there is in music to be enjoyed. If they hear a great deal of jazz out of school, this may be an argument for bringing them something different in school. If most of them have never heard music such as that in *South Pacific* or in the Gilbert and Sullivan operas, then it will be well to give them opportunities to do so. Certainly there is not one and only one basis for selecting music, but if one of your determining purposes is to help them discover what to listen to, this suggests as much variety as possible. You will find many suitable records in the list on pages 293-299. Start to go through as much of this material as you can and turn to other sources as well, such as catalogs of recording companies. You will find such musical explorations a personal pleasure, and they will probably open your eyes and ears to much that is unfamiliar to you. Obviously there are many different kinds of music—vocal solos, choral numbers, selections from grand operas, light operas, and oratorios, instrumental solos, orchestral works, string quartets, compositions by old-time classical composers, romantic composers, modern composers, American composers, folk music of many types. It will do you no harm at all to begin making discoveries for yourself, so delve in and have a good time. When you find anything that you yourself enjoy, consider whether you would like to bring it to your children and whether you could do so successfully. You may present it to them quite casually, as something that they might enjoy. You can, if you like, build up an elaborate psychological stage setting for it. You may hitch it up with expressive bodily movement, or dramatization, or singing along, or with the use of simple instruments; or you may think of it as an opportunity for quiet listening. Never be afraid of being simple and direct. Never be afraid of your own enthusiasms. Your children will not always like what you like, or even what you think they are going to like. But you will learn from experience, and I am quite sure you will find the experience enjoyable. After all, a pleasure shared is always sweeter.

Encourage individuals in your group to make their own musical discoveries and to share them with the rest. Perhaps you present something which everybody enjoys and then, a few days later, a child comes in with a piece of music which he thinks very much like the one you chose, or quite different. There is a living proof that you are succeeding in your attempt.

It may be—and here I am referring particularly to work with older children—that a piece of music which you yourself enjoy, and which you have every reason to consider lovely, does not at once arouse a favorable response. For instance, I once saw a sixth-grade group become extremely bored with an exquisite slow movement from a Mozart symphony, although it was well and sympathetically presented. The teacher asked them why they did not like this music. They said it sounded thin and seemed to have no tune in it. This latter comment would seem most amazing to anyone who knows anything about music, for Mozart is usually thought of as one of the most melodious of composers. I was interested to see how the teacher would handle the situation. She hesitated for a moment, with a look of considerable surprise. Then she told the class that she herself had played it over time and again the night before and had hated to stop, because it had seemed to her so beautiful. She went on to say that many people loved the music of Mozart, that the children were missing something if they could not accept him, and that perhaps the trouble was that they were used to music of a very different kind. But instead of trying to force the music on them, she asked if some of them would not be willing to give it a further trial out of school. If so, she would lend them the record, which belonged to her, so that they might play it over to themselves from time to time during the coming week. This seemed to them quite reasonable and six of them accepted the suggestion. I do not know how the plan worked out, for this was my only visit to this classroom; but it seemed to me that the teacher had dealt with the problem in a manner that was both wise and promising.

There is only one kind of music which should *always* be avoided. This is manufactured, made-to-order music, without any real expressive appeal, any poetry, any charm. The use of such alleged music is inevitably a waste of time.

2. How much background information should be given

to children concerning the music to which they listen?
Enough to serve for purposes of identification, to arouse
interest, and to help understanding. The point is certainly
not to teach them an array of historical facts about music,
which must be memorized and retained. But names and
information can have important and interesting psychological effects. You have probably noticed this yourself. If,
for instance, when driving across the country you come
upon an unfamiliar range of mountains, it means something to be told the name of the range. Something more
is added if you are also told the names of the principal
peaks, their heights, by whom they were first seen or
climbed, and so forth. One does not in the literal sense
see any more, but one looks at a natural scene with new
eyes and probably with a new appreciation if one knows
at least the names of its most conspicuous features. And
of course one can refer to, talk about, and even think about
those features much better later on if one knows "what they
are." This may be a human peculiarity, but it is applicable
not only to this familiar experience; but is just as true of
pieces of music as it is of rivers, mountain ranges, water-
falls, and canyons.

So it would nearly always be a mistake to enable children
to listen, even with great enjoyment, to a piece of music
without telling them *something* about it. How much you
should tell them will depend on various circumstances,
some of which we shall consider in a short time. But in
any case it should be exact from the standpoint of identification as far as it goes. One would never speak of "Haydn's
Minuet," for instance, for such a careless title is not only
quite absurd but in fact misleading. Haydn wrote a great
many minuets and it is certainly of some importance for
children to know just which of them they are enjoying.

On the other hand it would be unnecessary and unwise to
be pedantic and insist on the memorization of the opus
number of this minuet. But if there is a descriptive title
such as "Dreaming," or "Soldier's March," it should be
given; and if the minuet is the Minuet in G or the Noc-
turne in E flat, the children should be told so, for the purpose of designation and reference, even though they may
not know the meaning of G, or E flat, or understand, for
the time-being at any rate, the concept of key.

Children should also be told the name of the composer,
and it is often well to explain, informally and incidentally,
enough about him and his work to enable them to respond
to the piece with at least some understanding of its human
setting. This tends to make the composition under immediate consideration more meaningful and interesting, and
also gets it before the children as an example of a certain
type, or genre, of music. It gives them a chance to find
out eventually that they like not only this piece, but all the
music of Mozart, or Johann Strauss, or whoever the composer may be. To establish this attitude and interest is
clearly in line with your purpose of stimulating musical
discovery and exploration. You will find many good
sources of interesting information about music and musicians among the items in the bibliography at the close of
this book. Such information often appears, also, on the
envelopes of records and in pamphlets in record albums.

3. Is there any place for musical memory contests or any
variations of them? Not a large place certainly, but possibly some. These devices should under no circumstances
be used simply for the purpose of finding out what the children know. But once in a while it may stimulate and
focalize interest to play fragments of a dozen to twenty compositions, challenging the children to name them. I have,

indeed, seen a teacher employ a procedure which at the
first glance would appear extremely questionable, but
which actually seemed to have desirable effects. This
teacher had on hand the themes of a considerable number
of songs and instrumental pieces, notated on newsprint
and large enough for the whole class to see. These she displayed one by one on an easel, asking anyone who could do
so to identify them. There had been no formal teaching
of notation as part of the general program, but a good
many of the children took either class or private music
lessons, and it was clear that most of them were by no
means wholly at a loss. There was a definite interest and
eagerness, and it seemed to me that on the whole the procedure had an excellent influence, although it could very
easily be overdone.

4. Many opportunities for the discovery of music can
arise in connection with other subjects in the curriculum.
For instance, I have before me reports of units organized
by classroom teachers on "The Westward Movement,"
"The Old South," "Our South American Friends," and
"The Ancient Greeks and What They Gave Us." As part
of the work on these units, committees were set up among
the children to look for appropriate music, which they
brought to school, presented, and explained. These projects involved considerable searching, listening, and selecting, and the children made contact with a great deal of
material beyond that actually chosen. Topics in science,
too, can often have very significant musical ramifications.
In one such case the children were investigating the physical characteristics of rooms of various types—air temperature, wall temperature, ventilation, lighting, and so forth.
The question of acoustical characteristics also came up
and, among other matters, the children set to work to dis-

cover how music would sound in various kinds of rooms—
with and without drapes, carpets, furniture. In all such
cases it is obviously desirable to give the children as much
responsibility as possible for investigating, exploring, looking for material, trying it out, and searching for explanations if your purpose is to promote the discovery of music.

5. What are sometimes called "content units" can also
be usefully organized around musical topics. Not infre-
quently classroom teachers guide their children in developing dramatizations and plays based on the life of some
famous composer, or on the evolution and use of some
musical instrument. In the bibliography at the end of this
book you will find numerous items which have a very practical and helpful bearing on such undertakings.

To round out this discussion of specific issues by a return
to our basic consideration, what we want is by no means a
systematic presentation of musical history or literature as
such. Our aim should be to organize experiences and contacts sufficiently varied and sufficiently stimulating, so that
they reveal to children what there is in music, and arouse
in them a desire for further discoveries.

## IV

In the third place you will wish to help your children *to
discover what to listen for*. One of the fundamental ideas
which you need to understand about listening to music is
that it depends upon three things—attending, noticing,
and selecting. The reason why you often come to enjoy an
unfamiliar composition better after hearing it several times
is that, perhaps almost unconsciously, you learn to attend
to it selectively. At first it seems nothing but a confusing
mass of sound; but gradually you become aware of appealing and beautiful melodies, rhythms, and harmonies, and,

more important still, you accommodate yourself to its mood. Many of us find a good deal of so-called "modern" music hard to appreciate, largely for the reason that its musical components are unfamiliar. Anything you can do to help your children identify and respond to the various factors on which the appeal of music depends will tend to enrich and deepen their pleasure in listening.

But do not think that you are therefore committed to attempts at giving your children systematic lessons in musical analysis. This is a mistake which constantly appears in books and courses on music appreciation, and it is made also by not a few teachers. I know of one such course intended for elementary school children which is organized around a list of various musical forms, beginning with those that are supposed to be simple and going on to more complicated ones—the two-part form, the three-part form, the rondo, the sonata, the fugue, and so forth. In another instance, the various instruments of the orchestra are introduced one by one over a period of three years in a systematic way, beginning with the violin and ending with the English horn. Probably if your own musical training has not been extensive, you would find such subject matter rather formidable. But in this there is no need for discouragement, because such an approach is wrong in any case. It amounts to a mistaken application of a sound idea. That listening is a selective process, and that musical enjoyment depends on response to the constituents of a composition, is perfectly true. But this does not mean that we must proceed from this fact to list these constituents one by one, to attach technical names to them, and to teach them systematically. All you need to do is to help your children to notice and respond to elements of beauty and appeal in any composition to which they may be listening.

1. The first and most important of these elements is
mood. If anyone is to enjoy a composition, it is absolutely
necessary for him to "tune in" on the type of feeling embodied in it. Unless this is done, the most glorious music
can seem like nothing but meaningless and annoying noise.
But if this adjustment is made, then everything else becomes possible.

There are a great many ways in which you can help
your children to "tune in" on the mood of music to which
they listen and to discover the value and importance of so
doing. Your own attitude and actions in presenting a piece
can in themselves exert a strong influence, suggesting that
here is something important, worth attending to, certain to
be enjoyable. I have seen listening experiences ruined by
the clumsy, casual, apparently entirely unplanned behavior
of the teachers who carried them on. On the contrary, if
you have everything ready and in order, and if it becomes
evident that the whole presentation has been well thought-
out, you will already have done much to set the stage for a
good response.

Titles of compositions can be used in a variety of ways to
help children to orient themselves to mood, and to discover
the importance of so doing. You may decide to announce
the title before playing the piece, and this can lead to a
preliminary discussion of the kind of music which might
be expected. Or you may play the piece and then ask the
children to suggest titles, or to tell what they think the
music is "about."

Another possibility is to choose compositions which express different or contrasting moods. For instance, one
might present "Soldier's March," by Schumann (*RCA
Victor Basic Record Library* E-72), together with "The
Swan," by Saint-Saens (RCA Victor record number 1143).

One might at the same time display pictures of marching soldiers and a swan. What do the children see in these pictures? What would soldier music be like? What kind of music might go with the rippling lake and the graceful swan? Could the children tell which was which if the two pieces were played? Then one might play both pieces right through and let the children try to distinguish between the two, discussing the reasons for making the choice. If you are using contrast to spot the mood, you probably would avoid answering any questions or telling which record was which until both has been heard.

Another procedure is to encourage children to think of stories suggested by the composition, or to tell what they believe it might be "about." Here a few cautions need to be noted. We may safely say that a musical composition is never, or hardly ever, intended to tell one particular story or to represent one particular sequence of events. It may suggest many stories which differ in specific content. Yet there will be a basic similarity among them, for all of them will be outcomes or expressions of the mood which it is the chief function of the music to create. Thus stories suggested by the children may differ, and yet they may all be "right." Also you should be careful not to establish in the minds of your children the idea that they must always try to invent some sequence of events or some happening which is the true and only meaning of the music. The story, whatever it may be, is nothing but an instrumentality for establishing mood, not a literal account of what the music says.

The same warning applies even to using the story-programs which composers have sometimes attached to their music, and about which you can gather information in many of the books listed in the bibliography, on the envelopes of records, and from other sources. When the composer of a piece of music himself actually indicates that it was suggested by some event (as Tchaikowsky did, for instance, when he let it be known that his *1812 Overture* had to do with Napoleon's Russian campaign), you have something of very special interest and the story connection has a special authority. But even so the music is not a literal account of the actual events, such as one would find in a history book. It conveys and projects their mood; and both for the composer and all his hearers the emotional response is the essential consideration.

Quite a different way of helping children to "tune in" on the mood of music, and to discover the importance of doing so, is the use of familiar and favorite compositions. In one third-grade classroom I saw on display a list of "Our Musical Favorites," lettered large on a sheet of newsprint. I was told that the list was very carefully selected, that pieces were only included after considerable deliberation, and that changes were made from time to time. Pieces on the list were in frequent demand and were much enjoyed. Their very familiarity made them acceptable, because slipping into the mood came so quickly and decisively. And of course the whole business of selecting the compositions to be listed and of making continuous revisions also had their good effects.

2. In addition to overall mood, children should be helped to listen for what might in general be called structural or constitutive elements in a piece of music—its intensity (loud, soft, medium, changing), its tempo (fast, slow, medium, changing), its characteristic rhythm (strongly accentuated or smooth meter), its pitch (high, low, up and down), its style (dramatic, lyric, florid, etc.), its broad structure or architecture, and so forth. The

point, however, is that it is by no manner of means necessary to give systematic instruction in musical form, but
simply to lead the listeners to notice elements of beauty
and expressiveness in the music which they enjoy, and thus
to enhance that enjoyment.

As an instance, consider what might be done with *To A
Wild Rose,* by MacDowell. Before the piece was played,
the teacher might raise for discussion such questions as the
following: "If you were going to compose a piece called
*To A Wild Rose,* how would you have the music sound?
Loud or soft? Fast or slow? Does a wild rose make any
movement that might be imitated in the music? Is this
movement gentle or vigorous? Would a strongly accented
or smooth rhythm be best for imitating it? Would the
music be high, medium, or low? What instrument would
be best for expressing the sweetness and grace of a wild
rose? If this instrument played the melody, what instrument would you use for the accompaniment? What else
might be in the picture besides the rose? Would the
melody be simple or complex?" One recording of this
particular composition is a setting for cello, piano, and
harp, and if this is used, the children will perhaps be surprised and interested to know that MacDowell's original
piece was written for piano.* Or again, a piece might be
presented with a minimum of preliminary comment, following which there could be a discussion of its most interesting and appealing features. Notice, however, that
what is wanted is not a comprehensive and complete
analysis, but rather an indication of high points. Technical
terms, also, do not matter. All you need have in mind is
the help your children need in order to notice and ap-

* Adapted from *Music in the Elementary School,* California State Department of Education, Sacramento, California, 1939.

preciate the beauties that the music contains, or at any rate
a few of them. This can be brought about by a process of
mutual interchange and discovery in which both you and
they share. You are not in the position of an expert, giving
information, but in that of a guide and fellow-learner.

Participation through expressive bodily movement, also,
is an excellent means of helping children to discover
structural elements which help music to be expressive. As
your children become used to listening to what the music
"tells them to do," to making their own choices, and following their own insights, it is amazing how discriminating
and perceptive their responses can become. A group of
children without any technical knowledge whatsoever of
musical analysis can grasp the content and message and
apprehend the subtle beauties of quite complicated music
with remarkable completeness, by the agency of this direct
and natural medium. Response in terms of expressive
movement, as we have seen, is a true form of musical
participation, one of its great advantages being that it
presents almost no technical barriers. This is why it can do
so much to help discriminating and selective listening.

So, too, it is well to tie listening closely to other forms of
participation. Listening to a song can merge very directly
into singing it. And often when children listen to music,
they can develop settings for the use of simple instruments.
You need never feel any doubts about the value of "rote"
singing or "rote" playing, because control both of singing
and playing by the ear is fundamentally right. The expert
and cultivated musician who uses the notation as it should
be used does not spell out the notes. His eyes tell him how
the music should sound, and his hands, or his voice produce that sound. So the back-and-forth connection between listening and performing is not only natural and

easy, but also entirely proper and desirable. In particular, you need not be afraid that, when the children follow along with a song or a piece which they hear, they will only "imitate." What they will tend to do is to select or to notice. And your business, which requires virtually no technical expertness, is to help them to notice and select at least some of those beauties which make both listening and performing more delightful.

If you wish to help your children to recognize and understand the various instruments of the orchestra, a good many of the records listed at the end of this book will be helpful to you. They range all the way from clever but perhaps rather infantile impersonations like *Tubby the Tuba* or *Pee-wee the Piccolo* to more serious but still excellent material such as *Pan the Piper* which is suitable for the lower grades, and *The Young Person's Guide to the Orchestra,* which is adapted for the older child. Or you may like to set up projects like the two already described, in which the music of Tchaikowsky's *The Nutcracker Suite* was used. Here, as always, there is no need for systematic treatment or for the "taking up" of various instruments in some predetermined order. Recognition of different instrumental qualities and understanding of the various instruments themselves should arise directly out of the enjoyment of this or that musical composition, and should be a means of enhancing enjoyment.

CHAPTER SIX

# Singing

## I

WHEN YOU BRING MUSIC TO YOUR CHIL-
dren, you should by all means do everything you can to
*help and encourage them to sing.*

It may very well be that, at first sight, this advice will
strike you as formidable, and even as something that is
impossible for you to heed. To many classroom teachers,
singing is the great stumbling block, the great obstacle
which too often prevents them from bringing music to
their children at all. They themselves have no vocal confidence. Even when they find themselves in a group of people who are singing, they feel inhibited and ill at ease, and
their attempts to join in seem feeble and give them no
pleasure. And when it comes to trying to lead or direct the
singing of others, they are daunted at the very idea. They
shrink from any suggestions that they might get their
children to sing, partly because they have a natural objection to looking and feeling foolish, and partly because they
feel that they are not capable of helping their children
avoid bad habits and bad methods of vocal production and
tone placement. Since to many such teachers music in the
classroom means singing and nothing else, the outcome of
all these vocal inhibitions is that their children have virtually no contact with music at all.

It has already been pointed out in these pages that music

should by no means be equated to singing. But even with regard to singing itself, there is no need for this defeatist attitude, wide-spread though it certainly is. To overcome it, two things are necessary—first, a constructive point of view, and second, a knowledge of and an ability to use certain readily available resources. Granted the fulfillment of these two conditions, a solution at once can be found for various practical problems connected with the promotion and encouragement of singing in your classroom.

## II

You may think it strange when I say that the right point of view is the first and greatest necessity for you, if you are to help and encourage your children to sing. I stress this point precisely because it is a mistaken point of view that holds back many classroom teachers from making any such attempt. From unfortunate experiences of their own and from the attitude of trained musicians, these teachers have picked up the idea that singing is difficult, that it must always be done "correctly," that no one can get anywhere with it unless he has a good voice, and that no kind of worth-while progress or achievement is possible without a long course of expert vocal training. They may admire others who can freely make music with their voices and envy them the evident pleasure that comes from so doing. But since they themselves lack the technical foundation which is supposed to be essential, they feel that it would be quite impossible for them to do anything about getting other people, including their own children, to sing.

There is, however, no necessity whatever for being inhibited or frustrated by this doctrine, because the doctrine is false. I will try to summarize and point up the true doctrine about singing by centering it around the following three propositions, by discussing each at length.

1. Singing is just as natural to children as talking. Students of child psychology have called attention to this truth often enough; and if you wish to hunt up the idea in their writings you will have no difficulty in finding it. But you need do nothing so laborious in order to convince yourself of the validity of the proposition. All that is necessary is to watch children, and to keep your eyes and ears open when they are acting in a natural, childlike way. You will find that they do lots of singing, and lots of humming and crooning which belong more or less in the same category. Observe a child when he is by himself and unaware of your presence, when he is wrapped up in some activity or perhaps just daydreaming. How often he hums and croons or goes over and over a snatch of some refrain! Observe a child when he runs to greet his father or is handed some enchanting gift. Notice how much music there often is in his exclamation of delight. Observe children on the playground and notice how naturally their feelings pour forth, not only in words but in the tones and cadences of their voices. You may have heard this little refrain coming from a group of children at play:

It falls into all sorts of rhythms and is hooked up to all sorts of words. No one ever taught this to children. It seemed to come to them by nature. Locate yourself close to a child at a church service where there is good and free congregational singing. Quite likely you will hear something that will make you wonder, and that may help you to understand. There the child stands and sings away, with-

out a thought, without an inhibition. You cannot doubt
that there is happiness in it, and self-forgetfulness, and
living beauty too. It is an amazing and revealing performance. It transforms that hackneyed old expression about
"singing like a lark" into something poignantly and vividly
authentic. Watch children for a little while and you will
not need any scholarly or ponderous psychological opus to
convince you that, for them, singing is a completely natural
activity.

When you come to think about it, this cannot be otherwise than true. Human beings have sung directly, naturally, spontaneously all through the ages and everywhere
on earth. Singing has always been associated with primitive religious and tribal ceremonials, with communal experiences and activities, with work and play, with love and
war and hope and fear and birth and death. That there
could be any issue, any problem, any difficulty in all this
never remotely entered anybody's mind. Nobody ever
even dreamed that all human beings should take voice
lessons before participating in the act of song. Even right
down to modern times one of the obvious working assumptions of public worship has been that singing is perfectly natural, and that it is possible for everybody and
valuable for everybody. Many of us who are adults have,
to our great misfortune, lost this spontaneity and unreckon-
ing, unquestioning confidence. But in your children's
personalities it still lives on.

Now it is precisely such free, natural, untrammeled singing that I have in mind when I urge you to encourage your
children to sing. You will, I am sure, realize at once that
the problem, looked at from this point of view, takes on a
completely new appearance. I can only hope that my suggestion of getting your children to sing has not called im-

mediately to your mind such questions as when to use "rote" songs or "observation" songs, how to go "from rote to note," how to get all the notes of a song just right, how to drill on tonal patterns, how to use the syllables, how to establish the so-called "head voice," and so on and so forth. I well realize that these are among the typical issues with which many music specialists are primarily concerned. These things are prominent and standard items in the conventional picture of grade-school music, as it has come to be understood and taught in many places. But just how much have they to do with free, spontaneous, happy singing? Not a great deal, surely! As one thinks about them, it seems very evident that they are based upon two assumptions; first, that singing is a means for teaching the "fundamentals" and for developing a facility with the notation; second, that singing itself is a difficult and skilled activity which must be taught from a technical approach. They are just precisely *not* procedures designed for the immediate promotion of the freest, happiest, most spontaneous singing possible among a group of children, they take no account of singing as an activity which is natural to them and full of value on its own account. If this kind of singing is what you are after—and it certainly should be— then you simply will not concern yourself about many of these conventional procedures and, in so doing, you will have overcome what may have been daunting and insuperable obstacles.

Of course the practical problem of ways and means still exists. You want to know how to prepare yourself, how to get songs started, where to look for suitable song material, on what basis to select the best kind of material, what sort of things might be done with a song after the children have become able to sing it, how to deal with children who find

singing not so easy, and so on. But all such problems now
take on a new look. They become manageable problems—
problems that can be handled by an ordinary human being
who is in no sense a technically trained expert, and who
may indeed have some musical and vocal limitations. For
what you are aiming at is not to teach a technical skill, or
to convey the so-called "fundamentals," or to build reading
ability. Your purpose is a far simpler one, and for you far
more feasible. *It is simply and solely to create situations in
which your children will be helped and encouraged to
realize to the fullest possible degree their natural tendency
to express themselves in song.* And this is something that
any person who understands children, and who has the
will, can certainly accomplish.

But is it enough? Does it not make singing a very flimsy
and trivial activity, devoid of all substance and solid content, and indeed of all respectable educational value?
Instead of arguing the point in the abstract, let me ask you
to consider your own case, even though I have to do so
on the basis of guesswork. When you were a little child,
singing came natural to you, too. Perhaps if you take a trip
back along the avenues of memory, you can recall that this
was so. But somehow, somewhere along the way, you lost
this naturalness, this spontaneity, this unreflecting self-confidence. Just how this might have happened in any individual case it is, of course, impossible to say. But happen
it very possibly did. And it was a great loss in two very important respects. First, it blocked you off from a very free
and direct contact with music. It created musical inhibitions and barriers and false attitudes which are the real reasons why you doubt your own ability to bring music effectively to your children. Second, it had effects upon your
personality which were, all of them, unfortunate. It

blocked you off from an avenue of free natural expression, so that today you are less expansive, more tightly tied in upon yourself than you would be if life had not deprived you of your natural gift of song. That, perhaps, may be putting it rather brutally, but if you make a self-appraisal you will probably come to feel that there is considerable truth in this diagnosis.

Was the loss of this gift of natural and spontaneous song inevitable? I do not believe so. At any rate I am quite sure that the gift could have been fostered and encouraged, so that very likely you could have kept it always. What you needed was not voice training, or technical training, or knowledge of the notation, or adeptness with the syllables; but rather constant and above all sympathetic and enthusiastic encouragement to sing and to enjoy singing. You might never have become a prima donna, but you would have had something precious forever in your life—the precious gift of song. Burl Ives, when asked when he learned to sing, once replied, "I started singing as soon as I could talk. It was just something that went in the family." That could have been your own experience also. Try to imagine what that could mean—group singing, community singing, singing in church and in school, singing with your friends and for your friends, singing all by yourself for your own pleasure at home, or on a walk, or when driving your car, or to create again some musical delight that had come your way. And these are only hints and suggestions! Such singing could have opened up the art of music to you, as a golden realm where you found yourself at home. And, by relaxing tensions and making self-expression possible, it could have been an influence for personal fulfillment.

Can you for a moment maintain that any school activity

which even remotely promises such values is negligible, or
trivial, or superficial? Consider the question in human
terms and it answers itself. We so easily think that solid
and respectable educational values mean only intellectual
grind, the ponderous acquisition of information, the laborious establishment of skills. All teaching suffers from
these heavy-handed interpretations, including the teaching
of music. But there is something that transcends them all,
and that is the freeing of the human spirit.

> Shades of the prison-house begin to close
> Upon the growing boy,

That formidable saying is all too pertinent to much that
happens in our schools. But when you encourage your children to sing spontaneously, naturally, joyously, you are
doing something at least to prevent those shades from
closing in. If you accomplish this and nothing else, your
work has solid, precious, and lasting values. Anyone who
calls it trivial is simply purblind. Your aim, above all else
and by all means, should be, through encouragement and
opportunity, to help your children to keep and use their
natural and precious gift of song.

2. In the act of song a person gains a very direct and
intimate contact with, and experience of, music itself. The
greatest of musicians have recognized this, almost by in-
stinct. Schumann once insisted with much emphasis that
every musician should sing, even though his voice was poor,
because of what it could do for his ear. While he was composing, Beethoven sang vociferously, albeit from all accounts most untunefully. From time to time microphones
have picked up the somewhat crow-like singing of Tos-
canini amid the complex of orchestral sound which his
baton was evoking. And as for the layman, he is urged by

Ruth Crawford Seeger, in her book *American Folk Songs for Children,* not to be prevented from singing the songs therein contained by any sense of vocal inadequacy.

Now I have argued in these pages that our emphasis should center on music, rather than upon expressive movement, or listening, or instrumental playing, or creating, or singing as ends in themselves. So the purpose you set before yourself in the encouragement of singing among your children should not be to make them into competent vocalists, but to bring them to the very heart of music itself. The heart of music is expressiveness, and singing is the most direct of all means of sensing and conveying expressive musical values. It is true that the expressive content of a piece of music depends upon and is embodied in a multiplicity of nuance—the rise and fall of melody, the alternation and shading of loud and soft, the instant's pause at the end of a phrase, the speeding up as a climax approaches, the slowing down as the end draws near. It follows that these factors of expressiveness must be studied, practiced, refined, if their full meanings and perfections are to stand revealed. But these problems should not be handled as technical problems, in their own right, but always dealt with as problems involved in *saying something* clearly and beautifully. For instance, I once watched the work of an elementary school choir to which the children came of their own choice, half-an-hour before the time for opening the daily session. The rehearsal was being conducted by two of the classroom teachers. One of the pieces was the well-known round "Dona Nobis Pacem." At one point the children fell noticeably below pitch. The teacher in charge did not thereupon simply drill them on the notes. She pointed out that the music did not sound as it should. By emphasizing in particular the wave-like rise and fall of the melody in its musical plea for the granting of peace, she stimulated the children to react to the meaning of the music, with the result that technical difficulties disappeared. On another occasion I observed a rehearsal of a nationally selected high school chorus, which was at work on the hymn "Jesus Lover of My Soul." Almost the entire emphasis of the conductor was upon the meaning, the emotion, the appeal of the words and the music. The results obtained certainly justified this approach. These examples may show you, as they have helped to show me, what it means to say that the act of song brings one straight to the expressive heart of music.

The boys and girls in the national high school chorus were experienced singers, and the children in the elementary school chorus were a selected group. They could go much further in the refinement of expressive nuance than will be possible for your children. But the kind of experience involved in the act of song should be and can be the same for your children as it was for these others. The primary and controlling purpose should not be to sing correct notes, or correct pitch, or to produce good vocal tone. Such things as these are means to an end—very important means, no doubt, but means nevertheless. The primary purpose should be always to sense, to feel, and to convey *what the music says*. Even a very imperfect realization of this purpose is enough to make singing musically and educationally worth while.

Perhaps I can bring this home to you by telling you of a device which a very fine pianist of my acquaintance uses in his own practicing. When he is working at a passage in a composition, he stops time and again to sing the tune over to himself. It is certainly no exhibit for an audience, for he has a poor voice and does not stay on pitch any too well.

But, to the understanding listener, what he is trying to do is very evident. He is reaching out for the music, feeling for it, endeavoring to sense it very closely and intimately. He says that by this means he can sense the expressive, continuous, stream-like onward flow of the melody far more subtly and convincingly than by the keyboard alone, which always tends to break it down into separate, discontinuous notes.

Try this for yourself when you are all by yourself. Sing a folk tune, or one of the Stephen Foster songs, or a theme from a symphony. Notice how convincingly this singing brings you right to the expressive heart of the music. Doing this is something that you yourself can enjoy. The primary purpose of acquiring what we call a vocal technique is nothing more than to make certain of being able to use the voice with all the flexibility, all the certainty of refinement and control necessary for making the expressive intention of the music apparent and enjoyable to others besides the singer. With such things in mind you can see at once what it means to say that singing can bring your children to the very heart of the music; and also you can understand that just such singing exemplifies a fundamentally correct approach to vocalism as well.

3. Singing is more than a purely vocal activity; it is an activity which involves the entire personality. Watch a canary singing. It is not merely working its lungs and its larynx; the whole canary sings, right from its claws to the tip of its beak. It converts itself into a living, breathing, feeling instrument of music. That also is how people sing when they sing naturally. There is a striking similarity here between a singing canary and a spontaneously singing child. The child, too, sings "all over"—body, soul, and spirit—or in modern terminology, with the whole self.

This proposition carries with it a number of very interesting and practically important implications. It explains at once the peculiar delicacy and difficulty of the teaching of voice, a point which deserves brief comment here, even though you yourself are not directly concerned with vocal instruction as such. Voice teachers have concocted an enormous, even incredible array of procedures, devices, techniques, methods, concepts, and nostrums. Moreover the best authorities among them are quite amazingly at loggerheads over the nature of the proper approach, and about the very fundamentals of their business. Some of them will tell you that you ought to practice breathing for a long time before singing a note, while others say that you should not give breathing a single thought. Some will insist that you must bring the voice forward in the face, while others retort that this is all nonsense. A few of them have even advocated taking honey to make the voice sweet, and beer to make it robust. There is no end to these astounding contradictions and peculiar ideas and to the damage which has been done by them.

The reason for this unfortunate situation is that singing, as an act of the whole personality, is so subtle and complex that to analyze the precise factors which make it go well is something about which there has been no certainty up to the present time. I mention all this partly because it is interesting, and partly to prevent your feeling too cast down if you think you do not know how to get people to sing. Plenty of professional voice teachers do not know either, even though they imagine they do.

Another far-reaching implication of the proposition that singing involves the entire personality is that the principal blockages to singing are not technical but personal. Remember this the next time you find yourself confronted in your classroom with a child who is what used to be called a monotone, but is now given the less derogatory label of a "hesitating singer." By dint of a little judicious bullying and humiliation, and a few challenges to attempt abstract tone-matching, doomed to certain failure, you can, in about ten minutes, transform this hesitating singer into a lifelong non-singer. Obviously you have not put a crimp in his technique, because he has no technique. The crimp has been put in his personality, by establishing a prejudice and a self-distrust which are reinforced and confirmed each time he opens his mouth to sing. On the other hand, by avoiding pressure as you would the plague and substituting encouragement, by creating situations in which this child will want to sing, feel free to sing, and be moved to throw himself wholeheartedly into the act of singing, you can help him to develop confidence and to find a world of pleasure in the use of his voice. The plain and indeed very obvious truth is that everybody, or almost everybody, can sing, because everybody has the necessary physical equipment. Some people will sing better than others, because nature has given them a better instrument. Thorough training, years of hard work, and long experience can be expected to bring with them a better vocal control. But the actual mechanism of singing is a gift of nature to us all and, granted the right personality orientation, anyone can use that mechanism quite well enough to gain both benefit and enjoyment for himself, and to share fruitfully with others the act of song.

Yet another extremely important implication is that singing is dependent upon and inevitably reflects the total personality values of the situation. When a person stands up on a platform and sings a solo to an audience, he manifests not merely a technique, but also, and more

significantly, a personal adjustment to the whole setting.
This produces one kind of singing, and a perfectly good
kind too, in its own way. But it is not the kind of singing
you are after. Here, incidentally, is the reason why the
concert soloist is not likely to be a good vocal model for
your children. Again, when a highly selected group of
high school students appears in seemly robes and projects
a studied interpretation of a motet by Palestrina, they
too are manifesting a personal adjustment to a particular
type of situation. What they give forth is a certain type
of singing, excellent of its kind no doubt, but once more
not the type of singing with which you are primarily
concerned. You realize it is important to cultivate the
talents of the gifted child who may be in your midst. But
first of all you want all your children, through the medium
of song, to realize the educational and personal values that
can come to them through music. You want their singing
to reflect individual and group enjoyment, to be inspired
by a spirit so contagious that everyone will feel invited
to join in, to be so convincing and stimulating in its freedom that it will carry beyond the boundaries of classroom
and of school and will indeed tend to establish them as
singers for life, to serve them as a means of experiencing
and responding to the manifold beauties and expressive
meanings of the art of music. This is the kind of singing
which you should certainly want to get. And this fact
should encourage you—it is the easiest of all kinds of singing to get. What you have to do is to create personality
situations which favor it and then to touch them off by
one or another of the devices soon to be discussed.

So to sum up, the controlling point of view in terms
of which you should approach the practical problem of
getting all your children to sing amounts to this: *Every-*

*thing turns on the creation of what we have already called singing situations*—situations, that is to say which favor free, enjoyable, natural, musically expressive song. The finest type of congregational singing (which does not occur any too often nowadays) is an admirable illustration of what I mean by this phrase. There is momentum and incitement. No one is concerned about voice production, or vocal quality, or tonal patterns, or even about carrying the tune with anxious perfection. No one is trying to learn the fundamentals of music. There is not the slightest thought of public display. Everything centers upon the meaning of the words, the appeal of the music, the great and fulfilling sense of togetherness. This singing is done for the inspiration of man and the glory of God. I have, of course, used congregational singing only as one illustration of my meaning, and the singing situations which you create in your classroom will obviously not be identical with it in detail. Indeed, details can vary extensively and flexibly, and ought to do so. But those situations will always be identical in purpose, in intention, in the conditions that are essential. They will be situations designed above everything else to establish and arouse in your children *the will to sing.*

### III

This discussion of the controlling point of view has now brought us to the practical question of how you might go about organizing suitable singing situations in your classroom.

1. For many classroom teachers the first and most crucial problem to be solved in organizing such situations is the inability of these teachers to sing, or at any rate to sing well. Unless some way for helping them deal with this

difficulty can be found, there will not be much singing in their classrooms. However a good practical solution is right at hand; they can make use of records. This we now proceed to discuss.

There are two reasons for dealing at some length with the use of records for singing. First, the instrumentality is of great practical value in itself; and you as a teacher should thus know how to use it with discrimination, good sense, and judgment. You need to understand the characteristics which make any given record or set of records suitable or unsuitable for the purpose at hand. Second, a study of some of the available recordings will throw considerable light on a number of important issues connected with the management and encouragement of children's singing in general. With these two aims in mind, let us proceed to review some of the available material.

First let us consider "Singing Activities" which is part of the *RCA Victor Basic Record Library for Elementary Schools*. The singing program consists of four albums, each containing four ten-inch unbreakable records, on which there are a large number of children's songs. One of these volumes is intended for the primary grades, and the other three for the upper grades.*

Play the records through and see what you think about them. I believe that you will at once find them enjoyable. The music is charming. The text of the songs is poetic and imaginative. (The text itself is given in the first of the albums, but not in those subsequent.) Each performance, for the most part, is sensitive and artistic, although in one or two cases the singer does not enunciate the words as

---

* To save you some possible confusion I should warn you that the numbering of the albums is not consistent. They begin with number one, and then skip right on to numbers four, five, and six.

clearly as one could wish. Moreover on the albums are comments, provided by the editors, about these songs, which are interesting and attractive, and which certainly could be adapted for classroom use.

Now these are very genuine values. Indeed, one can go further and say that they are essential. If you want to organize singing situations which will arouse the will to sing, the very first requisite is to have songs with a living and direct appeal. Children are very responsive both to musical appeal and to poetic and imaginative intimations in the text. You do not have to make a fuss about such things or to talk about them a great deal. If they are present they are likely to speak for themselves; and you should remember that they often make a far deeper impression on children, and even on quite young children, than is apparent on the surface. These values are most certainly present and richly present in this singing program that has been recorded.

But to what extent are these songs singable for children? Here the answer is not so favorable, at least in quite a good many instances. For example, the opening song on side A of record 1, Album I is "Little Bo-Peep." Here is a charming tune and a charming poem. But the song has two serious disadvantages and one other that is probably less important. (a) For little children it is rather tricky; they may well find it so difficult that they simply give up. (b) Children are likely to find the song pitched too high for free and enjoyable singing. (c) The singer seems to present it rather as though it were an encore on a concert program, instead of singing it as though she were trying to get a group of children to sing along with her.

Let me dwell for a moment here on the thought that this song is pitched too high for its purpose of getting children to sing. This is a very common fault in songs intended to be used by children in school. For many years there has been a sort of superstition that children must "get their voices up" at all costs. But it has done a great deal of harm, for we know definitely that the kind of high-pitched singing so often required is not natural to them. Songs pitched too high tend to block just that kind of spontaneous, expressive singing for which you should always aim before anything else.

So we have already arrived at some general criteria and understandings. These, of course, are more important for our purpose than specific evaluations of specific records. To recapitulate, we have found that a song should be, above all, beautiful, expressive, appealing, both in its music and its text. Here is certainly the paramount consideration. But besides this, the song should not be too intricate in its melodic line, it should be comfortably pitched, and it should be intimately presented. You will find it interesting and instructive to go through all the records in the four albums of the "Basic Singing Program" with these criteria in mind. I think you will come to feel that the first condition is abundantly fulfilled, but that the material is somewhat uneven with regard to the other three. Perhaps I might venture to give you a hint or two to guide you, although I can only express my own opinions with which you may well disagree. Thus all the songs on record 4, Album I seem to me to range from good to very good from the standpoint of singability. The same appears to me to be true of "Blow the Man Down" (record 2, Volume IV), "Night Herding Song" (record 1, Volume V), and a good many others. However when we turn to "Loch Lomond" and "The Land of the Sky-Blue Water" (both on record 4, Volume IV), it is a different story. The songs are beautiful. Your children would certainly enjoy singing them. You could do all sorts of things with them—dramatizations, projections in expressive movement, and so forth. But they are presented as though the artist were singing from a concert platform, rather than trying to get others to sing along with him. So you may regretfully conclude that they are not as practical as they might be when it comes to organizing dynamic singing situations in your classroom. I believe that if you will follow up this kind of critical evaluation, you will find it both enjoyable and repaying. You will learn a good deal about how to judge material, which is the first step in learning how to use it. Also you will see clearly that a fine musical training is no guarantee whatever that a person is fitted to do an effective job of teaching in an elementary school. For many of the vocalists who have recorded the songs in these albums are obviously performers, first and foremost, and not promoters of the act of song, which is just what a teacher ought to be, and what you yourself can be.

Now let us pick up a handful of other records of a decidedly different type. We will choose the following: "The Gingerbread Boy" and "Chicken Licken" (Decca DU 88009), "Grandfather's Farm" (Children's Record Guild CRG 5004), and "Ship Ahoy" (Children's Record Guild CRG 5003). All of them are commercial releases. Several important things can be learned from studying these records.

(a) The music, although it is not "great," is nevertheless "good," i.e., expressive, appealing, poetic. The same is true of the text. (b) As to singability, they measure up very well. The melodies are not intricate, and the presentation is intimate and inviting. The range of pitch in one or two instances might be questionable. (c) From a strictly musical standpoint the presentation is not always impeccable. If you listen carefully you will notice that here and there the singer takes certain liberties, changes and slurs certain notes, and slides about the pitch. Various people have criticized these records very harshly on this account. Undoubtedly it is a defect, but I myself would not consider it a fatal one. After all, our great question is "Will these records make your children *want to sing?*" (d) Many of these songs are presented by the male voice. Is this suitable for children? Some very able and experienced persons doubt it. My general conclusion is that it makes far less difference than you might suppose, so long as the man sings intimately, warmly, and in a manner to encourage others to join in. Most certainly Frank Luther, who is one of the artists involved, does all this. (e) I have reserved what is perhaps the most outstanding point until the end. All these songs are of the "song-story" type, i.e., the music is embedded in a continuity or narrative. What about that? The answer is that it presents you with fine opportunities. The narrative itself can get the children singing, without any help from you. Moreover it suggests dramatization, imitative and expressive movement, and the introduction of mechanical sound effects. Children can participate otherwise than by singing, and such participation may be a very effective means of arousing the will to sing.

Now let us examine some "straight" songs, either deliberately intended for "singalong" purposes or usable as such. They are as follows: "Sing-Along" (Young People's Records, Inc. 722), "Another Sing-Along" (Young People's Records, Inc. 723), "Let's All Join In" (Young People's Records, Inc. 403), "Thirty-Three Children's Songs," sung by Frank Luther (Decca-DU 88004-88005, two records), "The Wayfaring Stranger," sung by Burl Ives

(Columbia Set C-103). Here again we have plenty to consider, plenty to learn.

(*a*) These records will give you many hints and pointers about how to get a group of children singing. Notice how the thing is done, particularly with the first three, which have been very successful. The music itself is appealing; this in itself makes you want to join in. It is sung in such a way as to promote the singing of others. The layout on the record is practical, in the sense that with a little care and practice you can get the needle down just about where you want it. (*b*) As to Frank Luther's singing of the thirty-three children's songs, it is direct, intimate, and inviting; and the songs themselves are worth while. But the record is crowded, and you would have trouble picking out any one particular song and getting the needle down just at its beginning. (*c*) I have introduced the Burl Ives records here for a deliberate reason. They may serve to open your eyes to the tremendous range of exceedingly attractive American folk material. You can use this material for all kinds of purposes. With your children it will be almost sure fire, and surely it is a legitimate part of their musical heritage, as Americans.

Let us now briefly summarize this rather lengthy discussion of the possibilities of records for the organization of singing situations. (*a*) Always choose songs primarily on the basis of their expressive significance and aesthetic appeal. Songs lacking in these characteristics are not germane to your purpose, which is to bring *music* to your children. There are plenty of good songs. Why use anything else? (*b*) Choose recordings in which the presentation is direct, simple, imaginative, and inviting. (*c*) **Pay attention to the pitch range, the upper limit of which**

should correspond approximately to that of the treble
staff. Beware of songs that go too high. (*d*) Beware of songs
which involve too much intricacy in the melodic line.
Younger children in particular will find them frustrating.

One final comment of importance should be made.
*Do not let the use of recordings hamper your own develop-
ment, or discourage you unduly in the use of your own
voice.* If your children can sing along at once and learn
to sing better through the agency of recorded music, so can
you. The best type of intimate, direct, imaginative presentation can be stimulating to your children. Do not avoid
this same stimulus on your own account. You may never
reach the point of being able to perform like a concert
singer, and there is no reason why you should. But you
certainly can come to find more and more pleasure in
using your voice for expressive song.

2. As to the actual management of the singing situation,
always remember that its controlling purpose is to arouse
the will to sing. In other words, the singing situation is
neither more nor less than an opportunity for your children to enjoy beautiful and appealing music through the
use of their voices. Do not, therefore, point it towards
ulterior aims. You are not trying to teach the fundamentals, or proper methods of voice production, nor should
you be particularly interested in trying to get your children
to learn to read. You simply want them to experience
music through song. If the material you use has genuine
musical vitality and worth, that experience in itself can
have great significance and value.

It follows from what has just been said that the more
direct, natural, and informal your procedures, the better
things are likely to go. There is, for instance, no need to
assign children to special "singing seats," as is so often

done, with the good voices at the back of the room and the poor voices in the front. The purpose of such a plan has always been to make the tone produced by the good voices audible to everybody, and to place the poorer singers where they will be accessible to the teacher. This practice, however, clearly implies an emphasis on tone and tone-production rather than upon singing itself, and you may be sure that such an emphasis is conveyed by suggestion to the children. If you are going to change the seating arrangement at all, it would be better to let the children gather around in the front of the room where they can hear the music well, taking any position that they please. Do not think of them as pupils who are going to be taught a lesson, but as small human beings who are about to lift up their voices in song with pleasure and profit to themselves.

So much for the general picture of the singing situation. Now let us consider some of the specific points involved in handling it.

(a) You will always be wise to let the song itself do as much of the teaching as possible. Do not pick it to pieces beforehand. Do not stick in your thumb and pull out a couple of tonal patterns for preliminary study. Never mind about neutral syllables, or *tonic-sol-fa* syllables, or numbers, or note names. Teach the whole song. Do not teach the material little bit by little bit, or even phrase by phrase. Remember always that *the song itself is the thing*. Think of the song as something to be sung and enjoyed and treated as such, simply and directly.

Good records are exceedingly well suited to this "song-wise" approach, because they provide the supremely valuable elements of impulse and inspiration. Even if you are a good pianist and quite competent in using your voice, it is very doubtful if you can rival Burl Ives, Frank Luther, or Charity Bailey in singing a song in such a way as to make children want to join in. If Ives, or Luther, or Bailey could visit your classroom, they would have your children singing in just about thirty seconds flat. It is true that some of their magnetism cannot be captured on a recording, but the records are very effective, nevertheless. In any case, the vital consideration is to get the song rolling. If you happen to be a very good song leader, use your own talent most of the time and use records only occasionally. If your own vocal powers range from reasonably good to vestigial, rely extensively upon records, using your own voice to pick up the tune and to draw everybody else in by example.

Do not pussyfoot in your approach. If you have found a song which interests and charms your children, let them pick it up when and as they will, fragmentarily at first, and then with more and more completeness and confidence. You will be surprised to find how fast they can learn a new song in this way, and how well they can sing it. This is what I mean by letting the song itself do as much as possible of the teaching.

(b) The time for analysis, for calling attention to this or that specific detail or aspect of the music or the performance, is after the children have become able to sing the song, and not before. Attention to such details as rhythm, pitch, or loudness should always be for the purpose of making the singing of the song more enjoyable, more expressive.

Here is an instance from a second-grade classroom. The teacher began by inviting the children to choose a favorite song to be sung, which at once produced an easy mood and a relaxed feeling. They chose "Rain Drops" from

Book 2 of *New Music Horizons,* which they proceeded to sing through. Then the teacher asked them to look at the picture on page 86 of the book, which shows four drops of water coming down, the first and third being larger than the others, with the first the largest of all.

"How many rain drops do you see?" inquired the teacher.

"Four."

"Are they all the same size?"

"No, some are bigger than others."

"Which is the biggest . . . the next biggest?"

"The first . . . the third."

"All right! Whenever we come to the first and the third, let's make big tunes." (sic!)

The song was then sung again, this time accompanied by clapping, and it certainly had an added verve. The accent-pattern of four-four time was conveyed, not as a problem in arithmetic, but as an element of expressive beauty.

However, the teacher still had something more to say. When the song was finished, she remarked, "Oh my! I'm not sure whether that was a rain song or a hail song. Class, how does the rain sound?"

There was a little fumbling, but soon an answer satisfactory to all emerged.

"Lightly."

"Then let's sing our song *lightly.*"

Which they proceeded to do, with good success.

(c) The use of familiar favorite songs, which was involved in the instance just given, deserves a word of special comment. Some teachers have found it a very good idea to compile a list of such songs on the basis of the votes of the children, revising it as occasion demands. The use of such songs can often be very helpful in creating good singing situations. This is similar to the list of favorite compositions suggested in our chapter on listening.

(d) It should be obvious that the text of a song provides many opportunities for establishing a good singing situation. If the text is as poetic and imaginative as it ought to be, then nothing more complicated than a brief discussion of it, or even the expressive reading of it, is needed to set the preliminary mood in effective fashion. And in the course of developing the song, you can often return to the text and its meaning for the sake of making the singing more beautiful, more suitable, more expressive.

Or again, the text can be dramatized. Thus a first-grade group was using "The Ice Cream Man," which appears on page 29 in *New Music Horizons* teacher's book for the first grade. They dramatized the song by bringing in the ice cream man with a slow wave of the hand (two measures) and by describing his truck by motions of both hands, first left and right and then above and below (third and fourth measure). During the next two measures, they rang the ice cream man's bell and, for the last two measures, repeated the motions with which they began the song.

(e) Let singing arise naturally in connection with listening and in connection with expressive bodily movement. When activities of these types are going on, let the children sing if they want to sing and when they want to sing. If a real singing momentum gets started at a time when you had in mind either listening or bodily expression, do not check it. On the contrary, take hold of it and shape it up. There is no more reason for insisting on a fixed posture in singing than for insisting on a special seating arrangement. Remember that it is the child rather than the voice that sings. And he will sing best when impulse and inspiration arrive which motivate naturally this singing.

(f) What about accompaniments? In recommending the use of "singalong" records I have obviously assumed that your children will do a good deal of accompanied singing. Yet there has been much insistence upon unaccompanied and even unaided singing. This insistence has, in fact, been made into somewhat of a fetish. The reason usually given is that such singing forces children to grapple with musical problems entirely without assistance, so that they are likely to learn better. This, however, clearly contemplates something very different from free, natural, enjoyable singing, and carries with it the implication that the function of song is to get children to master tone production and tonal patterns and grammatical fundamentals. There is, however, a very genuine danger in the use of an accompaniment, particularly on the piano, for it can completely submerge the singing. This should most certainly be avoided. The true function of an accompaniment is not to drown out the children, but to incite them to sing more easily and more expressively. For this purpose a good record may often be better than the piano, and the same may be true of the guitar, the accordion, a small group of flutophones, or various rhythm instruments. The autoharp, too, is an excellent medium for the accompanying of songs, because it is not obtrusive, and yet supports the voices very well. Moreover you yourself can learn to play it without any undue investment of time or trouble.

In summary, there is no general or universal answer to the question "What about accompaniments?" Remember the controlling purpose of the singing situation—to get your children to want to sing and to want to sing better. When a song is being started, accompanying it will almost certainly help. Sometimes when the song is being polished, the voices should sound alone. But in the later stages, a stimulating, imaginative, provocative, expressive accompaniment will be pretty sure to add to the pleasure of the experience.

(g) Should you yourself sing along with the children? Most of the time, yes; always, no. The singing of a good song should be a shared group experience, and you yourself are a member of the group, albeit the focal member. The issue closely resembles that involved in the use or avoidance of accompaniments. Those who lay down a universal principle that the teacher should never sing along with the children, because by so doing she might help them, are obviously contemplating something other than natural, enjoyable singing. But you wish to create and maintain a singing situation, and your own example, participation, and pleasure can have a strong and beneficial influence towards this end.

(h) Should the children use song books? There is no reason at all why they should never do so. There is no reason at all why they should always do so. It will often be helpful to them to have both the text and the score before their eyes. As to the score, it is true that you are not engaged in teaching them to read, but there certainly is nothing against calling your children's attention to this or that passage or detail as it stands in the notation, wherever so doing may seem advisable. Also many modern song books for children contain excellent pictures and interesting explanatory accounts. It would be very foolish not to make good use of such material. Books judiciously employed can help in the creation and management of vital singing situations.

3. The problem of what is often termed the "child voice" is one that frequently comes up in discussions of elementary school singing. This so-called "child voice"

is supposed to have certain desirable characteristics. It is supposed to be light, high, and soft, and to be what is often called a "head voice." From a purely musical and even a purely vocal standpoint these characteristics are dubious, to say the least. As to lightness and softness, there is no reason whatsoever why children should not sing this way upon some occasions, but also sing heartily and indeed loudly when this is demanded by the expressive content of the music. The idea that children's voices should always be urged upwards has been submitted to experimental investigations and observation; both tests and wide experience have proved that this premise is a fallacy, that all children do not sing naturally on a very high pitch level, that those who do are the exception rather than the rule, and that many of the songs in the older school music series are pitched definitely too high. As to the alleged "head voice," it is a perfectly meaningless and preposterous expression. It corresponds to nothing in reality, nothing in the vocal action itself. There is simply no such thing as a "head voice" any more than there is any such thing as a "stomach voice," which is another common although less familiar vagary of vocal teachers.

But our criticism of this concept of the "child voice" goes further and deeper than these purely musical and vocal objections to it. *For you are not dealing with voices, but with children.* You are not, or at any rate you should not be, trying to produce a certain style of vocal production, but rather to help all the children in your group to find enjoyment and self-fulfillment as persons in experiencing music through the act of song. This must always be the focal consideration, and it carries with it plenty of definite practical implications. You will try to overcome indiscriminate yelling, because it obscures all refreshing and repaying contact with music, although it may for the moment be fun.

For the same reason you will not work for the kind of whisper-singing so greatly admired in certain quarters. When from time to time you ask your children to sit up straight, breathe deeply, and sing, your central purpose in so doing will not be to make the vocal machinery work better, but to bring about a focusing of their personalities; and, as we have already remarked, this conventional singing posture is by no means a universal *sine qua non*. You will not be much concerned about ruining your children's voices—something which you will realize is beyond your capacity, in any case, whenever you listen to the use children make of these voices on the playground. But you will always be very much concerned about frustrating and inhibiting their will to sing.

When you try to help your children vocally, your aim will not be to produce better voices, but to enable them to find more joy in singing (which, by the way, is more likely than anything else to improve their vocal production). Dwell on the meaning of the text and the feeling of the music, and encourage the children to express these values as they sing. Do not let false fears about imitation prevent you from using records as models. Emphasize the importance of clear enunciation—"dear*est*" rather than "dear*ust*," "judg*ment*" rather than "judg*munt*," the sounding of the final "r" in words ending in "r," and so forth—for clear enunciation is a most valuable aid in singing. Teach your children to avoid sliding up to and away from tones instead of singing them squarely. Also teach them to avoid catching the breath in the middle of phrases. These are the crucial points to have in mind in the management of singing. You yourself can learn to deal with them. But deal with them always for the sake of releasing free, natural, expressive song, and not with the idea of establishing a vocal technique. Children naturally enjoy singing and can benefit from it in many ways. But both the enjoyment and the benefits can be increased if you help them to improve their singing. A great deal of such help you can give on the basis of your own good common sense and judgment. You can certainly get valuable pointers from some of the music specialists in your school system. But if some of these suggestions happen to be technical, remember that you must use them simply to release the act of song and to enrich and invigorate the experience of singing, and that you should never go one inch of the way towards transforming yourself from a teacher of children into a teacher of voice.

4. Numerous references have already been made in these pages to the monotone, or the non-singer, or the hesitating singer, but it is appropriate here to consider directly the problem he presents. The basic reason why a child's inability to sing is regrettable is not that he fails in a required accomplishment, but that he is blocked off from a whole range of delightful and repaying experiences. It is perfectly true that he can and should experience music in many other ways, so that the blockage is not fatal. But there is no doubt whatever that singing has certain peculiar musical and human values of its own, and for a child to miss them is a very great pity.

When a child does not sing, and cannot sing, or gives the impression that he cannot sing, the difficulty nearly always lies in his adjustment as a person rather than in some defect in his vocal organs. His inability may be due simply to inexperience with dynamic group singing situations; if this is the case the trouble is likely to clear up of its own accord, given time and patience. Or the cause may be the emotional and social negativism which certain children manifest as they develop; or it may be general indifference and unresponsiveness, arising out of spoiling and pampering out of school, or conversely out of under-privileged out-of-school conditions. If a child fails to sing after all uninhibited situations fail, he might well be checked by a physician for some physical defect.

All this indicates the proper line to take in dealing with the child who does not sing, or who does not sing well. (a) Persistently organize dynamic singing situations, re-membering that their influence on certain individuals re-quires time. (b) Open up for the child a variety of musical activities other than singing. (c) Never, directly or by im-plication, discourage the child from singing as well as he can when he is willing to do so. (d) Never subject him to humiliation, as for instance by using individual tone-matching drills in front of the class. Abstract tone-match-ing is difficult for a child in any case, and when the non-singer makes a public and ridiculous failure, any nascent impulse to sing is almost sure to be killed, and all block-ages against singing greatly reinforced.

Skillful and intuitive teachers, working in very favorable situations, have found it possible to do much to help the non-singing child to solve his problem by giving direct vocal aid. Non-singing children are taken in small groups of three or four, and special singing situations are created for them. Easy, expressive enjoyable songs are chosen. Everything possible is done to give encouragement and in-centive and to maintain a will to sing. The children are not disheartened by the presence of others who sing much better. There is no tone-matching, no drill. The treatment simply consists in the singing of songs under these sympathetic, stimulating, and very helpful conditions, and some very remarkable results have been achieved. I do not describe this technique with the thought that you yourself will be in a position to apply it, for such may not be the case. My purpose is to show you what is actually involved in successfully transforming a non-singing child into a singer by focalized vocal assistance, and also to indicate how greatly the correct procedure differs, both in its human and its musical emphasis, from the clumsy and destructive tone-matching drills that go on in far too many classrooms.

One final word needs to be said before we leave this subject. *Never classify the non-singing child as an unmusical child.* Singing is a lovely and rewarding thing for any child, but music itself is far greater than song. Even if some apparently unconquerable inhibition prevents a child from singing, he may still respond profoundly and to his lasting benefit to the manifold and varied appeal of the musical art.

5. Do what you can to organize singing opportunities outside the classroom. Community singing in the school assembly, or with two or more grades or groups brought together, can be very stimulating and helpful. There is the element of novelty and also the momentum due to sheer numbers and the resulting mass of tone. Do not, however, emphasize performance as such, but make such occasions genuine, dynamic, informal singing situations, directed always toward the benefit of the children. For instance, if not too many are present and the physical conditions of the room make it possible, a circular seating arrangement may be helpful. The participation of the school band or orchestra can also add zest to such large-group singing.

Some classroom teachers have been able to organize an elementary school chorus or glee club. Naturally, these must be selected groups, to some extent, although they should be set up on what is called an opportunity basis, which means that children should feel free to seek membership on their own initiative rather than simply being chosen by the teacher. Selective requirements for admission should include the child's own interest, his ability to make the necessary social adjustments, the quality of his voice, his capacity to control pitch, and his ability to sustain a part. Also the balance of parts in the organization must be considered. Eligibility should be limited, though not rigidly, to fifth and sixth graders, though some fourth-grade children will also be found suitable for membership. The two crucial questions to consider about any such organizations are (a) what effects does it have on its members as persons? (b) what is its over-all influence throughout the school? There is no doubt that membership in such an organization can be a rich and memorable experience, both musically and personally, and for this reason it belongs in the pattern of a child's general education and can constitute a constructive force in his development. Rehearsals, accordingly, should be effective and regular, taking place at least for two periods a week in school time, and should include some memorized songs, some new songs, and some half-learned songs. There is no objection at all against working towards stated public performances, so long as the children are not exploited, and so long as they are not endlessly drilled on a very small repertoire. To display one's achievement to others, and to share with others the joy of singing are natural desires and powerful incentives, and no apologies are needed for using them.

# CHAPTER SEVEN

# Making Music with Instruments

I

IN BRINGING MUSIC TO YOUR CHILDREN YOU should by all means give them rich and varied opportunities for *making music with instruments*. Such opportunities open up avenues of personal participation other than those afforded by singing or expressive bodily movement and highlight various aspects of music which are not emphasized elsewhere. No program of music for your children can be rounded and complete unless it includes the experience of music making by instrumental means.

Here, as so often happens, the conventional words and phrases which we are almost compelled to use in talking about musical matters convey quite misleading suggestions. To speak of playing a musical instrument seems at once to indicate the use of some "standard" instrument such as the piano, the violin, or the clarinet; and also it raises the formidable problem of technique, for the "standard" instruments are difficult to use. Is it really proposed that your children should be offered lessons on these instruments and that they should set to work to gain the necessary skills for dealing with them? Could work of this kind properly be said to provide "rich and varied opportunities for making music with instruments"? Would it really be a good thing for a majority of your children, even if it could be arranged at all? Above all, could you

yourself carry it on? You may very well ask these questions, and the answer to each and all of them is no!

Let us look into this matter of musical instruments and
see what it is that we can and should do. What, first of all,
is a musical instrument? Disregarding its name, and strip-
ping it of all conventions, it is in essence nothing more nor
less than a machine—a mechanical means for the making
of music. This characterization is true of pianos, violins,
organs, French horns, and so forth, which are complicated
and delicate machines. But it is true also of far simpler
machines, such as rhythm sticks or homemade flutes and
rattles. Since these provide mechanical means for the making of music, they are genuine musical instruments. Now
the peculiar values that a person can get from working
with a musical instrument do not come from the complexities of the machine, which indeed may prove frustrating.
These values come from the sheer fact that he is using a
machine. For instance, a child who is taking piano lessons
will be almost sure to learn the notes far better than he
could from just singing. The piano, of course, is a complicated machine; but the child could learn the notes just
as well from a homemade zither, or a set of water glasses,
or a dollar flute, which are all quite simple machines. Let
me hasten to say that I mention the learning of the notes
only as one illustration of the many valuable musical insights that a person can certainly get from working with an
instrument. The point is that these insights or understandings arise not from the complexity of the instrument,
but from its machine-like character, which requires the
child to manipulate it in this or that way to produce a desired effect. It follows, therefore, that in organizing opportunities for your children to make music with instruments,
you should not limit your thought to the standard instru-

ments but think, rather, of other simpler mechanical means for the making of music.

All this suggests our line of attack upon the problem of technique. If it were possible, by some magic procedure, to teach your children to play the piano, or the violin, or the clarinet really well in three easy lessons, it would be wonderful. They would have available to them means for exploring and experiencing music very richly, and also all kinds of opportunities for personal self-fulfillment and group cooperation. This, of course, cannot be done; but we can put into the hands of children machines for the making of music which are very easy to operate, such as tuned water glasses, drums, marimbas, small flutes, sand blocks, harps of various kinds, and so forth. Admittedly a person cannot go so far into music or do so much with it by these simple means as he can through the use of standard instruments. But such easily manipulated machines can bring to a child entirely authentic and very valuable musical experiences, and also personally valuable experiences in the way of participation. Many teachers, including both classroom teachers and music specialists, are discovering and utilizing the very valuable possibilities offered by easy-to-operate mechanical means for the making of music. But it is very important for teachers to understand just why the use of such simple instruments can be beneficial, if the benefits are actually to accrue. This is my reason for beginning with a rather careful and lengthy analysis of just what is involved.

Various terms and labels have been attached to the kind of music-making devices to which I have referred. Sometimes they are called "toy instruments"; but this seems a needlessly disparaging expression, for if one thinks of their potentialities, they well deserve to be taken seriously.

Sometimes they are called "social instruments"; but this seems to carry the rather odd suggestion that the standard instruments are non-social, which certainly should not be the case. Sometimes they are called "pre-band" and "pre-orchestral instruments." All the suggestions and implications of these terms are thoroughly bad and thoroughly wrong. The point of introducing simple instruments is just precisely not to prepare your children directly for complicated ones; but rather to open up for them the art of music in a new and easily available medium. To speak of these music-making devices as "simple instruments" comes closer to what we ought to have in mind, but the word seems a little ambiguous and indefinite. We shall do best to call them "easy-to-play musical instruments," for this is exactly what they are, and the term suggests precisely the values we hope to get from them.

## II

What kinds of easy-to-play musical instruments can we have? In dealing with this question, and indeed in our basic planning for the organization of experiences with music-making by instruments, a good starting point is to consider the various ways in which music is actually produced by mechanical means.

*First,* music can be made mechanically by percussion, that is, by striking objects together. Here a subclassification is necessary. Sometimes the objects struck together to produce music are capable of producing only one pitch; examples of this include cymbals, rattles, sticks, and some kinds of drums. Sometimes we have arrays of such objects, capable of producing many different pitches, such as sets of bells, chimes, marimbas, or the piano with its strings. *Second,* music can be produced mechanically by friction and plucking, as in the case of sand blocks, the various types of harps, the guitar, the violin, and the old-time harpsichord. *Third,* music can be mechanically produced by blowing, which makes the column of air within an instrument vibrate, examples being Panpipes, flutes, reed instruments, and the pipe organ.*

All standard instruments depend in one way or another on some one of these three processes of hitting, rubbing, and blowing. But all of them are hard to play. Our practical problem, therefore, is to produce easily manipulated devices which also utilize these processes, and which sound reasonably well. This reduces the subject to its ultimate simplicity. If you look at it in this way, you will see very clearly what is involved. Moreover your own inventiveness will be stimulated, for you and your children can devise many excellent means of utilizing hitting, rubbing, and blowing for the making of music. This is what we should have in mind when we talk about giving children rich and varied opportunities to experience music through the use of mechanical means or, in other words, of easy-to-play instruments.

A wide array of such instruments can be purchased.** Also many types of them can be made by your children. Quite apart from cost, there are many obvious advantages to be gained from encouraging children to make their own instruments. They can learn much about music in the

* Of course music can also be produced electrically, but we need not concern ourselves with this.
** Among the firms supplying them are Gamble Hinged Music Company, Wabash Avenue, Chicago, Ill.; Lyon and Healy Company, Jackson Boulevard, Chicago, Ill.; Lyons Band Instrument Company, 223 West Lake Street, Chicago, Ill.; Peripole Products Company, 2917 Avenue R, Brooklyn 29, N.Y.; Oscar Schmidt-International, 87 Ferry St., Jersey City 7, N.J.; Walberg and Auge, Worcester, Mass.

process and profit from many opportunities for cooperative planning and action.

Naturally if you are going to set up instrument-making projects with your children, both you and they will need guidance and help. In looking for such help, your best single source will be *Creative Music for Children,* by Satis N. Coleman (G. P. Putnam's Sons, New York, 1922). Also you will find valuable suggestions in *Creative School Music,* by Lillian Mohr Fox and L. Thomas Hopkins (Silver Burdett Company, New York, 1937), and in *Music in the New School,* by Beatrice Perham (Niel A. Kjos, Chicago, 1937 and 1950). A great deal of experience with regard to this type of work has accumulated, and there is available a wealth of practical and specific suggestions. This is not the place to give you exhaustive instructions about making simple instruments, and I will not undertake to do so. But it seems worth while to indicate possibilities by a few illustrations.

There are many types of easy-to-play, single-pitch percussion instruments. Rhythm sticks, for instance, are simply sticks of wood of various lengths and thicknesses, to be struck together or used for tapping on floor or desk. They can be bought, but it is easy to make them out of dowel sticks which can be had in various thicknesses and cut to the desired lengths. Gourds and moraccas are Cuban instruments of the rattle type. These too can be purchased, but also are easily made, for instance by using a small can or a cardboard box containing dried peas or BB shot. There are various types of jingle sticks, all of them being essentially rattle instruments, with the rattle attached to a handle. Drums of many kinds can be bought or satisfactorily made in a variety of ways; for instance, from tin cans of various sizes, by covering the open ends with inner tubing attached with rubber bands. Cymbals, which are clash instruments, are not very readily made, because a good clear tone calls for a specific kind of metal. Homemade cymbals have, however, been constructed out of saucepan lids and suchlike articles. The triangle is an inviting and intriguing instrument for children, and it has many good uses in the classroom. It is not easy to make at home, because of the need for bending the metal, but with cooperation from interested parents or the school shop this has been done.

Turning to multiple-pitch percussion instruments, the easiest to construct is the set of tuned water glasses or bottles. Dr. Arthur Fultz of the Boston State Hospital uses tuned water glasses in his work and has a very interesting name for them. He calls them "tunable tumblers"! Bottles have definite advantages over open glasses, because they can be corked or otherwise covered to prevent evaporation, and also because they can be hung in order on a rack. The marimba is an array of wooden bars tuned to the scale and struck with hammers. The construction of a good marimba is a somewhat ambitious project, because the sticks must be cut to just the right length and the proper kind of wood and varnish must be used if there is to be a satisfactory result. Mrs. Coleman gives instructions on the making of marimbas in *Creative Music for Children*. The xylophone is an instrument similar to the marimba in general type, but using metal instead of wooden bars. I have already given an account of the making of a xylophone in school with the help of one of the parents who had metal-working facilities. The collection and arrangement of sets of bells of many kinds offer numerous possibilities. Here you will find valuable suggestions in the two listed books on bells by Satis N. Coleman.

As to friction instruments, sand blocks are no doubt the
very simplest example. They are often regarded as percussion instruments, but I prefer to mention them in this connection. They can easily be made by attaching sandpaper
to pieces of wood. More important are the various types
of harps. There is the psaltery, a modification of the
zither. Psalteries have been made in school, though it is
not easy to do so. Instructions for making them will be
found in *Creative Music for Children*. Then there is the
autoharp, to which numerous references have already been
made. (Anyone who is not familiar with these instruments, and others that are mentioned, would find it helpful
to send for the profusely illustrated catalogs which are put
out by the various instrument companies listed on page
208.) The autoharp is a harp-type instrument with a
number of bars which can be pressed down to produce
chords when the strings are swept. It comes in two sizes,
with five bars and twelve bars. A five-bar autoharp is sufficient for most of your purposes. Indeed the very presence
in the room of a twelve-bar autoharp has been known to
tempt teachers beyond their endurance to give formal lessons in harmony. The instrument is easy to learn, produces a good tone, and is excellent for accompaniments.
An excellent source of instruction both for learning and
using this instrument is *Autoharp Accompaniments to Old
Favorite Songs,* by Lillian Mohr Fox (C. C. Birchard and
Company, Boston, 1947).

Among wind instruments, the most widely used are the
tonette, the recorder, and the flutophone, with the last
named instrument generally the favorite. Instruction
books for learning to play them are supplied by the manu-
facturing companies. Wind instruments of various types,
such as Panpipes, shepherd's pipes, whistles, and simple

flutes have been successfully made and played with enjoyment by children in school.

This brief introduction to easy-to-play instruments is very far from exhaustive. Indeed its only purpose is to indicate a few instruments that are available and to suggest what can be done. Many other kinds of easy-to-play instruments will be found listed in the manufacturers' catalogs. Also endless ingenuity has gone into the making of such instruments by children and teachers. Oatmeal containers, wooden kegs, mixing bowls, flower pots, pie tins, bottle tops, lengths of hollow bamboo are among the simple materials which have been put to an astonishing range of musical uses. Often school-made instruments are lovingly decorated and carefully fashioned, and both their construction and use give great satisfaction.

## III

Before we consider classroom procedures in connection with music making by means of easy-to-play instruments, it is first necessary to be clear about the values and benefits you should want your children to derive—about the *why* of these instrumental experiences and activities. Until this basic question has been answered, you cannot proceed intelligently to deal with the *how* of using simple instruments. We will consider first the broadly human values which ought to be contemplated and, second, the more definitely musical values, although of course the two are by no means rigidly separable.

1. The use of easy-to-play instruments at once opens for your children a great many avenues for enjoyment, self-fulfillment, successful achievement, cooperative group action, initiative, and leadership in connection with music.

(a) It is clear that instruments provide a wide range

of opportunities for pleasure and success in the performance of music. Children who cannot sing are given
chances to play. Children who for the moment prefer to
play have the chance to do so. Singing itself can be
enriched and enhanced by instrumental accompaniments
played by some of the children. Instruments can also be
used in complete and independent ensembles which play
pieces of music along with the phonograph or the piano;
the albums entitled "Rhythmic Activities" in the *RCA
Victor Basic Record Library for Elementary Schools,* as
well as many standard commercial records, provide material very well adapted for this purpose. Instruments can
be used by some of the children in connection with expressive bodily movement. Interesting projects and demonstrations can be carried on. All this is very valuable
because it implies a great many opportunities for personal
pleasure and success in the making of music.

(b) The various activities just mentioned provide many
opportunities for individual and group planning, choosing,
and initiative on the part of the children. What instruments could best be used to accompany a song, to go along
with a pattern of expressive bodily movement, to orches-
trate a piece? Why would certain instruments be better
than others? How could instrumental expression best be
arranged in connection with projects on Indian life, or
Spanish life, or cowboy life? Would it be well to obtain
certain instruments not already possessed? Where could
one obtain them? How much would they cost? Could
any plan be made and carried out for raising money for
buying them? Where should the instruments be stored?
What plans should be made for keeping them in good
condition? All these problems should be handled by the
children themselves as far as possible. Obviously they sug-

gest responsibilities and projects for individuals and sub-
groups, as well as active discussion and study by the group
as a whole. These are by no means mere busy-work activities. If you doubt that problems connected with the use,
selection, and care of instruments have an authentic musical relevance, ask any musician. And you can hardly doubt
that in carrying such responsibilities, children can learn a
great deal about working and planning together, or that
individuals among them may reveal themselves in new and
enlightening ways and benefit by challenges to initiative
and leadership.

(c) It is quite evident that the actual making of instruments also involves a great deal of individual and group
planning, initiative, and discrimination. The construction at home or in school of simple instruments can be a
most interesting challenge to ingenuity, and the outcomes
can be a source of pride and satisfaction to the makers.
Individuals or small groups can be asked to see what they
can do to provide instruments of such and such a kind.
Everyone can contribute suggestions. The workers can
bring in progress reports and, finally, they can demonstrate the finished product and explain the problems which
arose in making it. Cooperation and help can be obtained
from interested parents and others. It is, of course, possible
to spend too much time on the making of instruments; but
such work involves musical challenges, constructional challenges, and also challenges along the lines of personal initiative, cooperativeness, leadership, and good judgment in
dealing with others.

(d) The use of easy-to-play instruments tends in many
different ways to extend the musical activities of your children beyond the classroom and beyond the school. This is
already clearly evident in what has been said. For instance,

if instruments are to be purchased, letters can be written
to manufacturers, catalogs can be examined, perhaps samples can be borrowed here and there and tried out, the
opinions of experts can be solicited, and so forth. The
making of instruments, too, carries over immediately into
home life. I have already suggested the numerous potential values of having such an instrument as the autoharp
available to the children out of school time. Doubtless,
too, you will recall the examples of the boy who practiced
the flutophone so assiduously at home, of the girl who
studied the guitar independently in order to contribute
to an instrumental ensemble. There is no doubt that the
judicious use of easy-to-play instruments offers many opportunities for making music a very realistic influence in the
out-of-school living of many children.

2. Turning now to the distinctively musical possibilities
of simple instruments, there is at the outset a fallacy which
needs to be recognized as such and scotched. Because such
instruments are easy to play, and because the musical effects they can produce are limited and imperfect, it is often
assumed that they are trivial and inconsequential, and that
nothing of much importance can be learned from using
them, however enjoyable children may find it to do so.
But this disparaging conclusion does not follow at all from
the premises. No doubt the piano or the violin would have
a great superiority if they could be made as easy as the
flutophone or the autoharp; but in any case the virtual
elimination of the technical problem is a tremendous advantage. Consider, for instance, what a child is likely to get
from studying the piano. It is quite unusual for him to
become aware of anything much in the actual content of
the music—its rhythms, its harmonies, the flow and expressiveness of its melody, its form. The reason is that his

attention is entirely taken up with the notes and the problems of playing them, that is to say he must be preoccupied with technique, for the piano is a technically difficult instrument. It is true that the best modern methods of teaching elementary piano do stress musical values and musical content as much as possible. But such methods are very far from being available everywhere; and even so the technical problem still remains formidable. Clearly, then, if a child can be given an instrument which greatly reduces this problem, he can put his mind on the music he is making instead of on the exacting but after all mechanical business of getting his fingers to strike the right keys. So here is the great and central musical advantage of easy-to-play instruments, which have a proper and valuable place in the experience of children, and indeed of older beginners also.

(a) Through the use of easy-to-play instruments your children can learn a great deal about musical rhythm. Moreover they can do so without even being introduced to measure bars, time signatures, or indeed any of the features of the standard notation, but simply by sensing how the rhythm of various pieces of music ought to go. For instance, they can experiment with the accompanying of a lively song by using rhythm sticks and tom-toms. They find that every so often one of the beats which are being played by the rhythm sticks needs to be stronger or heavier than the rest, and this they can indicate by having the tom-toms play at these points. They discover that many rhythmic patterns seem to go in fours, threes, or twos, that some are fast and light, others slow and heavy, that an accentuation can often be made by a musical tone on a bell or a water glass instead of by a tap or a thump. Such experimentation with rhythm, the possibilities of which I have done no more than merely suggest, can be very valuable indeed. It is difficult, perhaps impossible, in the medium of a standard instrument. But with easy-to-play instruments it can be managed readily.

(b) Children can get a very clear understanding of how the notes of a melody fit together by accompanying songs on some such melody-producing instrument as the flutophone, the recorder, or the psaltery. This adds something specific to the experience of singing, because the voice always tends to emphasize flow and continuity while the instrument emphasizes notes. It is surprising how much real musical insight children can pick up by nothing more complicated or ambitious than just playing along by ear with a number of songs, using simple melodic instruments.

(c) For sensing chords and harmonic effects, the best of all the easy-to-play resources is the autoharp. Children who are studying the piano usually develop very little in the way of harmonic awareness—the sense of chords and chord effects—because they are completely taken up with notes and technique. But with the autoharp they can try out various chord sequences and choices for the accompaniment of songs or the background music provided for expressive bodily movement. Experimentation with chords can be an exceedingly valuable influence in anyone's musical development, but far too little of it is done because of the difficulty of the standard instrumental media. Here again, there is not the slightest need to teach children the technical names of chords, at any rate for quite some time. The point is for them to become familiar by ear with their effects and satisfactory uses.

(d) Once again, easy-to-play instruments can be very helpful in enabling children to sense and recognize musical form. Many pieces (*The Chimes of Dunkirk,* for example) have a middle section which contrasts with the beginning and the ending. When children are experimenting with instrumentation, they can sense such contrasts and bring them out, by choosing different instruments.

(e) The choice of instruments can underline in the minds of your children the mood effects and suggestions that constantly occur in music. The children are asked to choose the instrument which best brings out the swish of the wind, the heavy tread of the elephant, the patter of rain drops, the differences between loud and soft, fast and slow, heavy and light, and so forth.

(f) Notice particularly that I have constantly spoken of *experimentation* in connection with the various musical learnings we have been considering. The great, the outstanding musical value of easy-to-play instruments is precisely that they make such experimentation possible. When children learn by experimentation, exploration, and discovery, they will not learn systematically. They will not cover everything. There will be plenty of gaps and omissions. *But what they do learn they will learn very well, and it will tend to stay learned.* This, surely, is the important thing. As a matter of fact, one of the great defects of conventional musical instruction, both in classrooms and private studios, is its failure to provide opportunities for free musical experimentation. The use of easy-to-play instruments can do much to supply this lack. And since musical experimentation can be absolutely non-technical, but simply turns on listening to a piece of music, thinking about it, and trying to identify and bring out the effects that make it beautiful and interesting, it is well within your capacity to organize and manage the business, even though you have very little musical training.

(g) One final point needs to be emphasized, because it is a most important warning. *Never regard easy-to-play*

*instruments primarily as a means for introducing children
to or preparing them for standard instruments.* Easy-to-
play instruments have personal values and musical values
entirely in their own right. They have no specific relationship to the playing of standard instruments. They are
means of music making through which children can learn
a great deal, and from which a great deal of musical stimulation can come. They should be considered as contributing to a general, over-all, dynamic musical development.
One of the outcomes of such a development may very well
be a wish to learn some standard instrument. This very
thing happens time and again. But easy-to-play instruments are not preparatory devices in the specific sense.

## IV

This discussion of the values, personal·and musical, that
can be derived and should be expected from experience
with easy-to-play instruments points straight towards procedures for using them in your classroom.

A good way to start is with simple percussion instruments, a few at a time. These can be introduced for accompanying songs or patterns of expressive movement. It is
well to have at least two types of percussion instruments
on hand (purchased or homemade) as early as possible, because the children can then invent many interesting rhythmic combinations, instead of merely tapping out the beat
of the music in a mechanical fashion. For instance, one
line of a song might have a rhythmic background as follows:—

This   is   how   the   big   tall   Indian
—         —        —        —        (big drum)
   . .            . .              . .          . . (small drum)

Another rhythm pattern for a four-four measure might be:

Tick            Tick            (tiny block)
        tock            tock    (big block)

Here are a number of percussion patterns, all of them possible with any piece of music in four-four time, i.e., march time:

Many others can also be invented. Such patterns can also be developed for music in three-four time, i.e., waltz time. They can be used either singly or in various combinations. Give your children a free hand with the invention and, indeed, the extemporization of such rhythmic patterns. Also let the children decide which pattern would be best suited for gong, big drum, small drum, rhythm sticks, wood blocks, tambourines, and so forth; and which instrument would be best for the accompanying of any given song or piece or movement pattern. Do not always stick to one instrumentation. Encourage children to invent and try out variations and changes. Remember that the point is to give them opportunities to learn and grow musically through experimentation and exploration.

As to simple melody instruments other than wind instruments, i.e., water glasses, tuned water bottles, harps, marimbas, xylophones, bells, or chimes, all of them can be very effectively and helpfully used in connection with songs and movement patterns. The number notation already explained (see pages 89 to 93) can be used very readily and conveniently with such instruments. Do not hesitate to modify this system, using symbols of your own if it does not enable you and your children to put down on paper everything that is wanted. Once again, encourage your children to choose and to decide which instruments to use, and how to combine them.

As to wind instruments, there are two ways in which they may be introduced. The first is to make the choice entirely by yourself. You order a number of instruments, all of the same kind. You intimate to your children that they are to learn to play this instrument and that you have so decided because, after investigation, you have found it satisfactory. (In case you want information about the most commonly used of the easy-to-play wind instruments and instruction about how to play them, see *Melody Fun,* by Forest Buchtel, for information about the tonette (Lyons Band Instrument Company, 223 West Lake Street, Chicago) and *Flutophone Classroom Method,* by Merrill B. Van Pelt and J. Leon Ruddick (Trophy Products Co., Cleveland 15, Ohio).)

Quite a different approach is indicated by the following report of what happened in one classroom.

A nucleus of a dozen or so children in a fifth grade had been making daily use (outside the regular school music period) of such simple instruments as psalteries, autoharp, xylophones, and marimba. The group spoke of the fact that they needed some wind instruments in their ensemble. The music teacher said that she had been considering buying several for the children, but that she had not made up her mind what kind to get. Would the group help her decide? *Would they!*

The next day the teacher brought in three varieties of simple wind instruments and asked the children to try them before making a definite choice. She showed half a dozen boys how to finger the instruments, suggested that they teach others who might wish to learn, left a bottle of alcohol and some cotton for disinfecting the mouthpieces after using, and said she would be back in a week to get their report.

The children's report at the end of that time stressed their reasons for choosing a particular instrument. In their own words the reasons were:

"It's easier to play and doesn't stretch my fingers as much as the others."

" . . . it's easier to get a good tone on."

" . . . it's cheaper, and that makes a difference."

" . . . you can't break it, and that's important." *

In general, always stress learning through experimentation, exploration and discovery rather than because of your own fiats and previous decisions, and always be willing to learn along with your children. This, of course, is one of the chief reasons for encouraging the making as well as the playing of simple instruments. When children set to work to make an instrument, they have to find out about the sound-producing characteristics of various materials, about pitch, tone quality, and so forth. All this is far removed

* Much of the above material on procedures is adapted from *Music in the New School,* by Beatrice Perham (Neil A. Kjos, Chicago, 1937). The seven percussion patterns cited on page 220 are from page 72 in that book, and the story cited above is from pages 77-78.

from busy-work or from a purely manual arts type of activity. It can lead to quite far-reaching and repaying research, and can result in much genuine and valuable musical learning as well as many repaying self-fulfillments.

Always emphasize choice actually made by the children themselves in working out instrumentations for the accompaniment of singing or expressive movement, or to go along with whatever record you choose to use. Let the children try out various effects and decide for themselves. Suggest a variety of group patterns, with everyone playing sometimes, some playing sometimes, and someone playing an occasional solo. It is often interesting to compare the easy-to-play instruments with their standard counterparts, perhaps using instrumental records such as those already suggested elsewhere in this book, or perhaps inviting performers to come for actual demonstrations. If at all possible, have an autoharp on hand both for classroom and out-of-hours use. Since you wish to encourage experimentation, work towards building a large and varied collection of instruments. As a matter of fact, the collection will tend to grow as the children become interested and find that their initiative is respected and encouraged. Remember always that your job is not to tell the children what to do, not to produce a stated and predetermined effect, still less to teach this or that easy-to-play instrument for its own sake. Your job is to create situations in which children will be stimulated, helped, and encouraged to learn and grow both musically and as persons.

I will bring this discussion to a close by mentioning a number of *don'ts*, by giving a few warnings, the point of which should be perfectly clear in the light of all that has been said.

(a) Don't lean too heavily on rhythm band books or toy

orchestra books which present developed orchestrations, seating charts, and so forth. I say this because such books give you cut-and-dried plans pointed straight towards predetermined outcomes in the way of performance. This is just precisely what you do not want. Such a procedure tends to sabotage all the real values, both personal and musical, of using easy-to-play instruments. Refer to good books for suggestions and ideas, but do not feel bound to follow the plans you find in them. Work out the plans best suited to your situation, along with your children. Everyone will learn more and get more out of the whole experience.

(b) Don't let anyone, yourself included, disparage child-made instruments as "mere toys." Some instrument manufacturers make much of the point that the instruments they produce are "not toys" but are, in fact, of superior quality. This in itself is all to the good. To have an instrument capable of true pitch and pleasing and characteristic quality is obviously desirable. But these characteristics should be discovered rather than presented ready-made. Beware of the implication that you want results in the way of performance rather than experimental learning by the children.

(c) Don't gear your work to the objective of having a rhythm band or a toy orchestra. Your primary aim is not to develop a junior performing organization, but to enrich and vitalize the musical experiences of your children. At least one of the manufacturers of simple instruments distributes catalogs showing pictures of uniforms for members of toy orchestras, similar to those used by high school marching bands. Have nothing to do with any such atrocity. You are not staging a cute display, nor exploiting your children for publicity. The simple instruments are primarily for them, and if they want to share their pleasure and their discoveries with others, let those others be parents and friends who love them and have their true interests at heart, as you yourself should do.

(d) Don't use simple instruments for the giving of lessons in music reading, or harmony, or musical form. Use them as agencies through which your children can come to a deeper enjoyment and a better understanding of music by bringing out and emphasizing the values and points of interest of actual songs and pieces. If enjoyment and understanding are achieved, such things as reading, harmony, and formal analysis will all emerge in their own good time.

CHAPTER EIGHT

# Creative Activities

## I

WHEN YOU BRING MUSIC TO YOUR CHIL-
dren, stimulate, help, and encourage them to carry on
creative activities.

But what are creative activities? What makes them
creative? How do they differ from activities which are not
creative? We must have understandable and as far as possible definite answers to these questions before we can talk
sense about this subject, and before we can tell what to do
and what to avoid when it comes to practical procedures.

But the whole idea of creativeness is very difficult to pin
down and define. It has a way of refusing to stay within
bounds and escaping from analysis. When one tries to be
specific and to say that this and that kind of thing alone
deserves to be called a creative musical activity, one finds
oneself omitting much that ought to come into the picture.
For instance, what about the composition or extemporization of original songs and instrumental melodies? Are
these creative activities in music? Certainly they are! So
far, at least, we are on firm ground. But are they the only
kind of musical activities which should properly be so
described? Here is an entirely different question, and I am
sure that the only honest answer must be no. When children evolve an interpretation of a song in dramatic action
or expressive bodily movement, are they carrying on a crea-

tive process? When a child selects the biggest, deepest drum available because he wishes to convey the impression of an elephant's heavy tread, has he made a creative decision? When a little boy asks for the recording of Debussy's *Clair de lune*, listens to it raptly, and comes back with a sigh as though from another world when the magic ceases, is not this a creative experience? To all these questions the only answer I can find is yes!

So the word "creative" covers a great range of territory; and when I urge you to encourage and help your children to create, I am not advocating one specific type of activity, as separated from everything else. Yet I am sure that the word is full of meaning which can be captured and understood, and that advice can be given that points to something so definite that you can see how to follow it in practice, and that all this will help you to find a criterion to help you decide what to do and what not to do.

I think that the best way of presenting the whole matter to you will not be to begin with generalizations and definitions. Therefore I shall follow what seems to me a more helpful and perhaps even a more honest plan. I shall bring before you a collection of instances of creative work that classroom teachers have done with music. Most of them seem to me to be good and really deserving of being called creative activities. But, for the sake of contrast, I shall also describe a few that seem to me not so good, and indeed unworthy of belonging in this classification. Then, having considered these cases, the next step will be to look for generalizations and a few practical guiding principles.

## II

1. The first practice is very simple and direct. A music supervisor was visiting a first-grade group in a country

school. When she walked into the room, she found the
children huddled around a table, "chattering like little
monkeys." Noticing her, finally, a child spoke up and said,
"Oh Mrs. Martin, come and see the flowers growing."
They had brought a large piece of clinker, set it in a bowl,
poured in a mixture of water, salt, ammonia and bluing,
and the chemical reaction had produced little flowers of all
colors. The children were delightfully excited. One of
them said, "Mrs. Martin, let's make a song about the pretty
flowers." The supervisor asked her to start it, which she
did. Others added to it, and soon the group had a song:

> See the pretty flowers growing
> On a piece of coal.
> Oh, what pretty colors have the
> Flowers on the coal.

The music was very simple, but to the children it seemed
wonderful.

2. Next we have an instance of a song made by a third-
grade group according to suggestions found in their reader,
which was the Gates-Huber text *Wide Wings,* Book Three.
On pages 294-295, there is the story called "Fairy Fort,"
with a scene describing a spring singing itself to sleep.
The children made a poem about this, which was discussed
and improved. It came out in final form as follows:

THE LULLABY FOUNTAIN

> Go to sleep, my fairy fountain,
>   In your bed so deep.
> High above is Mother Mountain
>   Singing her little ones to sleep.

Then the group tackled the problem of setting the poem
to music and making a song out of it.*  The children decided that it ought to be a lullaby, that is should be soft
and in waltz time.  They developed a tune line for the first
line of the poem, which was put on the board.  It looked
like this:

Then the teacher (who in this case could handle the conventional notation) put the staff on the board, found the
note on which the song began, and identified the notes
which had already been suggested, after which the various
lines were worked out, with the following result:

* This instance is from *Salem Public Schools: Course of Study in Music.*
Salem Music Committee, Salem, Massachusetts, 1945.

Two comments are in order here. First of all, the song could have been put on the board by means of the number notation already described, although such indications would not have been so accurate or complete. Second, it is very interesting and suggestive to find a musical activity which no one could hesitate to call creative arising directly out of another area in the curriculum.

3. Now we come tc a more elaborate and ambitious example, which I describe in the words of the classroom teacher who carried it through.

It all started with applesauce. Now applesauce in itself certainly doesn't sound music-provoking, but it led to one of the most satisfying and thrilling musical experiences that any teacher can hope to experience with her children.

The first graders were scheduled to make applesauce one morning last fall. Their cooking was a great success and all of us thoroughly enjoyed the results. *Life Magazine* seemed to be cooperating with the project because that week it carried several delightful pages devoted to our apple industry. The caption under one of the pictures mentioned Johnny Appleseed. None of the children knew about him. I told them the story and they seemed to like it very much. By the next day I had several books to read from, as I thought they would like to hear a written story as well as a told one. I read Stephen Vincent Benet's ballad and a story called "Johnny Appleseed," by Josephine Scribner Gates.

After finishing the reading, I could sense a musing and thoughtfulness in this ordinarily squirmy group of six-year-olds that I have never felt before. Johnny Appleseed had captured their imaginations. We talked a bit about it and then I began to hear chatterbox Johnny singing-talking about him in a non-rhythmical and chanting sort of way. The talking had become a singing and gradually I could hear some voices lifting and singing the name "Johnny Appleseed." I felt that if I had ten ears and ten hands, only then could I catch and keep the wonderful quality of chanting song that I was hearing. I was afraid that, if I made the children conscious of what they were singing and how they were saying these things, the spell would be broken and nothing would be left but twenty youngsters all talking at once.

John was singing the loudest and I could hear "I begin the story of Johnny Appleseed." Sally near him was singing "He was a good man and I like him."

I put these words on the board and naturally they all wanted to know what the words were. I thought surely then that the mood was broken. However, they all had a song to sing, and I scribbled madly to get the words down, feeling that they were so much a part of the chanting melody that if we had them, the melody could not help but come forth again in somewhat the same way. Besides, there really was no choice for me as I certainly didn't have the facility for translating their music into notes on the piano.

Very much excited at the turn our little cooking venture had taken, I spoke to Evelyn Ouelette, the elementary music teacher, and she arranged to come in and see if she could get the song down. It seemed sheer magic to me the way she drew the song out. Each child sang his part and although the words were on the board they came out slightly different and more rhythmically. They enjoyed the phrase "more apple trees" and used it more than in the original version. The song took on a clearer form but through their own choice, and they felt it as a whole piece rather than in separate phrases.

I asked them if they would like to sing their song at the assembly that week, and oh! the enthusiasm! The prospect of being on the stage was thrilling to them. Immediately they thought of having a play, too, as that seemed to them a very proper thing to do if they were to be on a real stage. They wanted Johnny Appleseed to row his boat, and they wanted to have him plant the seeds and then come back and see them sprouted. Music and body movement are synonymous with children, I am firmly convinced. I had seen them sway as they sang and felt that a complete expression would only be obtained if they had an opportunity to move to their music.

When Miss Ouelette came in to play the song for them, I suggested that they might be the seeds. They began to move and "sprout" and as they assumed tree shapes they swayed as if the wind were softly moving them to and fro. It was so beautiful that we held our breath as we watched, wondering at the great beauty that is in the child.

The same day, Mrs. Riva Evans, the elementary physical education instructor, and I sat down and talked the whole thing over, and on Wednesday, during our regular rhythms period, we spoke of their plans for the play. The play was to follow the song and as Miss Ouelette played they rowed away in their little boats, they "sprouted," and they moved in the breeze.

The play as it was finally presented still retained the simplicity of the original expression. Scenes and acts were added for the exciting sound and in order that the curtain might be drawn and opened as often as possible.

One of the boys wanted to be the announcer who informed the audience about what was happening. They all insisted on having a boat on the stage and I must admit I wasn't too enthusiastic about that. The play was to be given on Friday and they decided on the boat on Thursday. However, I need not have worried about it, as in ten minutes they had the boat built. They used heavy mural paper, cut lengthwise and folded in the front and back. Then they tacked it on a small, low stool which stood in the center of the boat. The boy who was Johnny Appleseed made a sign for the boat, and, of course, the name of the boat was "Johnny Appleseed."

In the first act Johnny rowed his boat to the accompaniment of some rowing music used in rhythm class. The second act showed Johnny planting the seeds. The children were all lying flat on the floor on their stomachs and as Johnny scooped imaginary dirt about each child, he would curl up into a little ball. As Johnny left the stage they would begin to "sprout" and assume the shapes of trees. Then he returned and walked around the stage looking at his apple trees, and—crowning effect—he actually picked some apples, for each child had an apple concealed in his hand, which he lifted as he grew to be an apple tree.

In the third act all the children sat on the stage and sang their song. They hummed the melody as the curtain was drawn.

We rehearsed the play once as a whole in the room. A few minutes before the audience arrived we ran through it on the stage. Although the children had never done anything on a stage before, they didn't seem to find any difficulty with the mechanics of the stage, and they thoroughly enjoyed the whole event.

The entire experience has sharpened my perceptions. Children make music all the time, maybe not on such a grand scale as when a Johnny Appleseed story kindles their imaginations, but in little ways all day long. Little children, like a two-year-old I know, sing the new words they like. They get a rise and fall, a rhythm and lilt in their voices. They don't yet know that we separate talking and singing. They are not aware of the adult and his "music period" kind of music.*

4. A third-grade group was studying about Italy. With the help and encouragement of their teacher they hunted a number of the songs of that country and learned to sing them. Also they looked for and found many interesting stories about Italy, and about how the people there lived and worked. These stories were told to the class. A large model of Vesuvius was made out of plaster of Paris and put on display. Murals of Italian scenes were painted and hung up. All this work was brought to a focus in a surprise

* Muriel Mangeau, "Our Singing Children." *Music Educators' Journal,* volume 34, 1948, February-March, pp. 30-31.

program for the music supervisor, when next she came to visit them.

5. A fourth-grade teacher led her children to develop additional verses to the song "Polly Wolly Doodle," *New Music Horizons,* Book 4, p. 8. These verses were developed by individual children at home, and then sung to the class by the children who had written them. The teacher found this an excellent way of getting some of the boys in her class to sing. Here are a few sample verses.

I came to a river and I couldn't get across,
  Singing Polly Wolly Doodle all the day,
So I spent my money for a blind old hoss,
  Singing Polly Wolly Doodle all the day.

A goat goes butting to and fro,
  Singing Polly Wolly Doodle all the day,
But you never know how far he'll go,
  Singing Polly Wolly Doodle all the day.

My Sal she goes to bed at eight,
  Singing Polly Wolly Doodle all the day,
She does this 'cause she never has a date,
  Singing Polly Wolly Doodle all the day.

There were many more!

6. The essential idea of so-called "creative dance," as carried on in the schools of Passaic, N. J. by Mrs. Humphreys, is to give children freedom, help, and encouragement in expressing the values of music in expressive bodily movement. Everything centers on having the children do what the music "tells" them to do—to listen, to respond, to choose, to express.

7. The subsequent undertaking, and the one that follows, are both comprehensive creative projects. In each

case I quote the report of the teacher in charge. The first was carried out by a fifth-grade group; the second was an all-school undertaking.

The children's interest in the making of puppets was aroused through the work of a previous 5B class. We made famous folk and fairy tales our center of interest. Through much experience in telling and writing stories we decided upon *Hansel and Gretel* for a puppet show. The reasons for selecting the story of Hansel and Gretel as used in the opera by Humperdinck were: it was a story familiar to the entire class; there was music already created for the story, with simple melodies; it limited to a minimum the number of characters on the stage at any one time, yet allowing many to participate in the chorus and background music; and it afforded easy interpretation of characters by the children.

After the selection was made, we divided ourselves into groups. It was not too difficult to place each person in the group in which he would work best because of different interests. The pupils were arranged into groups as follows: making of puppets; making of stage; painting of scenery; writing script; singing and announcing. There were pupils who worked in more than one group at different stages of development. All groups worked simultaneously.

A group was selected to go to the library to find what records and books were available for their use. They secured the *Columbia Masterworks Album, Hansel and Gretel,* and the story. Additional records were obtained from the Department of Education, Music Division Circulating Library of Records.

From the very beginning the class became familiar with the music. After several listening periods, pupils were introduced to the words of the melodies. Another teacher offered to help with the rehearsals of the chorus, duets, and solos. Much practice was given in singing and interpreting the songs. During an English and literature lesson a selection of characters was made. These persons were the ones who made the puppets. One pupil in the group drew costumes that would be suitable for the characters in the story. With suggestions and the cooperation of the sewing and manual training teachers, the puppets were soon ready for stringing.

When all the groups had completed their task it was necessary to fit the parts together. These rehearsals called for concentrated effort on the part of the characters, the chorus, and the stage band. The pupils had difficulty in coordinating the speaking, the singing, and the manipulating of the puppets. However, after a great deal of practice, much of the awkwardness was eliminated.

When the pupils felt they were ready, permission was given for the use of the community theatre. The theatre's lights, and sound equipment were used during the dress rehearsal.

Due to the use of the large auditorium the entire school was able to see the performance. This performance was enjoyed immensely by all, especially by the primary grades. Through compliments given to the children, their work and efforts were rewarded.

8. We, at Montebello School, felt the need of another school song. We chose, through discussion, to make it a school project—asking all classes from grade three to grade six to contribute a creative song. The music teacher took a poll of each class and found that most of the grades composed both the words and the music, while a few composed words to familiar tunes. A date for the deadline of writing the song was set. Shortly thereafter, an assembly was held for all the participating classes. Each group presented the song to the school in its own creative way. Some groups had pupil accompaniment; while others had the teacher or music teacher accompany the song. Several classes had chosen members of the class to lead the song. After each song was presented to the entire assembly, a vote was cast by the judges. This group of judges was composed of a representative from each participating class and several teachers. Naturally, before the assembly all directions

were given to the judges as well as to the audience. In the assembly hall, on a movable blackboard was listed the number of votes cast by the judges. When all the judging was completed, the winning class repeated its song to the audience and the assembly was closed by a few final remarks. The following day, the winning school song was written on a large chart and exhibited in the main hall for the entire school to see. On an additional bulletin board there was exhibited a small copy of each composed song that had been entered. A copy of the winning song was mimeographed and sent to each teacher so that it could be taught to the class.*

9. I close with two examples which are questionable. Both are adaptations of Mother Goose songs, correlated with health and safety programs. The first song is a variant on "Little Jack Horner." The words are as follows:

> Little Jack Horner stood on a corner
> Watching the cars go past.
> He looked to the right, he looked to the left,
> And then he crossed safely at last.

The second modifies "To market, to market to buy a fat pig."

> To market, to market a toothbrush to buy,
> Home again, home again, Mother and I.
>    For I must take care of my teeth while I'm small
>    Then I shall never have toothache at all.
> I'll brush them at morning, I'll brush them at night,
> 'Twill keep my teeth clean and make my smile bright.

---

* The two foregoing accounts are quoted from mimeographed reports on file with the Board of Education, Music Division, Baltimore Public Schools, Baltimore, Md.

I have before me no report of the procedures by which these rhymes were developed, so that no final judgment can be fair. But both of them are topical in a very literalistic sense, and extremely pedestrian. They have, to an uncomfortable extent, the appearance of being made to order rather than flowing spontaneously from feeling. In fact, it is difficult not to regard them as moral rhymes instead of as true poems.

### III

These examples, no doubt, convey and suggest more than can easily be captured in any set of generalizations. Yet general statements, although prosaic, insufficient, and liable to misinterpretation, have their uses. So let us try to formulate some which will epitomize the meaning of creative activity in the light of the foregoing instances.

1. In every case where it is possible to feel that an authentic creative experience was involved, the children were being helped and encouraged to enjoy and use freedom—freedom to choose, to decide, to respond in their own way. They were not simply let alone, for this would be a spurious freedom. A situation was set up which made freedom possible, and within this situation they were given suggestions and help which enabled them to take advantage of it. And of course an essential part of this situation was the attitude of the teacher. The first three examples are excellent illustrations of all this. The chemical flowers, the story of the fountain, and the legend of Johnny Appleseed captured the interest of the children. It would have been easy for the teachers concerned to have taken note of this fact, approved of it, and then passed on to something else. But they were wise and perceptive enough to make a pause and to give time and opportunity for the children's reac-

tions to manifest themselves and develop. Moreover, the project that developed out of the Johnny Appleseed legend shows very clearly the importance and necessity of support, guidance, and help. If the children had been left to their own devices, this undertaking would certainly not have gone so far, and the same is clearly true of many of the other examples.

We have to contrast this organized and guided freedom with what at least seems to have been involved in the adaptations of the Mother Goose songs. One has the very strong impression that in these instances something was being virtually forced upon the children. It is very improbable that there was an actual formal assignment, but one can almost hear the teacher presenting the class with the proposition of taking the Mother Goose song in question and making up words about crossing streets or brushing teeth which would fit it. The difference is subtle, but its implications and effects are enormous.

2. In all the authentic instances the children responded in terms of feeling. They made a *poetic* response, in which they captured and conveyed some of the emotional values and meanings of experience. We find the children delighted, charmed, excited by the flowers blooming in their chemical bowl, by the story of the fountain, by the legend, by the tale of Hansel and Gretel, by the movement suggestions of one song and the sheer jolliness of another, by the sense of loyalty to their school. Then we find them translating this delight, this charm, this excitement into words, and tunes, and movements, and plans for dramatic action; and in so doing they produced the thing called beauty.

Children, as I have elsewhere remarked, are natural poets, sensitive to the appeal and the emotional and aesthetic meaning of experience. Therefore a most essential characteristic of their creative musical response is its true poetic quality. Recall the hushed wonder of the teacher at the lovely spontaneous chanting evoked by the legend of Johnny Appleseed. One finds the same charm, the same poetic and aesthetic quality in the following simple utterance by a two-year-old.

> I want a kitty
> A kitty with pink feet
> A kitty with pink hands
> A kitty with pink fur
>     But blue eyes like me.*

By way of contrast, look again at the following:

> Little Jack Horner stood on the corner
>     Watching the cars go past.
> He looked to the right; he looked to the left
>     And so he crossed safely at last.

Can you seriously doubt which is true creative expression, which type of response you should try to evoke from your own children?

3. Creative response, in all its forms and aspects, is an act of self-expression, a realization or projection of something that comes from within. This is its most central and essential characteristic. External imposition kills it, for "Creative music is not the setting down on paper of a series of notes which various children have sung 'because the class decided they would write a song.' Instead it is a child's own expression of his feelings, musically, which

*Our Singing World: The Kindergarten Book: "Teaching Suggestions," p. xviii. Ginn and Company, Boston.

provides emotional release and satisfaction in self-confidence and progress." *

Expressive bodily movement for the sake of learning about time-signatures, composing a song for the sake of learning how to use the notation, listening to a piece for the sake of identifying its form—all these are negations of the creative process. They are attempts to utilize it for ulterior ends, which inevitably destroy its intrinsic values. Precisely the same thing is true of the making of poems (or rather of rhyming verses) and songs, for the sake of conveying a moral lesson, or explaining or telling facts about a topic. This is fundamentally the objection to such a production as

> To market, to market a toothbrush to buy,
> Home again, home again, Mother and I.
>   For I must take care of my teeth while I'm small
>   Then I shall never have toothache at all.
> I'll brush them at morning, I'll brush them at night,
> 'Twill keep my teeth clean and make my smile bright.

Like too much of the material contained in many of our school music series, it is a painful and hackneyed versification rather than an authentic and poetic outcome of personal experience.

### IV

When it comes to practical ways and means of inaugurating and handling creative experiences and activities, we can see very clearly from all that has been said that there is no single right answer. No fixed or set method can be described or recommended as the one that is always best.

* Doris Lee and Murray Lee, *Creative School Experiences*, p. 13.

The first and greatest necessity is for you to have in mind
what you really mean by creative experience, for if you are
clear about this, the practical problems tend to solve themselves. Still, the question of procedure remains important.
The best way to deal with it is to tell you what various
teachers have actually done. No doubt a good many working ideas will present themselves as you reflect about the
instances already given, but it seems well to present a few
more illustrations which particularly stress the procedural
problem. I shall not attempt to classify or systematize these
additional examples. Indeed I shall deliberately avoid doing so, because the methods exemplified are not intended
as copies to be imitated, but simply as suggestions to stimulate and focalize your own thinking and planning. You
must find out what works best for you and for your children; and while it is very helpful to know what other teachers are doing, your management of creative activities can
only succeed if it is distinctively your own.

One approach centered on first-grade children who had
difficulty in singing, and who had been playing simple instruments as accompaniments to songs. These children
were asked to imitate the sounds of bells, triangles, chimes,
or cymbals, all of which they had played during the singing. Then they were asked to imitate the sounds of animals
and sounds in nature. From these "sound accumulations"
they chose three about which to make a song. The results
were fragmentary, but it was a step in the right direction.
Through this simple creative project the hesitating singers
were stimulated with a spirit of fun and they became eager
to take part.

Nursery rhymes furnished a starting point in several second and third-grade groups. The teacher sang the first line
and the children sang a second line invented by them. All

the groups made one to three original phrases and are planning to create music for an entire poem. At first the children were slow to respond and produced phrases which were not very melodious, but these were written down nevertheless. But quite soon the phrases became much more interesting as the children gained confidence and experience, and almost every child wanted to create a song.

A fifth and a sixth grade worked together on a Thanksgiving program, creating poems and music which they thought their brothers and sisters in the lower grades would enjoy singing. The music was kept very simple, and short songs were selected and sung by the sub-primary and first-grade children, who were very proud when they found that a brother or a sister had made the song they were singing.

In one school a beginning on creative activity was made from the second grade through the sixth. The children created one phrase and then added a second and a third. Soon the fifth- and sixth-grade children were able to create whole melodies to given words.

By way of an interesting contrast to these careful simple-to-complex procedures, in a certain sixth grade the music supervisor wrote on the board,

> Oh! We are pirates bold!
> We sail the raging main.

"Will you please finish the poem and set it to music," she said. There was a gasp, for this was the first time that any such suggestion or request had been made to the children throughout their entire school career. However, the song was written and sent to the supervisor within a week.

Enthusiasms of the moment can often be admirable starting points for creative effort. Thus on a rainy day a child in a second grade asked if the class might write a story about the forest people in the rain. The children all saw the rain from the windows, heard it on the leaves outside, thought of things that happen when it rains, and of rabbits and squirrels and other woodland folk hurrying home. All this developed into a story, which grew into the following:

### RAINDROPS IN THE WOODS

Rabbits are hurrying off to their homes.
Squirrels are scurrying; so are the gnomes,
This is the reason they're scampering by—
Raindrops are pattering down from the sky.

Now all the raindrops are laughing with glee
Chasing the animals under the tree.
Now you can hear them with voices so clear
Telling the woodland folk winter is near.

Various individuals and sub-groups experimented with music, and finally the following emerged.

The instances presented here are just a few random samples, for there are endless ways in which a classroom teacher can promote creative musical activities with her children. Suggestions for starting points can be found in the daily experiences of children, in reading, in English, in social studies, in music which they hear. Many teachers in the lower grades like to encourage children to sing extemporized phrases in response to such greetings as "Good morning," or "How do you do?," or "Where are you?" But creative response is not limited to the extemporization or composing of poems and songs. It can occur in connection with expressive bodily response, the choice and use of instruments, the development of dramatizations. Listening, too, can be a creative experience. This does not mean that children must always act out or tell in words the meaning of the music which they hear, but essentially that they must capture and be captured by that meaning, which is often inexpressible in any other medium, for it consists in the living beauty of the music itself.

Thus when you are organizing and promoting creative response you are not setting up a self-bounded, limited, lesson-wise activity. Everything turns on helping children to be free to feel, free to express, free to be themselves. And so, in encouraging and enabling your children to carry on creative activities, you are doing nothing less than taking hold of an idea, and exemplifying a spirit which can and should permeate all of your work.

CHAPTER NINE

# Musicianship

## I

WE HAVE NOW DEVELOPED WHAT I HOPE
you will consider a fairly clear and comprehensive picture,
a program of music for your children which is practical
from your own standpoint as a classroom teacher. That
program should consist of expressive bodily movement,
listening, singing, the playing of instruments, and creative
activity, five phases of musical activity woven together and
organized in all kinds of patterns and arrangements. It
should be a program of musical experiences rather than
music lessons. And always it should be geared very directly
and realistically to the actual human needs of your children. It may seem to you that such a program proposes
something very well worth doing, something you would
like to do, and something you feel able to do.

But is it adequate? Is not something of great importance left out? Has it any solid substance? What, after all,
will your children be learning about music itself? You can
see how music may be brought to them as a means of personal and social fulfillment and of cultural enrichment.
But, in planning to achieve these values, have we not
blithely and irresponsibly tossed out of the window almost
everything indicated by the term musicianship?

There is no doubt that many people would be inclined
to criticize our proposals precisely on this ground. They

would be apt to say that what is here suggested adds up to a program of mere trivialities. As for the kind of activities and experiences I have described, children may like them and even get something out of them—for the time-being. But wait a few years! These same children will then discover that they have no usable competence, no solid training, and in fact that there is nothing left. Specialists in music are particularly likely to raise objections such as these, and similar doubts may occasionally have invaded your own mind also. Such questionings are far too serious to be ignored. To bring music to your children might still be worth while even if it did mean nothing more than providing various pleasing but superficial musical treats. But if, on examination, the proposed program turns out to be no more than an attractive but essentially frothy educational soufflé, then it certainly cannot be taken very seriously and probably has no future, from the standpoint of your children themselves.

I am sure, however, that this very disparaging interpretation is quite incorrect. It is due to a misunderstanding both of the nature of musicianship and of the way in which children really learn and grow. Indeed I will go so far as to say that *a program of varied and personally repaying musical activities provides the best possible setting for a child's development of vital and substantial musicianship.* I have from time to time hinted, and indeed rather more than hinted, at this very idea. But now the time has come to pull all the threads together and to face this somewhat perturbing issue head on.

## II

In order to back up the broad assertion I just made, I have to find an answer to two closely related questions,

"What is musicianship?" "How can it best be acquired?"
Those who might be inclined to criticize our proposed
program because of its seeming lack of solid musical content have a very clear-cut answer to both these questions.
By musicianship they mean specifically the ability to interpret the musical notation. They sometimes call this "musical literacy." And they believe that children can best
achieve this ability by being taught the "fundamentals of
music" (i.e., note names, note lengths, rests, sharps and
flats, keys, key signatures, time signatures, measure bars,
clefs, etc.), presented in a series of topical lessons. It is, I
think, a much better and fairer statement of that position
to say that what is contemplated is an ability to interpret or
understand the notation, rather than to assert that music
reading is the determining aim. The ability to read music
well is none too common even among professional musicians, and for the enormous majority of sixth-grade children it is hopelessly out of the question. I doubt if those
whose thinking is in the direction I have indicated really
have actual reading in mind, although they constantly and
incautiously allow themselves to use the expression. Essentially their idea is that a good program of music in the elementary school ought to produce a competent understanding of the notation, which can best be developed by a long
series of lessons on the so-called fundamentals. This undoubtedly is what our critics are thinking about when they
complain that the program here recommended will not
produce musicianship, whatever other values it may have.

The plan of an orderly sequence of lessons on the so-
called fundamentals, culminating in a practical understanding of the notation, looks very sensible. But, as a matter of
fact, it does not work out. It has been tried all over the
country for many years, yet the contemplated results are

not forthcoming. The commonest complaint of directors of high school bands, orchestras, and choruses is that children come to them without any ability to interpret the score. There is no doubt that they are right, and quite probably your own experience in the grades bears them out emphatically. What then is the conclusion? Surely that something is radically wrong with the plan itself! No other inference seems possible, for when people set out to work for a certain outcome, keep on working for a long time, and then fail to get results, this is proof positive that something must be wrong. Indeed a little analysis makes the trouble very clear, and an understanding of the problem will help us to clarify our own position and to see more completely the meanings and possibilities of our own proposals.

1. To think of musicianship as essentially the ability to interpret the notation is to think of it far too narrowly. This is exactly the way in which teachers fifty years ago used to think about reading the English language. They saw that in order to read English a child must be able to interpret printed symbols—words, word-patterns, and sentences. Of course this is perfectly true as far as it goes. But the trouble was that teachers saw nothing else. They concentrated on word-meanings, grammar, and spelling, because to do so seemed the sensible way of getting children to understand what they saw on the page. It did not work very well. Reading nowadays is taught and learned far better than it was fifty years ago, at any rate up to the fourth grade.* The reason very largely is that teachers now operate in terms of a much broader concept of reading ability. They have come to realize that if a child is going to learn to read effectively, he must be interested, he must want to read, and that getting him to want to read is more

* This, I may remark, is a well-established fact.

than half the battle. So a wide variety of reading materials, attractive in format and content, are provided. The child is introduced to printed English in a setting of perfectly normal experience. He finds in his primers not merely a series of drills, but all kinds of items which have a real appeal and meaning for him. Pains are taken to orient the child to school life in general and to reading in particular. There is far less direct drive and far more general stimulation and encouragement. And here, as always, the ultimate proof of the pudding is the eating. Up to the fourth grade we are producing English literacy far better nowadays than teachers managed to do fifty years ago, for all their grooved and narrowly focused efforts.

Exactly the same is true of musical literacy or musicianship. Here too, orientation, interest, and will are of supreme and determining importance. By far the best way—indeed the only good way—of getting a child to understand the notation is to get him to want to understand it. It is not the slightest use trying to pound into his head a lot of stuff which he finds abstract and complicated, and which strikes him as essentially pointless, although of course he does not put the matter to himself in any such terms. This is the certain road to failure. On the other hand, if you can create in a child a real personal orientation to music, a desire for it, an "at-home-ness" with it, then there will not be much trouble in teaching him anything he needs to know about the notation.

It is this personal orientation towards music, this acceptance of it as a delightful influence in life, this desire for it, that the program we have worked out is supremely adapted to bring about. Let me try to be specific. John enters the first grade. At once he finds himself drawn into a whole range of musical activities and experiences. He listens to music which, although simple, is charming and attractive. Along with the other children he gets right into a good deal of this music by means of expressive bodily movement. Pretty soon he is tapping out patterns with rhythm sticks or playing on a set of water bottles, which he does his best to keep in tune. He is encouraged to sing. Perhaps he hesitates a little about this, but the songs are naturally appealing and before long he is joining in with the others. He makes up little tunes of his own. As he proceeds through the school he runs into similar though increasingly complex and far-reaching experiences in every grade. By the time he is in the sixth grade he has absorbed a great deal of music. He has discovered it, made friends with it. Music has become part of his life, both in and out of school.

Is it not quite correct to say that, by the time John is in the sixth grade, he has become a real musician, though no doubt in a limited sense of the word? Has he learned anything much about the notation? Perhaps so, perhaps not! Does it matter? He has now reached an age at which the symbolic language of music will not be particularly difficult; and he has absorbed so much music that this language will be meaningful to him. If he gets into an elementary school choir, or joins the orchestra or band when he enters junior high school, he will already have a good musical orientation. He will have assimilated taste, standards, interest, an intuitive understanding of what it is all about. Can you really believe that he will have much trouble with the score, even though no one has ever given him formal instruction in reading it?

This is the kind of musicianship which you, as a classroom teacher, can certainly promote. It is a far sounder foundation even for future musical specialization than any

amount of formal grammatical drill on the so-called fundamentals. And, what is far more important, you will have
established music as a constructive influence in John's
whole life.

2. The concept of musicianship which centers everything
on a direct drive for understanding the notation is not only
indefensibly narrow. It also involves a basic error. As we
have seen, it stresses a sequence of lessons on the so-called
fundamentals. But are these alleged fundamentals really
the fundamentals or essential elements of music at all?

Well, specifically, what are they? I have already listed
them several times, but let us do so again. Quarter notes,
half notes, whole notes, eighth notes, note names, key signatures, symbols for two-four, three-four, four-four, six-
eight time, measure bars, symbols indicating rests of various lengths, slurs, dots, treble and bass clefs—these perhaps
are enough instances. I will ask you now to notice something of the utmost importance. *These are really elements
of a symbolic language or code; they are not elements of
music at all.* They are devices for telling a person more or
less what to do when he plays or sings, or how to write down
any musical ideas he may happen to have. *They are signs
for something, but they are not the thing itself.* They can
have no meaning and no value to a child unless he has had
plenty of experience with the thing itself.

Consider a parallel case. Suppose you are teaching a
group of children who have lived all their lives in the middle of the great plains. You want to tell them something
about mountains. Not only have they never seen any mountains but, let us suppose, they have not even seen any pictures of mountains. You can explain the word "mountain"
to them after a fashion and, in a very superficial sense, they
will seem to understand. But they will never really grasp

its meaning, because to grasp that meaning they must go
from the thing to the symbol and not from the symbol to
the thing. There, of course, is precisely the objection to
calling the so-called fundamentals the true fundamentals of
music. They are nothing of the kind. They are only symbolic devices, very useful for taking hold of and manipulating experience and for directing action, but in and of themselves just the elements of a code. It follows, therefore, that
when we concentrate on these spurious fundamentals we are
not teaching musicianship at all. We are only teaching sym-
bol-juggling.

3. Should we then stop talking about the "fundamentals
of music"? Is the idea simply a pack of nonsense? I certainly do not think so. *The real fundamentals, the real
essentials are those elements which make any piece of music
beautiful, interesting, appealing, meaningful.* Of course
they ought to be stressed; of course they ought to be and can
be emphasized, and taught, and recognized, and learned.
And the program we have developed in these pages provides
an ideal setting for accomplishing these very things. Moreover the teaching of these true fundamentals does not re-
quire a great deal of technical knowledge. It is something
which you, as a classroom teacher, can certainly accomplish
if you will keep your ears open, and dismiss your fears and
doubts, and simply use your common sense.

(a) First of all consider rhythm. What is rhythm in
music? It includes two different yet closely related factors.
First there is the swing, or pulsation, or scheme of accentuation that runs right through a piece. Then there are groupings or sequences of fast and slow notes in various combinations. Much of the appeal, the interest, the beauty of
any composition—all the way from a simple folk tune to
a complex symphony—depends upon its rhythm. When

a listener notices or responds to the rhythm, his pleasure is likely to be increased. When performers bring out the rhythm, the effectiveness and enjoyableness of their performance are enhanced both for them and for any auditors they may have. Rhythm, therefore, is one of the true fundamentals, the true essentials of music, one of the elements upon which its beauty and expressiveness depend. All this you can very readily verify in and through your own experience with music.

So it follows that one should try to help children to catch, respond to, and realize the rhythm of music when they listen, when they play, when they sing, and when they create. How can this be done? Very simply and directly indeed. Let them experience music through expressive bodily movement. Many of them will pick up the broad features of the rhythm right away, with hardly any instruction or guidance, although some will benefit from a little help. Tie expressive bodily movement to the use of simple instruments, such as rhythm sticks, drums, triangles, and so forth. Let some of the children accompany the movement-patterns being created by the others on such instruments. Give children opportunities to develop instrumentations which call for the use of easy-to-play instruments to accompany pieces of recorded music, bringing out accentuation, pulsation, alternations and groupings of fast and slow. Tie such activities to singing also, so that the songs acquire the swing and pulsation which the children have come to feel. As such experiences continue, the children will develop a better, surer, more discriminating response to the essential factor of rhythm. At first it is likely that only the broader and more obvious aspects of rhythm will be noticed; but as time goes on there will be an increasing recognition of the details and nuances which go so far to make a piece of music beautiful and interesting. To carry on such activities you yourself do not need to be an expert technical musician, because everything depends on a direct and natural feeling for what is in the music, and for what it "says." By these means it is entirely possible for you and your children to grow together in rhythmic awareness. That is how our proposed program takes care of the fundamental element of musical rhythm.

Contrast this with the approach that stresses the wrongly termed "fundamentals." Children are taught that there are quarter notes, half notes, whole notes, eighth notes, sixteenth notes, and so forth. But this, surely, is a curious and roundabout way of talking. When a person steps out the onward pulsation of a march, he does not naturally or immediately feel that he is stepping in *quarter* notes. He is not aware of a *quarter* of anything. He merely feels the pulsation upon which the power and expressiveness of the march depends. Then again, children are taught about time signatures, four-four, three-four, two-four, six-eight, etc. But, when they catch through expressive movement the sway and pulsation of a waltz, they do not naturally or directly think of threes or sixes but merely of sway and pulsation, which they can catch and realize very well without bothering about arithmetic at all. Our musical notation very cleverly uses arithmetical conventions (such ideas as quarter notes and eighth notes are conventions only) for telling people what rhythmic patterns and arrangements should be sensed when they play or sing or listen to a piece of music. But those conventions are not the rhythm itself. They are only symbols for it. To try to develop a living sense of the thing itself from a study of its symbolization is about as absurd an instance of putting the cart before the horse as one can well imagine. Worse, it doesn't work.

What actually happens when children are introduced to rhythm through the study of note lengths and time signatures is that they never sense it at all. Then later on, band directors and orchestral directors complain that these same children have no rhythmic grasp. They are apt to follow this grumble with two quite inconsistent complaints: first, that elementary school music teachers should place more emphasis on note lengths and key signatures; second, that a sense of rhythm is a special gift granted to but a few. Both these claims are absurd. An emphasis upon the symbols is a very bad way of developing a sense for the thing itself; and a sense of rhythm most certainly can be developed by appropriate measures, which happen to be quite simple and direct.

Certainly your chief concern is not to please directors of high school bands and orchestras, but to make music meaningful and valuable to your children. However, the greater aim can also include the lesser if you help your children to discover and realize the pleasure, the interest, the manifold beauties of musical rhythm—something which it is well within your power to accomplish. And in doing so you will have helped your children to understand one of the real fundamentals of music.

(b) On what besides rhythm does the beauty of music depend? Other important fundamentals are melodies which rise and fall and flow, and harmonies which move and merge into one another like the shifting colors of a kaleidoscope. I once heard a very able and distinguished band director complain that when a group of high school pupils played a piece of music, they made it sound "just like a lot of notes." What he wanted them to do was to make it sound like *music*. Then how absurd it seems to insist on teaching children nothing but notes, notes, notes.

But since music is made up of notes do we not have here the most fundamental of all fundamentals? Surely it is absolutely essential for a person to master note names and symbols if he is to get anywhere with music at all! In the standard notation these are indicated by the lines and the spaces. Their letter names are A B C D E F G. Their numerical names are 1 2 3 4 5 6 7 8. Their syllable names are *do re mi fa so la ti do*. Each of these symbols can be modified by one of two special signs, indicating that it is to be interpreted as "half a step" up or down from its standard position, i.e., sharp or flat. All this is very interesting, and very sensible, and when it comes to writing music, very convenient. But are these facts the fundamentals of music itself? They are nothing of the kind. The notes, designated and identified by symbols, are only convenient devices. They are not really fundamentals at all. The true fundamentals of music are rhythm, melody, and harmony.

Now our whole program, our whole approach, is designed to give children a living grasp of these true fundamentals. Let us return to one of our previous instances, the one in which the teacher introduced the recording of "Rock-a-bye, Baby," letting the children move about and sing just as they pleased. These children were not singing notes. They were supremely unaware of notes. Yet they felt, realized, and projected the beauty of the music. Again, when the group of rural school children made up a simple song about the flowers in their chemical garden, their emphasis was not upon notes, but upon expressive melody. These children, on their childish level, were operating just as the very greatest of composers have always operated. When Bach, or Beethoven, or Mozart, or Chopin composed their loveliest and most exalted music, they were not putting notes together, carpenter-wise. Composers have always made music not out of notes, but out of rhythms, melodies, and harmonies. Listeners have always responded to it as such. And when you help your children to sense these things through expressive bodily movement, through listening in all its varieties, through singing, through playing simple instruments, and through creative activities, your procedure is profoundly right. You are developing musicianship in your children because you are emphasizing true, not spurious fundamentals.

Of course I do not say that note designations, note names, and note symbols are not enormously convenient, or that they are not worth learning. But I do insist that all such matters should be made incidental and peripheral rather than central. If you do the opposite you are grasping the shadow and neglecting the substance. For the very core and substance of your program is music itself and its true fundamentals. Let us suppose that your children have created a song, and that they want to write it down so that they can remember it and sing it again. How can this be done? They must employ some system of symbols. What shall it be—syllables, numbers, standard notation? *Whichever one is most immediately convenient!* Numbers may do the trick very well. But there may be some details in the tune which cannot be indicated by means of numbers. Then something better must be found. Let your children discover this better system for themselves, and go along with them yourself in their exploration. Quite likely they will find that they cannot do without some of the conventions of the standard notation. Admirable! They will have learned those conventions in an excellent and most meaningful manner.

Or again, if your children are working out an instrumen-

tation for easy-to-play instruments, they will need some
kind of device for registering their decisions in written
form. Exploration and discovery once more! Or yet again,
they (and you with them) are singing a song along with a
phonograph record. Would it be well for them to have
their books open, if the song occurs in those books? This
might be so. But do not use the books for note-pointing.
Perhaps some curve, or turn, or subtle nuance of the tune
is hard to catch from the sound alone, but when children
see it on the score it comes through at once. These are just
a few instances to show you what I mean by emphasizing
the substance rather than the shadow, making note names
and note symbols incidental and peripheral, and centering
always on the true fundamentals.

Notice how much mental anguish you can save yourself
by this way of thinking and acting. All the wrangles about
the relative advantages of syllables, numbers, and standard
note names become almost meaningless. You are teaching
your children to feel and respond to the true fundamentals.
When they need some device for writing down or recognizing melodies or harmonies, or bits of them, the most convenient device is the best. The standard notation is capable
of conveying more than any other system of musical symbolism, and so your children will be led towards an understanding of it because of its sheer practical advantages. But
always remember that the essence of musicianship consists
in sensing and feeling the expressiveness of the music, and
not in being able to manipulate the symbolism by means of
which we deal with it.

All this is true also of the way to deal with key signatures,
which are always supposed to belong among the so-called
fundamentals. Here once more we see the falseness and
futility of equating notational elements with musical essen-

tials. To teach key signatures to children so that they will have any genuine and vital musical meaning whatsoever is, to speak bluntly, a virtual impossibility. The whole business almost inevitably works out as nothing but a series of lessons on a set of abstract, quasi-mathematical conventions.

Yet there can be no doubt whatsoever that the key of any piece of music is a vital factor in its beauty and appeal. You and your children will discover this quickly enough if you start a song too high. It becomes at once more or less unsingable, and its expressiveness is reduced or destroyed. It has to be shifted downwards; and this, to put the matter technically, means transposing it into another key. Here, then, is an elementary but significant experience of the musical reality which is conveyed in a key signature. Instrumental activities can afford many additional experiences of the same reality. For instance, your children make and tune a set of eight water bottles. Some melodies can be played on these bottles without any alteration at all. Other melodies have to be shifted either upwards or downwards. Still other melodies contain certain notes which cannot be played at all on the eight bottles, a difficulty which can lead straight to further experimentation, exploration, and discovery. The best approach your children can make to an understanding of key and key relationships is to work as best they can at such musical problems.

(c) Harmony (i.e., chords and chord effects) is usually not considered as belonging to the "fundamentals," but to the later and advanced phases of music study. As a general thing, children are not helped or encouraged to learn anything at all about it. The study of harmony is supposed to be suitable for young people only when they begin to specialize in music, when they are about ready to enter a college or a conservatory. It is usually introduced as an extremely theoretical and abstractly technical subject, and students are apt to find it difficult because they approach it without any background whatsoever.

Here is another of the absurd and mischievous results which flow from confusing the fundamentals of music with the elements of the notation. The chord effects in any piece of music are most certainly vital factors in its beauty and appeal. It follows that children ought to be helped to realize, respond to, and appreciate these harmonic effects and values. But how can such a thing be done; and above all can it be managed by a person like yourself, who probably has no technical knowledge whatsoever of harmony? As always, the right answer is quite surprisingly simple. Just create situations in which your children have opportunities to experiment with chords and chord effects.

The autoharp is of obvious use in this connection, if opportunity for musical experimentation is offered. If children are using the autoharp to accompany singing, or instrumental playing, or movement experiences, let them try various effects and let the players and the group join together in discussing those effects and deciding which seem to be best. Similar possibilities also present themselves in the use of the guitar or the accordion, or in free chording on the piano. Always remember that the children who are using these instruments need not and should not be held to the playing of pre-determined "right" sequences of chords, but that so far as possible they should discover by experimentation and trial and error which chords and sequences are pleasing and which are not. Simple melody instruments, too, can offer very considerable harmonic possibilities. For instance, if a child is using a xylophone, or a set of chimes or tuned water bottles to play along with a song, there is no need for him always to play the tune of the song. He and everybody else may find it very interesting to work out a melody which fits well when played along with the tune of the song.

As your children discover certain chords they wish to use with a song or a piece, they may want to name them. That is a perfectly sound idea, for labels are always useful. All chords have names, as a matter of fact, and quite complicated ones at that. But there is nothing against inventing names of your own, for practical identification.

All such experimentation with chords adds up to very good teaching indeed. That it offers many opportunities for cooperation, leadership, and intensive thinking is very obvious. But, in addition to this, it is anything but trivial musically speaking. It is just the kind of experience with harmony that children ought to have and rarely get. All that you and your children have to do is to try out this and that effect, and to decide what you like and do not like, on a basis of feeling. Such preferences, after all, are the basis for every rule in the harmony textbooks; for the rules are nothing but condensed statements about what effects people tend to like and not to like.

(d) Musical form, or structure, or architecture, is, like harmony, not numbered among the conventionally accepted "fundamentals"; and yet it is a most important factor in the expressiveness and beauty of even the simplest music. It is an odd and interesting thing that the study of musical form has given rise to some very acrimonious conflicts of opinion among experts, for the reason that there are several different systems of musical analysis, each with its enthusiastic, not to say fanatical, partisans. I have known two presumably qualified experts to come almost to blows over the proper formal classification of such a simple piece of music as "The Old Refrain." The impression left on any layman would be that he could pay his money and take his choice, and that it did not matter much anyhow.

What, then, to do about it? Should you decide to have no dealings whatsoever with musical form? Tempting, I must admit, but hardly justifiable. Form is too important an element in musical appeal and expressiveness to be ignored. Here is what I would advise. First, have nothing whatsoever to do with technical terms. They are traps for the unwary, and I have known some fairly wary individuals to fall into them as well. Specifically, do not let yourself be drawn into wrangles about just what a phrase is, just what a two-part form is, and so forth. All this is word-juggling, and you want to help your children make contact with reality. Second, remember that the living realities of musical form are basically simple. As you listen to a piece of music you will quickly notice that some parts or sections of it are repeated. Such repetitions may be complete in every detail, or there may be variations and changes, ranging all the way from small ones to quite extensive ones. Also you will notice that new and perhaps contrasting sections are introduced from time to time. For instance, the simple song "Hush, my Babe" is built in this way: It begins with the music saying the same thing twice over; then something quite different is said; and then the first statement comes in again, somewhat altered. I would not care a snap of my fingers what technical label a person might attach to this form, for this simple description outlines the living reality of the musical architecture of this little piece. If anyone senses this structure he will probably like the piece better and be able to sing it more expressively and with truer feeling. For the form of the piece is part of its beauty.

So the way to deal with form as you bring music to your children is to help them to notice complete identities or repetitions, identities or repetitions that contain some variations within themselves, and contrasting or differing ideas which we might term musical statements. One of the very best of all ways of responding to these identities and differences is through expressive bodily movement. As children freely convey in movement what the music tells them to do, they can sense its shifts, its changes, its returns to previous ideas and statements. Another great resource is the use of easy-to-play instruments, for children can choose one instrumentation for one of the musical ideas of a piece, shift to another instrumentation when a different idea comes up, and perhaps return to their original choice when the first statement recurs again.

Let us bring everything to a head in a point by point comparison of the conventional scheme of lessons on the so-called fundamentals on the one hand, and on the other hand the program proposed in these pages, as judged from the standpoint of the development of musicianship. (*a*) The conventional scheme is precisely a sequence of topical lessons, with material specially devised to bear on the lesson topics. Our scheme consists of the widest possible variety of significant and appealing musical experiences and activities. (*b*) The conventional scheme is based on the assumption that an understanding of the notation can be built up bit by bit, through the sequential study of its separate elements. Our scheme is based on the assumption that any competent understanding of the notation can only come from growth, and that it is best developed incidentally in connection with many significant musical experiences and activities. (*c*) The conventional scheme is based on a false concept of the fundamentals. What are regarded as the fundamentals under the conventional scheme are not really the essentials of music at all, but only the elements of the notation. In fact the conventional scheme does not include among its fundamentals two of the most essential factors in musical expressiveness and beauty, namely harmony and form. Our scheme is directed entirely towards helping children to recognize the beauties which are the very stuff of music, and thus towards making their singing, their playing, their listening, their creative activities, and their movement-realizations more musically significant and satisfying. (d) The conventional scheme is pointed at understanding the notation, and it misses its aim. Our scheme is pointed at a fine and sensitive feeling for music itself and goes on the assumption that, once such a responsiveness is developed, the notation presents no very serious problems. (e) The conventional scheme requires the teacher to possess a specialized and peculiar technical equipment. Our scheme can be handled by any intelligent person who is willing to discover in and through her own experience how basically simple music really is.

It is astonishing how badly and stupidly music is commonly taught to children, not only in school classrooms but in private studios too. There is a fixation upon skill, technique, technical terms, technical symbols, and an ignoring of musical realities and musical values. As one surveys the scene one cannot but feel convinced of the crying need for the sort of general music program here envisaged and described.

### III

In bringing this discussion of musicianship to a close there are four general questions which I must consider. Very probably they have occurred to you long ere now.

1. If the notation is to be picked up incidentally in and through a variety of musical experiences and activities, will not this lead to very spotty and incomplete learning? Yes, it will. But what of it? Is not that the way anybody learns anything? He sees bits of it here and there. These points of clarity become foci of growth. They spread, they merge, they come together more and more in a systematic whole. No one can begin with systematic completeness and comprehensive grasp, for these are end-results not starting points. Children are put through conventional lesson sequences on the "fundamentals." By the time they get to the sixth grade they have "covered" everything. How much good does it do them? What do they really get out of it? Not even spotty learning! Only a uniform grey bewilderment and indifference! Is this better than incomplete learning?

2. How is the program proposed in this book related to the familiar doctrine of going "from rote to note," i.e., the notion of using rote songs in the first two or three grades and then introducing the study of the notation? There are far more differences than similarities. It is worth while to check off these differences and similarities, because this may help to define and sharpen the position taken in these pages. Let us begin with the differences, which are very striking and far-reaching. First, we have insisted that a child's experiences with music should be distinctively *musical* experiences which are good for him as a human being. Whether or not they are wholly "rote" experiences at any point (that is, lacking in any kind of symbolic content) really does not matter much. In some of the illustrations I have presented there has been a considerable symbolic content, and in others little or none; but this is not the important point. Second, a child's musical experiences

should include a great deal more than singing, whether
"rote" or "notewise." He should have opportunities to
express music in bodily movement, to listen, to play on
instruments, to create; and in any or all such musical doings he may or may not make use of symbols. Third, we
maintain that there is no set level at which standard notation should be introduced. It can arise quite incidentally
in connection with all kinds of musical projects and activities. Fourth, our aim in setting up an organized program
of musical activities in an elementary school should certainly not be to lay a foundation for studying the notation.
Our purpose should be very much wider than this—to introduce the art of music itself as a constructive influence
in children's living, both now and later on.

So much for the differences between the position I have
tried to present in this book and the "rote to note" doctrine. Those differences are so great that it may seem to
you that there can be no similarity at all. Here you would
be nearly right, and yet not entirely so, I believe. For with
all its limitations the "rote to note" idea does after all
recognize that music must come first. The contemplated
range of musical experiences is extremely narrow. The
purpose for which those experiences are organized is exceedingly limited. There is supposed to be quite a rigid
transition to notational study at a certain level. But for all
that, the claims of music are not entirely ignored. One
might say that there is that much validity in the "rote to
note" doctrine, and that the position taken in this book is
a great expansion, liberation, and indeed transformation
of it rather than an entire and complete repudiation.

3. Would it be proper to regard our proposed program
as intended to promote what is called "music reading readiness"? You will probably feel that the answer to this ques-

tion is already foreshadowed in what has just been said, yet it is worth while to consider the "readiness" issue rather carefully in its own right.

The concept of music reading readiness has been taken over in music education from other fields of work, and particularly from the teaching of English reading and of arithmetic, and it has come to be quite widely used and discussed. It is now well understood that a child's ability to read the English language or to do sums grows out of a great wealth of previous experience, and that if this development has not taken place the desired ability is very hard and perhaps impossible to establish. Specialists in the teaching of music have taken over this doctrine; hence the idea of a "readiness stage" which must be achieved before one tries to teach a child to read the musical notation.

Well, is the position taken in the present book in agreement with this doctrine or is it not? If I had to make a very brief answer I could, in honesty, only say "Yes and no." Which would be most unsatisfactory! So let us look into the question with some little care.

(a) The first thing that strikes one is that the ability to read music has not even remotely the same importance as the ability to read one's mother tongue. If a person cannot read English he suffers a tremendous practical handicap, and is shut off from innumerable avenues of enjoyment and personal development. Moreover he himself is pretty sure to feel inferior and humiliated. But a child or an older person can enter into a vast range of musical pleasure and, in fact, can participate rewardingly in music with very little reading ability. As to feelings of humiliation and inadequacy, it is only the professional musician who is likely to be afflicted by them because of an inability to read. As a matter of fact, there are plenty of good pro-

fessional musicians who are very poor readers. Thus music
reading is vastly less important, both musically and personally, than English reading. So the idea of organizing a
program for the specific purpose of promoting readiness
to read music seems to put a most exaggerated emphasis
upon music reading.

(b) The second important point is that the concept of
readiness as now understood by the best teachers of English
reading means vastly more than specific preparation. A
child must have matured physically and mentally to a certain point, he must have achieved a certain emotional
stability, he must have become oriented to school, he must
have developed a real interest in written and printed material and in the content of such material before he is considered ready for deliberate reading instruction. English
reading emerges out of a many-sided personal development, and often one would find it hard to say exactly where
and when reading starts. All this is true also of music reading. Music reading, too, must emerge out of many-sided,
long-continued, and above all personally satisfying and
rewarding experiences with music. It is only in this very
broad sense that one can talk correctly about "music reading readiness."

Now let us put these two ideas together, and see how
the result bears on the position taken in this book. The
program here recommended is not specifically designed to
produce music reading. It is not in any definite way tied
to music reading. You can carry it on to admiration without a thought in your head about music reading. Yet
strange to say it is the most hopeful procedure for developing music reading. Its keynote is not "music reading readiness," but "more-music readiness." And yet the
greater can contain the less. The intention of our program

is to develop in the child an eagerness for music, an interest in it, and a growing understanding of it. And this eagerness, this interest, this understanding can be transformed into reading ability if and when the necessity arises. Nor need the transformation be particularly difficult.

So you see why I have to give the very unsatisfactory answer "Yes and no," if you ask point blank whether the position taken in this book is in harmony with the notion of music reading readiness. The notion certainly has its dangers, and grave dangers too. If you take it as suggesting that all a child's musical experiences should be focused on the one outcome of getting him ready to read, I believe that it is dead wrong and in fact pernicious. But if you interpret it as meaning that a broad, varied, convincing range of musical experience is the best possible psychological setting for the development of any reading skill a person might need, then it is entirely in line with the thinking in these pages.

4. Notice, finally, how human values and subject matter values come together in our proposed program, as they always must in any sound educational scheme. You are teaching children? Yes indeed. But you are also teaching music. You are developing musicianship in your children —a living musicianship, which means an orientation towards music, an ability to enjoy and use it in all kinds of situations and for all kinds of human ends. For musicianship is not an affair of compartmentalized expertness or isolated skill. When a person possesses it, he becomes not merely a technician, but a musical person—a person in whose life the art of music functions for worthy and constructive ends.

In closing let me point out how this whole approach affects you personally. You yourself will be learning musicianship right along with your children, by sharing with them free and happy musical experiences. Even if you have good technical facility on the piano (let us say) the discovery of musicianship can come to you as quite an eye-opener. You will find that real musicianship does not primarily mean a hard grind on so-called theory, but rather an insight into the factors which make music beautiful and expressive. And if your own performing ability is almost zero, you will find that a person can become a sensitive and intelligent musician in a very genuine sense without being any kind of keyboard acrobat. So our approach here has much educational richness not only for your children but also for you, and by means of it you can grow into a better teacher and an individual whose personal culture is deeper, fuller, and better rounded—a person more able to understand and enjoy the art of music.

# CHAPTER TEN

# Some Outstanding Issues

THERE ARE STILL A FEW LOOSE ENDS TO BE tied together before we are done. This will not take us very long, but it is necessary if you are to gain a comprehensive understanding of the implications and bearings of what I have proposed in these pages.

## I

First, there is the question of standards. How can you, or your principal, or your superintendent, or anyone else tell whether and to what extent you are succeeding or failing? By what criteria should your work be judged?

The paramount standards are always human standards. When I see a child who is achieving a better personal adjustment and finding avenues for happy and fruitful self-fulfillment, when I see a group of children functioning together more happily and effectively, when I see a school that is patently a better school, all because of the music, then and only then am I willing to admit that the job is being done as it should be done. These human values cannot be registered by tests and cannot be expressed in marks. But they are unmistakably visible to the naked eye. Music can be a highly constructive influence in the individual and social living of children. To recognize this does not call for any kind of statistical proof. When it happens it is obvious, and I have seen it happen. When educational procedures transpose into better living, their values are so manifest and so convincing that he who runs may read. Consider what is happening to the children in their doings, their activities, their choices, their individual and social living. Here is your ultimate criterion. By this your work must stand or fall.

Purely musical standards, however, need by no means be ignored. In developing a group of children who are personally oriented towards music and interested in it, you are providing the best of conditions for musical achievement. Your work is virtually certain to have a powerful influence in this direction if you persist in bringing music effectively into your classroom. Your children will learn a great deal about music, not systematically perhaps, but in a vital fashion. Many of them will discover that music has attractive and inviting possibilities for them, and will seek to realize such possibilities and manage to do so. A program of activities and experiences such as we have been considering is a seed bed for musical amateurism, both in and out of school. By this we mean a practice of the art of music for the sheer love of it, without any thought of financial reward. If you and your fellow teachers persist in carrying on a program of this kind, good musical organizations become possible, a demand for class instruction in piano and instruments is likely to arise, and the private teachers of the community can hardly fail to feel the effects.

Even here, as you see, we are thinking of standards in terms not of measurable test results but of tangible human behavior. On any common sense ground this way of thinking about standards is eminently sound. And even though they cannot be expressed in statistics they are unmistakably recognizable, and the attainment of them is a very solid satisfaction.

## II

What is the relationship of your work to the music program in the secondary schools, and more particularly to the band, the orchestra, the chorus and other similar organizations, and also to the work of the private music teachers of the community? Briefly and in general terms the answer is this: You are providing a breadth of vital and stimulating musical experiences which none of the special organizations can furnish, but which is both exceedingly valuable and greatly neglected. In so doing you are making very tangible contributions to solving many of the problems of the high school music staff, and of the director of the band, or orchestra, or chorus.

(a) The whole tendency of your work is to bring into being a very large pool of individuals who are musically interested and who have well begun the process of finding themselves musically. This goes far towards solving the ever-present and quite awkward problem of recruitment for the high school musical organizations. It does away with the need for high-pressure salesmanship and undue influence which are often such unfortunate features of secondary school musical activities.

(b) You cannot guarantee that every pupil who enters high school will be able to read the notation. As a matter of fact it should not be your purpose to bring about any such result, even if it were possible. But there is every reason to believe that the long-term cumulative effect of a program such as the one here described is to bring large numbers of pupils to the seventh grade with enough understanding of music to be able to learn to handle the notation very quickly when the need arises. The difficulty of interpreting the notation has, in general, been grossly exaggerated. That difficulty is due very largely to attempting to teach the elements of the notation (the so-called fundamentals) with virtually no organized background of musical experience. A child who has had extensive, varied, focalized contacts with music through expressive bodily movement, listening, singing, playing easy instruments, and creative activities, and who has achieved a strong positive orientation and some real understanding of the expressive values of the art, will not have much trouble with the score when he begins to play clarinet in the junior high school band. So also a child with the kind of background your work can provide is in a very favorable position to make the most of private music lessons.

(c) Your work has very little to do with the direct development of musical skills and techniques. About this you need not feel in the least apologetic, for music teaching tends to overemphasize sheer skill quite beyond all reason. The very things that you can do excellently are seriously neglected, in spite of the fact that they are recognized by all intelligent and thoughtful persons as highly worth while, not only on personal but also on purely musical grounds. But although you do not directly teach skill, you lay the foundations for the teaching and learning of it. Lack of background is a tremendous handicap in any kind of technical development. A child who is already musically intelligent, discriminating, and well oriented has a great advantage when he takes up the study of an instrument. Granted this personal equipment, many of the obstacles to the acquisition of skill are much reduced.

(d) One of the important cumulative effects of your work is to establish sound and healthy attitudes towards music in large numbers of boys and girls. This, undoubtedly, is the direction in which we have got to move in finding a solution to one of the most vexatious problems of the high school music staff—the problem of contests. Many directors of high school bands and orchestras belabor the contest system with great energy. They insist that it has deleterious effects on boys and girls. They wax eloquent in insisting that young people should enjoy music for its own intrinsic values. But—they work as hard as they can for awards, just the same! The truth is that in many parts of America the contest system has a tremendous dynamism. High school staffs find themselves in the grip of something much stronger than they. The demand is irresistible, and their jobs depend on satisfying it. What can be done about the situation? There is no quick and easy answer. As a matter of fact an extreme contest psychology is an expression of crude and naive musical attitudes in the student body, which reflect themselves and find support in the community. One of the great cumulative values of a vital general music program such as we have been discussing is that, over the years, it strongly tends to create better and more civilized attitudes, and so to provide an altogether more acceptable basis for the work of the high school music staff. A student body which has been consistently and persistently led to discover the vast range of possibilities which music has to offer will lose interest in contests, because other and more constructive interests assert themselves.

(e) There is no reason at all why work in piano and in band and orchestral instruments should not be offered in the elementary school on an opportunity basis. But such work is in no sense a substitute for daily and varied classroom musical experiences and activities. The teacher of clarinet, for instance, is concerned first and foremost with the production of competent clarinetists. But your primary concern is to produce musically oriented human be-

ings. Musically oriented human beings are apt to be superior candidates for clarinet study, and a good many of them
are likely to want to take it up. When such a wish manifests itself, you should by all means support and encourage
it. But both you and the clarinet teacher should cooperate in seeing to it that the acquisition of technical skill
does not overshadow a broad and vital musical orientation
which can certainly be a lifelong asset.

The attitude of high school band directors, orchestra
directors, and choral directors to the elementary school
music program is often very interesting. They tend to feel
that there is something wrong, something lacking. They
are prone to insist that music should be taught as a "solid"
subject, and taken very seriously. So far one can heartily
agree. But when the questions arise as to who is to teach
it as a solid subject and how it is to be taught, these gentle-
men usually have no answer at all. Indeed any ideas they
may possess on the matter are apt to be extremely unrealistic, both in the light of how elementary schools are actually run and of how human beings actually develop musical capacity. In case you ever find yourself in an argument
with any of these excellent people, here are a few brief suggestions which you may think useful. Ask them what they
think would really happen if all the children in the elementary schools were led to discover what music really is
and what it offers, to develop some genuine standards of
musical taste, and to establish at least a beginning competence in dealing with music in various ways. Point out that
such a result is by no means utterly beyond the capacity
of the classroom teachers of America. Point out further
that if anything of the kind is to be achieved, it can only
be achieved by the classroom teachers, because the prospect
of hiring a sufficient staff of specialists is hopelessly fan-

tastic. Point out still further that while classroom teachers cannot function as virtuosi of the *do-re-mi's,* and probably do not even want to, they can have an enormous influence in establishing positive musical orientations in great numbers of children. In closing you might state that if there is ever going to be a substantial program of music in the elementary school, this is the kind of program it has got to be, and ask these people, as intelligent men and earnest musicians, to get behind such a program might and main, and to stop their crabbing.

### III

Where do the proposals put forward in this book leave the elementary school music specialist? This, surely, is a question which has been hanging over our heads from the very start; and even though I am not writing for the specialist I must deal with it briefly.

First, no adequate program of music in an elementary school is even remotely possible if the music specialist does all or most of the teaching. This is true for a number of obvious practical reasons. (*a*) Under the best of circumstances the music specialist can visit each classroom briefly perhaps twice a month. A proposal to teach any other subject on this plan would be laughed out of court. Music is not being properly handled unless it is a daily classroom experience. The music specialist cannot make it so. (*b*) It is quite impossible for the music specialist intimately to know all the children in all the groups with which she has to deal. Therefore she cannot adapt musical experiences and activities to their needs, proclivities, and abilities. She is bound to confine herself to a standard stint and standard procedures if she herself carries the teaching load. (*c*) The classroom visits of the music specialist are brief. Therefore she cannot develop and organize any extensive musical projects, or indeed any activities extending beyond the twenty minutes or so while she is in the room. For this reason alone she could not carry on most of the specific undertakings described in these pages. Her only choice is to give a musical injection and then hurry on elsewhere. This does not add up to effective teaching.

Second, no adequate program of music in the elementary school is possible if the content and procedures are to be dictated by the music specialist and delegated, under specific instructions, to the classroom teachers. This instantly kills the initiative of the classroom teacher and nullifies her greatest asset, which is her close contact with her children, her understanding of them, and the opportunities afforded by her strategic position for working with them, guiding them, helping them, and organizing their experiences and activities in the light of her knowledge of them. To treat the classroom teacher as nothing but a human phonograph on which the music specialist places suitable records in a suitable order is an outrage and an insult. Supervision of this kind is enough to kill any subject, and it will certainly kill music.

Then has the music specialist no place at all? By no means. In dealing with music even the competent classroom teacher needs help and guidance, a knowledge of available materials and devices, and above all lots of good practical ideas. All these are things the music specialist can supply. The musically hesitating classroom teacher needs encouragement and advice; here the music specialist can act as a spark plug. When a number of classroom teachers in a school are working with music, there is a need for coordinating their efforts, even if each individual teacher is doing an excellent job; the music specialist can guide such coordination. Often classroom teachers need some special in-service training in music, perhaps along the line of developing this or that skill or technique; the music specialist can provide such training herself or arrange for it. I know, for instance, of one school system where the music staff set up opportunities for group piano study, for the classroom teachers, which met with an eager response. So there are still plenty of vital functions for the music specialist. Perhaps, if we can get the right kind of music program all through the schools, in twenty years time the music specialist may have organized herself out of a job. But that time is not yet, and it may never arrive!

Does this mean that the music specialist is relegated entirely to the background, to the performance of obscure service functions? No indeed, although there is some tendency for this to happen. In one or two school systems with which I am acquainted, the music specialists work largely in the libraries and suchlike places, accumulating ammunition for the classroom teachers to fire off. This is a most deplorable state of affairs. No educational worker can retain vitality or a sense of real issues, nor can she continue to give effective service, unless she has many contacts with the children and with the operations on the firing line. The music specialist should have a share in significant projects, carry on some teaching of her own, work intimately with the teachers on the actual job. Along with this she must have sufficient time to think, to coordinate, to keep herself up to date on new material and new ideas. The primary responsibility is always with the classroom teacher who is in actual contact with the children, and she must have elbow room to exercise it. But the music specialist can and should serve as her guide, philosopher, and friend.

# Bibliography

*All the items listed below are chosen from a much larger body of material for the reason that they have proved of great value in practical situations.*

*Songs Chiefly for Primary Grades*

BERTAIL, INEZ. *A Child's Book of Christmas Carols.* New York: Random House, 1942.

BERTAIL, INEZ. *Favorite Nursery Songs.* New York: Random House, 1941.

BRADFORD, MARGARET. *Keep Singing, Keep Humming; A Collection of Play and Story Songs.* New York: W. R. Scott, Inc., 1946.

COIT, LOTTIE E., and RUTH BAMPTON. *Follow the Music.* Boston: C. C. Birchard Company, 1948.

COLEMAN, SATIS N., and ALICE G. THORN. *Another Singing Time.* New York: Reynal and Hitchcock, 1937.

COLEMAN, SATIS N., and ALICE G. THORN. *The Little Singing Time.* New York: John Day Company, 1940.

COLEMAN, SATIS N., and ALICE G. THORN. *Singing Time.* New York: John Day Company, 1930.

HUNT, EVELYN H. *Music Time; Songs for Children from Two to Seven.* New York: The Viking Press, 1947.

LANDECK, BEATRICE. *Songs to Grow On.* New York: Edward B. Marks Music Corporation, 1950.

MARTIN, FLORENCE M. *Songs Children Sing.* Chicago: Hall and McCreary Company, 1943.

MACCARTNEY, LAURA P. *Songs for the Nursery School.* Cincinnati: Willis Music Company, 1942.

NELSON, MARY JARMAN. *Fun with Music.* Chicago: Albert Whitman and Company, 1941.

PERHAM, BEATRICE (Beatrice Krone). *Growing Up With Music.* Chicago: Neil A. Kjos Music Company, 1937. Vol. I.

WHEELER, OPAL. *Sing Mother Goose.* New York: E. P. Dutton and Company, 1945.


*Songs Chiefly for Upper Grades*

COLEMAN, SATIS N. *Christmas Carols of Many Countries.* New York: G. Schirmer, Inc., 1934.

LANDECK, BEATRICE. *Git on Board.* New York: Edward B. Marks Music Corporation, 1944.

PERHAM, BEATRICE (Beatrice Krone). *Growing Up With Music.* Chicago: Neil A. Kjos Music Company, 1937. Vol. II.

*Treasure Chest Community Songster.* New York: Treasure Chest Publications, Inc., 1936.

*Treasure Chest of World Wide Songs.* New York: Treasure Chest Publications, Inc., 1936.

VAN LOON, HENDRIK W., and GRACE CASTAGNETTA. *Christmas Carols.* New York: Simon and Schuster, 1937.

VAN LOON, HENDRIK W., and GRACE CASTAGNETTA. *The Songs America Sings.* New York: Simon and Schuster, 1939.

WHEELER, OPAL. *Sing for America.* New York: E. P. Dutton and Company, 1944.

WHEELER, OPAL. *Sing for Christmas.* New York: E. P. Dutton and Company, 1943.

WHEELER, OPAL. *Sing in Praise.* New York: E. P. Dutton and Company, 1946.

WYCKOFF, MARJORIE E. *A Child's Book of Hymns.* New York: Random House, 1945.

*Dances, Singing Games, Bodily Movement.*

BRIGGS, DOROTHY BELL. *Kindergarten Book;* Games, Rhythms and Songs. Philadelphia: Oliver Ditson Company, 1941.

BURCHENAL, ELIZABETH. *Folk Dances and Singing Games.* New York: G. Schirmer, Inc., 1909-1922. 3 volumes.

CRAWFORD, CAROLINE. *Dramatic Games and Dances for Little Children.* New York: A. S. Barnes and Company, 1914.

CROWNINSHIELD, ETHEL. *New Songs and Games.* Boston: Boston Music Company, 1941.

CROWNINSHIELD, ETHEL. *The Sing and Play Book.* Boston: Boston Music Company, 1938.

DURLACHER, ED. *The Play Party Book.* New York: Devin-Adair Company, 1945.

HAMLIN, ALICE P., and MARGARET G. GUESSFORD. *Singing Games for Children.* Cincinnati: Willis Music Company, 1941.

HUGHES, DOROTHY. *Rhythmic Games and Dances; Basic Activities for Elementary Grades.* New York: American Book Company, 1942.

HUNT, BEATRICE, and HARRY R. WILSON. *Sing and Dance; Folk Songs and Dances including American Play-Party Games.* Chicago: Hall and McCreary Company, 1945.

*An Index to Folk Dances and Singing Games.* Minneapolis: Minneapolis Public Library, 1936.

*An Index to Folk Dances and Singing Games: Supplement.* Chicago: American Library Association, 1949.

KOZMAN, HILDA C. *Character Dances for School Programs.* New York: A. S. Barnes and Company, 1935.

LA SALLE, DOROTHY. *Rhythms and Dances for Elementary Schools, Grades One to Eight.* New York: A. S. Barnes and Company, 1939.

MARTIN, FLORENCE M., and ELIZABETH BURNETT. *Rime, Rhythm, and Song for the Child of Today.* Chicago: Hall and McCreary Company, 1942.

DE NANCREDE, EDITH, and GERTRUDE M. SMITH. *Mother Goose Dances.* Chicago: H. T. Fitzsimmons Company, 1940.

SHAFER, MARY S., and M. M. MOSHER. *Rhythms for Children.* New York: A. S. Barnes and Company, 1938.

SUTTON, RHODA R. *Creative Rhythms.* New York: A. S. Barnes and Company, 1941.

WHITLOCK, VIRGINIA. *Come and Caper; Creative Rhythms, Pantomimes and Plays, with Music by Various Composers.* New York: G. Schirmer, Inc., 1932.

WOLLASTON, MARY A. *The Song Play Book; Singing Games for Children.* New York: A. S. Barnes and Company, 1928. Seventh edition.

*Folk Songs*

COLEMAN, SATIS N., and ADOLPH BREGMAN. *Songs of American Folks.* New York: John Day Company, 1942.

LOMAX, JOHN A., and ALAN LOMAX. *American Ballads and Folk Songs.* New York: The Macmillan Company, 1934.

LUTHER, FRANK. *Americans and Their Songs*. New York: Harper Brothers, 1942.

MARAIS, JOSEF. *Songs from the Veld*. New York: G. Schirmer, Inc., 1942.

SANDBURG, CARL. *The American Songbag*. New York: Harcourt Brace and Company, 1927.

SEEGER, RUTH CRAWFORD. *American Folk Songs for Children in Home, School, and Nursery School*. Garden City, N. Y.: Doubleday Doran and Company, 1948.

SIEGMEISTER, ELIE. *Work and Sing*. New York: W. P. Scott, 1944.

WILSON, HARRY R. *Songs of the Hills and Plains*. Chicago: Hall and McCreary Company, 1943.

*Instruments*

COLEMAN, SATIS N. *Bells, Their History, Legends, Making and Uses*. Chicago: Rand McNally Company, 1948.

COLEMAN, SATIS N. *The Book of Bells*. New York: John Day Company, 1938.

COLEMAN, SATIS N. *Creative Music for Children*. New York: G. P. Putnam's Sons, 1922.

COLEMAN, SATIS N. *Creative Music Series*. New York: John Day Company, 1930. Vol. 1, "First Steps in Playing and Composing." Vol. 2, "The Drum Book." Vol. 3, "The Marimba Book." Vol. 4, "The Psaltery Book."

DILLER, ANGELA, and KATE STEARNS PAGE. *How to Teach the Rhythm Band*. New York: G. Schirmer, Inc., 1930.

FOX, LILLIAN MOHR, and L. THOMAS HOPKINS. *Creative School Music*. New York: Silver Burdett Company, 1937.

Fox, Lillian Mohr. *Autoharp Accompaniments to Old Favorite Songs.* Boston: C. C. Birchard Company, 1947.

*Instruments of the Orchestra: Handbook.* New York: RCA Victor Company.

Lacey, Marion. *Picture Book of Musical Instruments.* New York: Lothrop Lee and Shepard Company, 1942.

Perham, Beatrice (Beatrice Krone). *Music in the New School.* Chicago: Neil A. Kjos Music Company, 1937 and 1950.

*Rhythm Band Instruction Book.* 223 West Lake Avenue, Chicago: Lyons Band Instrument Company.

Herfurth, C. Paul. *Instrumental Horizons; Course in Ensemble Playing associated with New Music Horizons.* New York: Silver Burdett Company, 1950. Score for piano leader and any or all of ten instruments.

*Instrumental Horizons; Rhythm Instruments; Scored for Songs Selected from New Music Horizons.* New York: Silver Burdett Company, 1950.

Churchill, Virginia P. *Triangles and Cymbals; Folk Tunes and Classic Pieces for Children's Rhythm Band.* Philadelphia: Oliver Ditson, 1930.

Votaw, Lyravine, Ruth Diederach, and Cora Mannheimer. *The Rhythm Band Series.* 223 West Lake Avenue, Chicago: Lyons Band Instrument Company.


*Operas*

Bacon, Dolores. *Operas That Every Child Should Know.* New York: Grosset and Dunlap, 1911.

Dike, Helen. *Stories from the Great Metropolitan Operas.* New York: Random House, 1943.

LAWRENCE, ROBERT. *Aida.* New York: Silver Burdett Company, 1938.

LAWRENCE, ROBERT. *The Bartered Bride.* New York: Grosset and Dunlap, 1943.

LAWRENCE, ROBERT. *Boris Godunoff.* New York: Grosset and Dunlap, 1944.

LAWRENCE, ROBERT. *Carmen.* New York: Silver Burdett Company, 1938.

LAWRENCE, ROBERT. *Gilbert and Sullivan's H. M. S. Pinafore.* New York: Grosset and Dunlap, 1940.

LAWRENCE, ROBERT. *Gilbert and Sullivan's The Gondoliers or The King of Barataria.* New York: Grosset and Dunlap, 1940.

LAWRENCE, ROBERT. *Gilbert and Sullivan's The Mikado.* New York: Grosset and Dunlap, 1940.

LAWRENCE, ROBERT. *Gounod's Faust.* New York: Grosset and Dunlap, 1943.

LAWRENCE, ROBERT. *Haensel & Gretel.* New York: Silver Burdett Company, 1938.

LAWRENCE, ROBERT. *Lohengrin.* New York: Silver Burdett Company, 1939.

LAWRENCE, ROBERT. *Siegfried.* New York: Silver Burdett Company, 1938.

LAWRENCE, ROBERT. *The Magic Flute.* New York: Artists and Writers Guild, 1944.

LAWRENCE, ROBERT. *The Rhinegold.* New York: Silver Burdett Company, 1938.

LAWRENCE, ROBERT. *The Twilight of the Gods; Die Gotterdämmerung.* New York: Silver Burdett Company, 1938.

LAWRENCE, ROBERT. *The Valkyrie.* New York: Silver Burdett Company, 1938.

*Victor Book of Operas.* New York: Simon and Schuster, 1949.

WHEELER, OPAL. *H. M. S. Pinafore; Story and Music Arrangements Adapted from Gilbert and Sullivan.* New York: E. P. Dutton and Company, 1946.


*Biography*

BAKELESS, KATHERINE. *Story Lives of Great Composers.* New York: Frederick A. Stokes, 1941.

BURCH, GLADYS, and JOHN WOLCOTT. *A Child's Book of Famous Composers.* New York: A. S. Barnes and Company, 1939.

BURCH, GLADYS, and JOHN WOLCOTT. *Famous Composers for Young People.* New York: Dodd, Mead and Company, 1945.

BURCH, GLADYS. *Famous Pianists for Young People.* New York: Dodd, Mead and Company, 1943.

BURCH, GLADYS. *Famous Violinists for Young People.* New York: Dodd, Mead and Company, 1946.

BURCH, GLADYS. *Modern Composers for Young People.* New York: Dodd, Mead and Company, 1941.

BURCH, GLADYS. *Richard Wagner Who Followed a Star.* New York: Henry Holt and Company, 1941.

COIT, LOTTIE E., and RUTH BAMPTON. *The Child Bach.* Philadelphia: Theodore Presser Company, 1943.

COIT, LOTTIE E., and RUTH BAMPTON. *The Child Handel.* Philadelphia: Theodore Presser Company, 1945.

COIT, LOTTIE E., and RUTH BAMPTON. *The Child Haydn.* Philadelphia: Theodore Presser Company, 1944.

COIT, LOTTIE E., and RUTH BAMPTON. *The Child Mozart.* Philadelphia: Theodore Presser Company, 1942.

EWEN, DAVID. *Haydn, A Good Life.* New York: Henry Holt and Company, 1946.

EWEN, DAVID. *The Story of George Gershwin.* New York: Henry Holt and Company, 1943.

EWEN, DAVID. *The Story of Irving Berlin.* New York: Henry Holt and Company, 1950.

EWEN, DAVID. *Tales from the Vienna Woods.* (Johann Strauss). New York: Henry Holt and Company, 1944.

HANSL, EVA E., and H. L. KAUFMANN. *Minute Sketches of Great Composers.* New York: Grosset and Dunlap, 1932.

MAUROIS, ANDRE. *Frederic Chopin.* New York: Harper Brothers, 1942.

SCHWIMMER, FRANCESKA. *Great Musicians as Children.* Garden City, N. Y.: Doubleday Doran and Company, 1929.

VAN LOON, HENDRIK W. *The Life and Times of Johann Sebastian Bach.* New York: Simon and Schuster, 1940.

WHEELER, OPAL. *Frederic Chopin, Son of Poland.* New York: E. P. Dutton and Company, 1948.

WHEELER, OPAL. *Handel at the Court of Kings.* New York: E. P. Dutton and Company, 1943.

WHEELER, OPAL. *Joseph Haydn, the Merry Little Peasant.* New York: E. P. Dutton and Company, 1936.

WHEELER, OPAL. *Ludwig Beethoven and the Chiming Tower Bells.* New York: E. P. Dutton and Company, 1942.

WHEELER, OPAL. *Robert Schumann and Mascot Ziff.* New York: E. P. Dutton and Company, 1947.

WHEELER, OPAL, and SYBIL DEUCHER. *Sebastian Bach, the Boy from Thuringia.* New York: E. P. Dutton and Company, 1937.

WHEELER, OPAL, and SYBIL DEUCHER. *Franz Schubert and*

*His Merry Friends.* New York: E. P. Dutton and
Company, 1939.

WHEELER, OPAL, and SYBIL DEUCHER. *Mozart the Wonder
Boy.* New York: E. P. Dutton and Company, 1941.

WHEELER, OPAL, and SYBIL DEUCHER. *Stephen Foster and
His Little Dog Tray.* New York: E. P. Dutton and
Company, 1941.


*General Books on Music*

BAKER, ELLEN. *The Wonderful Story of Music.* New York:
Crowell, 1931.

BALDWIN, LILLIAN. *A Listener's Anthology of Music.* New
York: Silver Burdett Company, 1948.

BALDWIN, LILLIAN. *Music for Young Listeners.* New York:
Silver Burdett Company, 1951. In four volumes.

BUCHANNAN, FANNIE R. *How Man Made Music.* Chicago:
Follet Publishing Company, 1941.

COOKE, JAMES FRANCIS. *Young Folk's Picture History of
Music.* Philadelphia: Theodore Presser Company,
1925.

CROSS, DONZELLA. *Music Stories for Boys and Girls.* Boston: Ginn and Company, 1926.

HARTSHORN, WILLIAM C. and HELEN LEAVITT. *Making
Friends with Music.* Boston: Ginn and Company,
1940. *World of Music* series.

KINSCELLA, HAZEL G. *History Sings; Backgrounds of
American Music.* Lincoln, Nebraska: The University
Publishing Company, 1948.

KINSCELLA, HAZEL G. *Kinscella Readers: Stories in Music
Appreciation.* Lincoln, Nebraska: University Publishing Company, 1930-1936. Eight volumes.

SALOMON, JULIAN H. *Book of Indian Crafts and Indian
Lore.* New York: Harper and Brothers, 1928.

*Victor Book of the Symphony.* New York: Simon and
Schuster, 1934 and 1941.

WHITCOMB, IDA P. *Young People's Story of Music.* New
York: Dodd, Mead and Company, 1908.

WRIGHT, FRANCES, and LAVERNA LOSSING. *Song Source
Material for Social Study Units.* New York: Teachers
College, Columbia University, Bureau of Publications,
1946. Third edition.


*Professional Books*

*Music in the Elementary School.* California State Department of Education. Sacramento, California: 1939.

COLEMAN, SATIS N. *Creative Music for Children.* New
York: G. P. Putnam's Sons, 1922.

COLEMAN, SATIS N. *Creative Music in the Home.* New
York: John Day Company, 1939.

COLEMAN, SATIS N. *Your Child's Music.* New York: John
Day Company, 1939.

FOX, LILLIAN MOHR, and L. THOMAS HOPKINS. *Creative
School Music.* New York: Silver Burdett Company,
1936.

*Growth and Development of a Child through Music; Music
Guide, Kindergarten and First Grade.* Philadelphia:
Philadelphia Public Schools. Mimeographed.

*Guide to Music Experiences.* Santa Ana, California:
Orange County Schools, 1950. Mimeographed.

HOOD, MARGUERITE, and E. J. SCHULTZ. *Learning Music
through Rhythm.* Boston: Ginn and Company, 1949.

MURRAY, JOSEPHINE, and EFFIE BATHURST. *Creative Ways
for Children's Programs.* New York: Silver Burdett
Company, 1938.

MURSELL, JAMES L. *Music in American Schools.* New
York: Silver Burdett Company, 1943.

MURSELL, JAMES L. *Education for Musical Growth*. Boston: Ginn and Company, 1948.

PERHAM, BEATRICE (Beatrice Krone). *Music in the New School*. Chicago: Neil A. Kjos Music Company, 1950. Revised edition.

*Music Contributing to the Education of Children; the Creative Dance*. Passaic, N. J.: Passaic Public Schools, 1948. Mimeographed.

SHEEHY, EMMA D. *There's Music in Children*. New York: Henry Holt and Company, 1946.

THORN, ALICE G. *Music for Young Children*. New York: Charles Scribner's Sons, 1929.


*Recent School Music Series*

*The American Singer*. New York: American Book Company. (John Beattie, Ed.)

*New Music Horizons*. New York: Silver Burdett Company. (Osbourne McConathy, Russell Morgan, James L. Mursell, Marshall Bartholomew, Mabel Bray, W. Otto Miessner, E. B. Birge, Eds.)

*Our Singing World*. Boston: Ginn and Company. (Lilla Belle Pitts, Mabelle Glenn, Lorraine E. Watters, Eds.)

*A Singing School*. Boston: C. C. Birchard Company. (Peter W. Dykema, Gladys Pitcher, Eds.)

# Some Suggested Records

It would be unwise even to try to make a comprehensive listing of suitable records. For this there are two reasons. First, any such list would be so enormously long as to become very cumbersome. Second, it is unfortunately true that recording companies often allow records to lapse from production, which makes them difficult to obtain. Accordingly what I have done here is to present a set of classified samples, all of which have distinct merit and interest, and which seem likely to be available for some time to come. The items are, in the main, records made expressly for children. Of course a great number of standard recordings are also suitable and valuable. I have listed records specifically made for school use under a separate heading.

*Singing Records*

*The Adventures of Daniel Boone.* Young People's Records, Inc., YPR 425. A lively narration with authentic period folk songs.

*The American Almanac.* Young People's Records, Inc., January, YPR 430; April, YPR 434; May, YPR 419; August, YPR 429; November, YPR 417; December, YPR 424. Traditional and historical stories for each month with authentic related songs, mostly ensemble.

*Animal Fair.* Columbia, Set MJV-59, two ten inch records. Folk songs about animals sung by Burl Ives.

*Building a City.* Young People's Records, Inc., YPR 711. Fine singalong record.

*Chisholm Trail.* Young People's Records, Inc., YPR 409. Western songs.

*The Concertina that Crossed the Country.* Young People's Records, Inc., YPR 414. A continuity of the gold rush, with songs of early American life.

*Cowboys and Indians.* Allegro Junior 14. Songs of both, well done.

*The First Day at School.* Columbia, MJV-66. Songs sung by Dinah Shore about the wonderful things at school, with story continuity.

*Folk Songs from Brazil.* Columbia, Set MM-812, four ten inch records. Well sung by a Metropolitan opera soprano.

*The Gingerbread Boy* and *Chicken Licken.* Decca, DU 88009. Song stories by Frank Luther.

*Goldilocks and the Three Bears.* Decca 74461. Song story by Frank Luther.

*Grandfather's Farm.* Children's Record Guild, CRG 5004. Appropriate songs with an attractive story continuity.

*Hymns for Children.* Columbia, MJV-65. Four hymns sung well and distinctly by Floyd Sherman, with organ accompaniment. *A long-playing record.*

*Jo Stafford American Folk Songs.* Capitol Telefunken, Set CC-75, three ten inch records. A number of fine American folk songs.

*Johnny Appleseed.* RCA Victor, Little Nipper Series, Set Y-390, three ten inch records. Story, singing, background music. All good. Illustrates synopsis of story in album.

*On Lemmer Lemmer Street.* Children's Record Guild, CRG 5006. An authentic setting in English of a 16th century Hanseatic narrative song. Text and description on envelope.

➤ *Let's All Join In.* Young People's Records, Inc., YPR 403. A singalong record.

*The Little King of Yvetot.* Young People's Record's, Inc. YPR 732. Story continuity with five folk-type songs sung by George Rasely.

*Little Johnny Chickadee* and *Peterkin Pillowby.* Columbia, MJV-73. Two charming and whimsical songs by Rosemary Clooney, orchestral accompaniment.

*The Little Red Hen.* Decca, DU 88015. Song story by Frank Luther.

*Little Red Wagon.* Children's Record Guild, CRG 1004. Well-known folk spirituals, with continuity and sound effects, well sung; has good singalong possibilities.

*Lore of the West.* RCA Victor, Set Y-388, two ten inch records. Also comes on 45 r.p.m. record WY-388. Roy Rogers, Gabby Hayes, Lore of the West Singers. Much information on western life, clothing, and equipment in booklet.

*Mother Goose.* RCA Victor, WY-34, two 45 r.p.m. records (also on conventional records). Sung by Jack Arthur, illustrated book.

*Mother Goose Songs.* Columbia, MJV-67. Burl Ives sings eleven Mother Goose songs exceedingly well.

*Mother Goose Songs.* Decca DU 90000, two ten inch records. Frank Luther sings a considerable number of Mother Goose songs with a narrative continuity.

*The Owl and the Pussy Cat.* Allegro, aj 22. Crane Calder sings this old favorite song along with three others.

*Playtime Songs.* Young People's Records, Inc., YPR 605.

Charity Bailey in a charming presentation of unusual
songs.

*More Playtime Songs.* Young People's Records, Inc., YPR
729. More of the same.

——*Ride 'Em Cowboy.* Children's Record Guild, CRG 5001.
Set of cowboys songs, excellently sung with continuity
and sound effects. Participation and singalong.

——*Ship Ahoy.* Children's Record Guild, CRG 5003. Set of
authentic nautical songs and chanties, with continuity
and sound effects. Participation and singalong.

*The Shoemaker and the Elves.* Decca, DU-88010. Song
story by Frank Luther.

*Sing Cowboy Sing!* Capitol, Album AC-77, three ten inch
records. Shug Fisher and Ranchman Trio in familiar
and authentic western songs, well sung.

——*Sing-Along.* Young People's Records, Inc., YPR 722. What
the name suggests.

——*Another Sing-Along.* Young People's Records, Inc., YPR
723. Same comment.

*Skip to My Lou.* Allegro Junior 5. Title song and three
similar ones sung by Crane Calder.

*Tex Ritter Sings for Children.* Capitol, DC-91, three ten
inch records. Very live collection of songs.

*Thirty-three Children's Songs.* Decca, DU 88004-5, two
ten inch records. Sung by Frank Luther. Distribution
on records makes them rather hard to use.

*Three Billy Goats Gruff.* Decca, DU 88012. Song story by
Frank Luther.

*The Wayfaring Stranger.* Columbia, Set C-103, four ten
inch records. Fine folk songs excellently sung by Burl
Ives.

*The Return of the Wayfaring Stranger.* Columbia, Set
C-186, four ten inch records. Same comment.

*What the Lighthouse Sees.* Young People's Records, Inc.,
   YPR 702. Good for participation and singalong.
*Working on the Railroad.* Young People's Records, Inc.,
   YPR 427. Dramatic treatment of building American
   railroads, with authentic songs.


## Miscellaneous Recordings

*Bozo's Jungle Jingles* and *The Laughing Hyena.* Capitol,
   DAS-3011. The first item is a story continuity with
   familiar tunes first on four different instruments, then
   combined. Continuity poor but music clever. Second
   item very poor.
*Cinderella.* RCA Victor, Little Nipper Series, Set Y-399,
   two ten inch records. Songs and continuity from the
   movie, with text and illustrations.
*The Emperor's New Clothes.* Young People's Records,
   Inc., Set 1007-8, two ten inch records. The familiar
   story with music in gay operatic style by Douglas
   Moore.
*The Golden Goose.* Children's Record Guild, CRG 5002.
   The fairy story with music by Bernard Wagenaar,
   each character with theme played on different instru-
   ment.
*The Great Big Parade.* Allegro Junior 25. Participation
   record, sound effects, narration by Crane Calder.
*Igor Strawinsky.* Young People's Records, Inc., YPR 407.
   Music of the composer.
*Iolanthe.* Allegro Intermediate, ak 57. Selections from the
   opera.
*Music of Aaron Copland.* Young People's Records, Inc.,
   YPR 408. Music of the composer.
*The Neighbors' Band.* Young People's Records, Inc.,

YPR 726. Story about four musicians playing four instruments and finally cooperating.

*Operettas from Vienna (Franz Lehar).* Capitol Telefunken, Set ECL-2501, three twelve inch records. Excerpts from four operettas played by Berlin Philmonic Symphony Orchestra.

*Picking Up Paw Paws.* Allegro Intermediate, ak 58. Three square dances, called by Kraus, with directions on envelope.

*Pinafore.* Allegro Intermediate, ak 55. Excerpts from the opera.

*Pirates of Penzance.* Allegro, ak 53. Excerpts from the opera.

*Rondo for Bassoon and Orchestra.* Young People's Records, Inc., YPR 1009. Music by Weber well rendered, featuring the bassoon.

*Round and Round.* Young People's Records, Inc., YPR 431. Fugal form explained and illustrated through its analogy to the round.

*The Runaway Sheep.* Young People's Records, Inc., YPR 721. Story continuity with interesting music on an authentic shepherd's pipe. Good explanation of the pipe on envelope.

*Said the Piano to the Harpsichord.* Young People's Records, Inc., YPR 411. Two instruments in entertaining dialogue, with explanations on envelope.

*The Skaters, Arkansas Traveller, Semper Fidelis.* Columbia Masterworks, 71957-D. Stirring performance by Carnegie Pops Orchestra of these old favorites.

*Singing Games.* MGM, S-6. Three songs well sung; can readily lead to participation.

*Square Dances.* Allegro ak 54. Good material.

*There Were Three Indians.* MGM, S-4. Story of three

Indians who return to the world after many centuries. Chanting, tom-tom effects.

*The Toy Symphony (Joseph Haydn)* Columbia Masterworks, 7242-M. Charming symphony with unusual instruments which children can identify.

*Tubby the Tuba.* Decca, DU-90011A, LX 4424, one twelve inch record. Outstanding impersonation of the instrument.

*Tubby the Tuba, Animal Fair* (Burl Ives). Columbia, MJV-69. Two numbers on a long-playing record. The new version of Tubby is greatly improved.

*A Visit from Saint Nicholas.* Decca, 18499. Fine setting of " 'Twas the night before Christmas" by Waring and his Pennsylvanians.

*Why the Chimes Rang.* RCA Victor, Y-357, two ten inch records. Appealing Christmas story, with organ music.

*Wonderful Violin.* Young People's Records, Inc., YPR 311. Narrative identification of the violin.

*Records specially for school use*

*RCA Victor Basic Record Library for Elementary Schools.* RCA Victor, Twenty-one albums, covering rhythms, listening, singing, singing games, Christmas, Indian, rhythm bands, patriotic songs.

*Songs from The American Singer.* Decca ASE. Six albums. Distributer, American Book Company.

*Songs from A Singing School.* Columbia.

*Songs from New Music Horizons.* Columbia. Six albums.

Reviews and appraisals of current record releases for children are published from time to time by Charles Leonard in *The Saturday Review of Literature,* and by Emma Sheehy in *Parents' Magazine.* The catalogs of many recording companies are organized in a very practical and helpful manner, with useful classifications of the material. This is particularly true of the catalogs of RCA Victor and Columbia. Two valuable reference books are *A Catalogue of Selected Educational Recordings*, published by the Film Library of New York University, New York, N.Y., 1944; and *A Guide to Children's Recordings* by Philip Eisenberg and Hecky Krasno, Crown Publishers, New York, N.Y., 1948.

# Index

301